PROBLEM

SOLVING

STRATEGIES

TEACHER'S

RESOURCE

BOOK AND

ANSWER KEY

CROSSING THE RIVER WITH DOGS
AND OTHER MATHEMATICAL
ADVENTURES

TED HERR
KEN JOHNSON

KEY
CURRICULUM
PRESS

2512 MARTIN
LUTHER KING JR. WAY
P.O. BOX 2304
BERKELEY
CALIFORNIA
94702

Limited Reproduction Permission

The publisher grants the teacher who purchases this Teacher's Resource Book the right to reproduce portions as needed for use in his or her own classroom.

Unauthorized copying of any part of this book constitutes copyright infringement and is a violation of federal law.

Published by: Key Curriculum Press, P.O. Box 2304, Berkeley, CA 94702.
Copyright © 1994 by Key Curriculum Press. All rights reserved.
10 9 8 7 6 5 4 3 2 1   97 96 95 94 93
ISBN 1-55953-069-3
Printed in the United States of America.

How to Use This Book

TWO LETTERS BEGIN this book: one to you and your colleagues and one to the parents and guardians of your students. Here we describe our philosophy and some of our expectations for the course. Share the Letter to Colleagues with your colleagues who want to know what the course is about. You might want to copy the Letter to Parents and Guardians for students to take home. A Letter to the Student begins Chapter 0 of the student text.

The rest of this book is organized into three main parts: Teaching Problem Solving, Teacher's Resources for Chapters 1 to 17, and Answers to Problem Sets.

1. TEACHING PROBLEM SOLVING

Here you'll find discussion about how to organize a problem-solving course, including suggestions for how to conduct the class on a daily basis, ideas and activities for fostering cooperative group work, and suggestions for assessing your students' problem-solving work.

2. TEACHER'S RESOURCES FOR CHAPTERS 1 TO 17

Teacher's Resources for Chapters 1 to 17 include:

Chapter Overview

A summary of the key points in the chapter, with some concepts amplified and comments on didactic strategies for these materials. Here you'll also find notes on problems from the text.

Problems from the Text

The problems from the text are reproduced together on pages that can be used as copymasters. When it's time for students to work on a text problem, you can ask them to close their books and instead work off this copy so that they won't be tempted to read ahead to the solutions without first trying the problem. Cut the copies in strips if you wish to hand out just one problem at a time.

Questions from the Reading

These are questions for reading comprehension and building group communication skills. Use them to be sure the students are reading the text. Questions are asked about the solutions to the problems in the text to be sure the students learned what they should have in reading the solution. There are Questions from the Reading for Chapters 1 to 3 only. These are meant primarily as a crutch and catch-up for students who have not yet developed their reading skills to the point where they can read simple technical text. You can use these questions however you want to, but we have two suggestions for using them effectively.

A. Hand the questions out to each group and have each group answer them, either individually or as a group to turn in or just to discuss.

B. Use some or all of the questions in a whole class discussion about the reading.

Problem Set A, Version 2

These problems are similar to the ones from Problem Set A in the text. Handing out a sheet of problems for the students to do has not proven effective. The students need to take time to ponder and discuss any problem that is assigned to them. Use these problems sparingly if and when you need an extra problem for groups or for a problem of the day. They can be written on the board, or, if the problems are really long, you can duplicate and distribute them. You can also use some of these problems for extra practice if your students are having difficulty with the strategy.

Problem Sets B, Versions 2 to 4

Like the Problem Sets B in the text, these problem sets call upon strategies from the chapter they appear in or from previous chapters. Students are expected to choose appropriate strategies. For this reason, Problem Sets B don't appear until Chapter 3. As Problem Set B is the most important component of student evaluation, these versions are provided so that you can use different problems in successive semesters. For example, you could use the Problem Sets B in the text for the fall semester, then use Version 2 in the spring. Reserve Versions 3 and 4 for the following year. Thus you have two years' worth of fresh problems.

3. ANSWERS TO PROBLEM SETS

All of the answers to Problem Sets are organized into two main sections: Answers to Text Problem Sets and Answers to Teacher's Resource Book Problem Sets. The first section includes answers to Problem Sets A and B for each chapter in the student text. The second section has answers for the extra problem sets found in this Teacher's Resource Book, also organized by chapter.

Answers to text problems whose solutions are described can, of course, be found in the text and are not included here.

Letter to Colleagues

This is not a book. It is a course. The course was developed at the Academy of Math, Science and Engineering at Luther Burbank High School in Sacramento, California. Written and oral communication skills are an important emphasis of the course. Students practice these skills in presentations, group interaction, and written solutions.

The course has been very carefully written and tested, and we are aware of no other math class like it. Teaching the course requires a high degree of interest on the part of the teacher. Taught well, this will most likely be your favorite class, and a majority of your students will say it was the best class they ever took. Your students will become much better problem solvers and more willing to take risks. Subsequent math courses with these students can be taught very differently.

This is not a course for you to show your students how smart you are. Although there will be times when you want your students to see you struggle with a problem you have not solved, for the most part you want to let the students solve the problems. Your role is to guide students in developing their math and communication skills. You should plan on solving all of the problems yourself, though, outside of class. We think you will enjoy it.

There will also be a significant change in your students' attitudes. Many will start to enjoy the challenge of this class and many will come to see themselves as mathematically enabled. The classroom atmosphere you create is an important consideration in this process. An atmosphere of competitiveness is very destructive. Students must feel that it's okay to be wrong and it's safe to ask questions—that they have permission to be different and that divergent thinking is not only accepted but encouraged.

You will often need to get out of the students' way. Students may do things differently than you would or even in ways you think are incorrect. But resist correcting them. This is a necessary part of the process for developing students' communication and problem-solving skills.

Good luck teaching this unique new course. We hope you have as much fun with it as we have.

Sincerely,

Ted Herr

Ken Johnson

Letter to Parents and Guardians

Your student is enrolled in a radically different math class. This class was designed around the concepts of problem-solving, critical thinking, written communication, and oral communication.

This class is like no other you or your student has seen before. Students who have taken this course have achieved tremendous amounts of growth in the above areas. There is no reason why the same shouldn't occur in this class.

Your student will be bringing home mathematical problems: some recreational and some serious applications. These problems all provide practice using real-life problem-solving strategies. As the course develops, you will find that the problems get much tougher. Furthermore, the book will highlight examples of real people who use these strategies in their work.

You may wish to work with your student on the assignments. We strongly encourage this, as we are developing the skill of working with other people, and parents and guardians are definitely considered people! You should be warned, however, that in order to best help your student, you will need to get in on the ground floor. Start the book as your student starts the book. You may find the problems fun to work and mentally stimulating. You may also find strategies that can be applied to your own job.

We encourage the students to get together to work on the problems and the solution write-ups. We also encourage the students to exchange phone numbers so that they can call one another to work on these problems. We hope that your student will be able to work with other students as much as possible within the confines of your family rules.

This course is an academic course. We estimate that each student will spend five to seven hours per week outside of class solving problems and writing up solutions. We believe that each student will develop skills that will last a lifetime.

Contents

TEACHING PROBLEM SOLVING

Philosophy and Goals

WE FEEL THAT problem solving is very important. We also feel that good problem-solving skills don't necessarily come naturally but can be taught. Students need lots of opportunities to practice problem-solving strategies. Then they need to learn how to choose an appropriate strategy to solve a given problem.

Our guess is that teachers reading this are somewhere between fair and good problem solvers. Most of us probably learned a lot of strategies on our own. We developed them from within with minimal outside impetus. It may seem that a student loses something by not being left alone to develop problem-solving skills. We disagree. Just as some athletes may be naturally good at what they can do, they are better when they're coached. This is also true of problem-solving athletes.

We often hear the call to "integrate problem solving into the regular math courses." Our response is that (1) it's hardly happening anywhere; (2) where it is happening, it isn't enough; and (3) students still see traditional math topics as the point of their math courses—not problem solving. This would be okay if students were already good at problem solving, but before that it gives them too many things to concentrate on. Should they concentrate on the math content, or on problem-solving strategies? They can't do both from the start. They *can* do both if they're already good problem solvers.

This course teaches more strategies than come up naturally in even the best problem-solving-integrated math courses. For example, an algebra course may employ guess and check, patterns, working backwards, and subproblems. Unit analysis may also be touched on. Geometry uses diagrams, subproblems, and eliminating possibilities. An advanced algebra course may touch on easier, related problems. But students may never be exposed to systematic lists, matrix logic, or using manipulatives. And strategies that do arise in other courses won't be explored to their fullest extent.

This course is designed to give students a firm problem-solving foundation. It also teaches them to think and work together, present solutions orally to the whole class, and write-up detailed solutions. In other words, it helps to prepare them for life.

Background

We developed and first taught a one-semester problem-solving course at Luther Burbank High School in Sacramento, California, in 1985. Ken Johnson has taught the course at Sierra Community College since 1991. We designed the course for upper-grade high school and community college students who have completed a year of algebra. The algebra prerequisite is not so much a content requirement as an experience requirement; the problem-solving course is not easy, and requires a certain level of maturity and "stick-to-it-iveness" for students to produce the expected outcomes. College-intending students should benefit greatly from the course, both when they take college entrance exams and when they take more advanced courses in which they employ the problem-solving strategies they've learned. And for students not intending to go to college, this problem-solving course is likely to be the most relevant mathematics course they'll take.

Overview of the Course and Textbook

STUDENTS USING *Problem Solving Strategies* learn a different strategy and its substrategies in each chapter. Each chapter is designed to take about a week, so by the end of the semester, students will learn 15 to 20 or even more problem-solving strategies and substrategies.

Each strategy is described at the beginning of the chapter, along with "real-life" examples of its utility. Students are then presented with a problem and asked to close the book and try to solve the problem. Complete solutions follow these text problems using the strategy presented in the chapter. Most solutions are presented from a student's point of view, using diagrams, charts, lists, or other mathematics symbols, with commentary and explanation provided at every step. These problems and solutions form the body of each chapter. Certain problems reappear at various places throughout the text in order to demonstrate multiple approaches to the same problem. It's important that students learn that there are often many ways of solving a problem. Require students to read the text. Assigning about four pages each night is reasonable, though the breaks should follow the natural breaks in the text explanations.

Using the Problem Sets

Besides the text problems used to model a strategy, two additional problem sets at the end of most chapters provide students with practice using problem-solving strategies as they learn them. Problem Set A consists of problems that can be solved using the strategy presented in the chapter. Students may work on them in groups during class, or individually at home as the Problem of the Day (POD). Problems of the Day are the subject of student presentations, described in more detail in the section Presentations and Problem of the Day that follows later in this book.

Problem Set B includes problems that can be solved by any of the strategies presented in that chapter or any previous chapter. For this reason, the first Problem Set B doesn't appear until Chapter 3. Problem Set B is intended to be used as a weekly problem set, with students required to write full explanations of their solution processes. The five Problem Set B problems may seem like too few. It's not—it's plenty. In problem solving, less is better than more. These strategies can be hard to learn and students need time to develop their skills. Don't overkill—make it fun. The students will probably spend 4 to 8 hours during the week on each Problem Set B. We have found it works best to assign Problem Set B on the Tuesday after you finish the chapter, to be due the following Tuesday. As you'll see in the Assessment section that follows, these problem sets are the most important component of a student's grade.

A Typical Week

In a typical week, you might start modeling the new strategy by working a few problems on the board. Let students try a problem from the text or Problem Set A in their groups. (If it's Monday and you didn't give a problem of the day on Friday, then there won't be any student presentations and you will have extra time for introducing and practicing the new strategy.) On Tuesday you could start with presentations, and then possibly have students do another problem or two in groups. On Wednesday, you will probably follow the same routine. We give one day a week, usually Thursday, to work on Problem Set B in class. The day before we don't give a problem of the day, so students have the whole period to work on their problem sets with their groups. On Friday, go back to more presentations and, if you so choose, another Problem of the Day. Since Problem Sets B don't appear until Chapter 3, you will probably have daily presentations for the first four weeks. A more detailed description of how you might conduct the first four weeks of class is found in a later section.

The Classroom Atmosphere

The focus throughout the course is on what students are doing, not what teachers can do. Students will spend a good part of their time engaged in problem solving, working in cooperative groups. Much of the first week of the course should be spent building skills students need to work effectively in groups. More discussion of groups, along with ideas for group-building activities, can be found in the Groups section of this book.

Most of the rest of students' class time will be spent presenting solutions and discussing those solutions. For this reason, it's essential that you establish a safe, supportive atmosphere so that all students feel comfortable in presenting. In a traditional class in which problem solving is the "hard part" of the course, students develop a lot of anxiety about it. And public speaking makes most people anxious. But students who feel supported by one another and who are given the opportunity to focus on improving their problem-solving skills without fear of reprisal when they're wrong will develop confidence in their ability and overcome these anxieties. Read the section on Presentations and Problem of the Day for more on how this safe atmosphere can be established.

Finally, we should mention that our students have accused us of using "bait-and-switch" tactics in this course. You and your students should be warned that the course starts out quite easy, but gets harder fast, starting in Chapter 3. Some students complain good-naturedly that they were "lured" into an easy course for the first two chapters before we "switched" it for a tough course. We feel the advantage to starting easy is that students gain confidence and overcome anxiety. These first two or three weeks can set the tone for the course. Once students feel like capable problem solvers, they're ready for the greater problem-solving challenges to come.

presentations and the problem of the day

ALMOST EVERY DAY (with the possible exception of Friday) in first quarter, and about half the time in second quarter, you will give a Problem of the Day (POD) at the end of the period. Assign the problem with about three minutes left in class and have the students copy down the assignment. PODs will generally come from Problem Set A or from the Problem Set A, Version 2 in the Teacher's Resource materials. Students should be told that they should expect to work on the problem of the day each day for about 10 to 20 minutes.

When Problem Sets B start, you may wish to give students one class period to work on the problem set in class (usually about two days after giving the assignment). In order to maximize the class time to work, you probably won't give a POD the day before. We also recommend not giving a POD the day before the Problem Set B is due. Thus, you'll usually assign about three POD's per week during the second half of the course.

At the beginning of the class period allow students who are doing presentations time to go to the board to prepare their solutions to the Problem of the Day. You will find that students start arriving for class early so that they can get a good space on the board. Note: You need a classroom that has lots of boards, preferably on every wall. During the first few weeks, have students write their names and say their name when they start presenting to help the class learn everyone's name. If your board space can't accommodate all the people who want to present solutions every day, you can pass out blank overhead transparencies and overhead projector pens. Whatever solution you find, don't waste time having students work on a single board one at a time, erasing between presentations.

During this time you may want to walk around the room and check off the Problem of the Day for everyone else who did it. Then have everyone sit down, and call up the students one at a time to give presentations of their solutions. Each presentation should last about one minute. Insist that each person give a clear explanation of how they solved the problem, not just their answer. Even if the student essentially solved it the same way as a previous presenter, he or she needs to explain the solution as if no one else had presented it. When the explanation is finished, allow the presenter time to field questions from the class. You may want to say something like, "Any questions for Tina?" If there are none, you can say, "Thank you, nice job," or something like that. Don't make any further comment, whether positive, negative, or correcting.

Presentations will probably take between 15 and 25 minutes of the period.

It is important that wrong answers are presented too. Don't allow the students to avoid presenting incorrect solutions. Often very productive debates center around what the right answer is. These debates would never occur if only right answers were allowed to be presented.

You must create a safe, supporting atmosphere so that all students feel comfortable in presenting. Don't allow students to criticize each other or ask questions like, "Why didn't you do it this way?" Questions should be directed toward what the student did.

Also, do not get in a dialog with each student as they are presenting. Let her or him talk to the class and the class only. This will build their confidence in public speaking and take the focus away from you. Remind the class often that they are to address the class and not you.

After all the presentations have been made, you may want to briefly summarize them, but do not give your solution. Even if the students could gain some valuable insight, the short-term opportunity is not worth the long-term loss. The students must not think that you are going to rescue them from incorrect solutions presented. Even if no student challenges incorrect work, you must let it slide. If they believe that the teacher will take care of mopping up messes, they won't be concerned about doing it themselves. You must not give your method for solving a problem, even if the students didn't come close to the most effective manner. In order for divergent thinking to be encouraged, you must value it. That includes not setting the stage for your thinking to be competing with that of the students. This approach will build confidence in your students, and they will start to look to themselves as problem solvers, rather than looking to you as the ultimate word on everything. Do mention the variety of solutions. It's nice to summarize the similarities and differences between the different approaches. Students will ask you if they are right or who is right if there are multiple answers. Resist the urge to tell them. If they are unsure who is right, let them discuss it in groups and maybe carry it over to the next day. Avoid telling them that their answers are correct. We have never given a problem that was missed by everyone.

Evaluating the Problem of the Day

The Problem of the Day generates two different grades: One grade is for doing the problem; the other grade is for presenting. Each of these grades can count for up to 15% of the total grade in the course.

To give the students credit for doing the problem, walk around the room during the first few minutes of class as the presenters are writing on the board. Simply check off in the roll book who did the problem. We do allow these problems to be made up after absences, as it is important for everyone to do every problem assigned. The solution does not have to be correct to get credit. If a student gives a less than honest effort, then he or she will need to re-work it and turn it in later.

The presentation points are separate. Give each student that presents a presentation a point. Write this in your roll book also as a 1 with a circle around it, differentiating it from the check that a student gets for just doing the problem. A circled 1 then represents a presentation and credit for doing the problem. We require a certain number of presentations for various grades. The standard we tell our students at the beginning of the semester is that they have to do one presentation every two weeks to get a C in presentations. If they do more, they get a higher grade. At the end of the semester, we usually give 7 points for each of the first 5 presentations and 1 point for each presentation after that, up to a total of 50 points. So a student who does 5 presentations gets 35 out of 50 points, which is 70%. Note, this is less than one presentation every two weeks. However, one every two weeks would work out to be about eight presentations, garnering 38 points ($7 \times 5 + 1 \times 3$) which is 76%—still a C. Ten presentations gets 80%, fifteen gets 90%, and twenty gets 100% for the presentation grade. You should adjust these grades as necessary depending on the size of your class and the number of opportunities for presentations. There will probably be opportunities for presentation about 50 times (roughly an average of 3 per week) during the semester.

If your class has more than 25 students, don't allow a person to present 3 days in a row. The reason for this is that there will be several students who want to present all the time, and they tend to monopolize the available board space. Some students are easily intimidated and won't go to the board without some prodding from you. Keep careful track and remind those students of their obligation to do one presentation every two weeks. The first few presentations are the toughest. After that, most students are willing to go to the board at any time. Creating the safe atmosphere described earlier is vital to many of your students' willingness to present. As you walk around the room checking for work, take notice of the student who has not done many presentations. If their solution looks interesting (and correct), encourage them to put it on the board. This will give shy students a chance to present their best work and will give them confidence in presenting.

groups

THIS CLASS IS BUILT around groups. The teacher's role is often just to stay out of the way. If you have rarely taught using groups, this will be a major change in approach.

This course emphasizes process more than answer. The journey is more interesting than the final destination. There are very few problems that can be approached in only one way. Mathematics teaching in general is often directed by a teacher, and students merely follow the teacher's examples. *Problem solving develops better when the students have to determine their own direction through a problem.*

Allowing the students to work together may seem strange. You may wonder what individual students actually can do by themselves. We believe after you have used groups for awhile, you will probably feel more comfortable about that issue. For this course, we recommend that you encourage the students to work together. You may wish to give an occasional quiz of one or two problems for each student to do individually, but we rarely find that necessary.

What are the benefits of using groups?

Students often feel intimidated about asking questions of the teacher when they don't understand. A small group of four students is much less intimidating, and most students will feel free to admit that they are confused among a small group of their peers.

Many problems in this course are very difficult, and most students could not solve them completely alone. However, when four minds get together to solve one problem, ideas feed other ideas and solutions are attained more easily. There is a tremendous benefit in observing someone else's thinking process. We teachers often fool ourselves into believing that the students always achieve this insight into thinking by watching us solve problems. The problem with that is we already know how to solve the problem and the students know this. When they observe a peer's thinking processes, they know that their peer is struggling to solve the problem just as they are. Groups also allow for more on-task behavior than standard seating. When a class is motivated and working, the students are close to 100% on-task. The learning in groups is active learning, not passive learning. Students are also learning valuable life skills and job skills. People who can work well with others have good tools for success in their careers.

Research into cooperative group work indicates that students learn more, retain it better, and have a better attitude about school and about themselves. You may also find that students used to working in groups are more likely to work together outside of class.

How should I arrange my classroom?

The physical arrangement of the classroom is very important. A sample class arrangement is shown below.

Suppose your classroom has six rows of desks, with six desks in each row. These thirty-six desks can easily be organized into nine groups of four. Students turn their desks sideways and face each other.

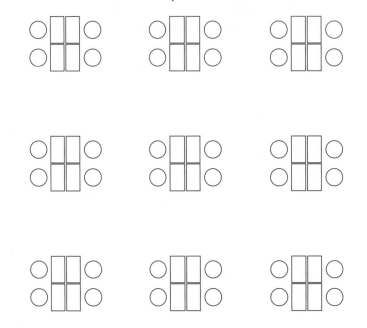

If you walk around the center group, you will walk next to every group and be able to listen in on every group. You should constantly move through the room in different ways though, to be sure that you are not ignoring anyone. Do not just stay at your desk or in one part of the room.

Suppose your class has eight rows of five desks. This causes a little more of a problem. If you have 32 students or less, just make eight groups (or less). If you have 36 students, you may want to add one student to each of the back groups and have four groups of four and four groups of five. You may also want to try to create a ninth group in whatever section of the room that has the most space.

Be creative if your classroom situation is less than desirable. But don't use a bad classroom situation as an excuse to not try groups. Virtually any classroom can achieve as good or better space and traffic efficiency with desks arranged in groups, whereas the class will really suffer if students are always sitting in rows. With practice, the conversion from rows to groups or from groups to rows can be done in less than a minute.

Desks must touch. You should not be able to walk between members of a group. If students are not sitting close enough together, then ask them to move or move their desks yourself. Every group member must be able to communicate with each other.

If the desks are close together, then you should also have room to walk between different groups. You should consciously set up a walking path around the room that brings you next to every group in one circuit around the room.

How should I select students for the groups?

We do it randomly, by one of the following methods. We change groups approximately every two weeks—more often at the beginning so students get to know more classmates faster.

1. Take a deck of cards and separate out enough cards for the number in the class. For example, if you have 24 students, you would use the Aces, twos, threes, fours, fives, and sixes. Then shuffle the cards and give a card to each student. All the aces are in one group, the twos in another, etc.
2. Have each student fill out a 3" by 5" card with their name, address, phone number, etc. Keep these all semester. Use these cards to change groups. Shuffle the cards and deal them out, four per group. Then call off the names of each group.
3. Go around the room and count off, giving each person a number according to how many groups you want. If you have 32 students and you want eight groups, count off 1 to 8, then start again at 1. Make sure the counting off happens randomly.

What if the number of students in my class is not a multiple of four?

In general, it is better to form groups of five rather than groups of three. A group of three loses a lot of communication avenues and is decimated if one person is absent.

What do I do about absences?

If one person is absent, leaving a group of three, it is probably okay for one day. If two people are absent, you will probably want to move the two remaining people to another group, or split them up and put them in two different groups. You may also want to do this if there are several groups of three one day.

How often should I change groups:

Change groups once a week for the first few weeks, then every two weeks or so after that. Changing groups often early in the course allows students to learn the names of more students more quickly. It also lets them experience multiple viewpoints and gives them the idea that everyone in the class can contribute something to the group process. If you leave students in groups too long at the beginning of the semester, they may get too comfortable and resist changing groups, fearing that a new group won't be as productive.

What is the teacher's role?

The teacher's main role is to get out of the way. You are no longer "The Sage on the Stage." Your new role is that of "The Guide on the Side." Avoid interrupting a group to input your opinion or give them direction. Do keep them on task, however. You need to guide, not direct. Steer them in a better direction if they get way off track and if you don't think they will get back on. However, lots of times students will get back on track by themselves, so you have to let them try. The kind of communication and thinking that occurs under these situations is invaluable. It is very difficult to know when to stay out of their way and when to interrupt. If you can't tell what to do, it's better to leave them alone. Ask questions, don't give answers. Avoid telling students whether or not they are right, because that tends to shut off their thinking. In order for the students to become better thinkers, they need to be able to evaluate situations (problems/answers) for themselves. If they find that the teacher will always be there to provide a crutch, they will learn to limp.

Group Building Activities

AT THE BEGINNING of the course, you should do some activities that encourage students to work together. Two very good activities are the Color Square game and the Digit Place game described separately. Some other good activities follow. The first three activities help students get to know one another and learn each other's name.

Interview: When you first move into new groups, have the students pair up and interview their partner. Allow about 1 to 2 minutes, and then have them switch. Then each person has to introduce the partner to the rest of the group.

Fascinating Facts: On the first day of class, have each student write down a fascinating fact about themselves. It can be anything: hobbies, interests, sports, places they have been, where they work, and so on. Insist that the facts be publishable. Put one in for yourself, too. Then type up the list of facts and distribute one to each student. Two or three times during the next few days, let them have some time to roam around the room and discover other people's facts. Don't let them just tell each other their fact. Treat it as a game, and model good questions. For example: "Does your fact have to do with travel? Does it have to do with pets? Does it have to do with hobbies or interests?"

Name Test: After three or four weeks give your class a low key name test. Have everyone stand in a large circle around the classroom or outside. Then pick someone to go first. They say their name. Then the next person says his or her name and the name of the person who came before. The third person has three names to say, the fourth four, etc. After the list gets up to fifteen or so names, cut it back a little by telling the next person they only have to go back as far as John, who is maybe standing halfway back. After finishing the entire circle, start back with the first people again so that the names from the last part of the circle get mentioned more times.

Teamwork: Have the students individually try to make as many words as possible out of the letters of the word "teamwork." After a few minutes, allow them to work together as a group.

Making Twenty-Four (or some other number): Have the students individually try to make 24 using one or more mathematical operations or symbols or functions. Then have them work together in their group.

The 1994 Game (or whatever year it is): Have them try to make the numbers from 1 to 100 (or some other smaller range) using the digits 1, 9, 9, and 4 in that order (you can eliminate the order restriction to make the game easier).

Examples:

$1 + 9 - 9 + 4 = 5$

$1^{994} = 1$

$1 + (9 - 9)4 = 1$

$(1 + 99) \div 4 = 25$

Keep a wall chart with the number and the solution. As students discover solutions for the numbers from 1 to 100, they can write them on the chart.

The Color Square Game (a.k.a. Rainbow Logic)

The Color Square Game is one of the best logic activities that we know. It never fails to excite the students tremendously. It can be played as a whole class, in small groups, or with a combination of both, which is the way we use it. It is an easy game to understand, but it is very challenging to play.

The reasoning that students do is quite sophisticated. They also get practice in explaining their reasoning to others.

The rules of the game are simple. Use a three-by-three square like the one shown at right. Color the squares with three colors—red, blue, and green—with three squares of each color. Squares of the same color must be contiguous (joined on a side). Do not show students your colored squares but draw a blank three-by-three square on the board or overhead projector. It is up to the students to logically figure out what is in each square.

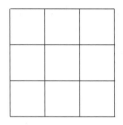

Students begin asking for the colors in particular rows or columns. For example, a student might ask, "What is in row 1?" You might reply, "Row 1 contains 2 blues and 1 green" and write "2B, 1G" next to row 1. Do not divulge the order of the 2 blues and 1 green. It is best if you can always reply in alphabetical order. Ask if anyone knows the color of a particular square. Tell students not to guess, but rather figure things out logically. Always ask why the student believes the square is that color. If the student can prove that a square must be a particular color, then fill in that square. We like to let the students explain their reasoning to their group. After all squares that can be filled in are filled in, allow the students to ask another question about another row or column. Continue the game in this fashion until the students deduce the colors of all nine squares. They should be told that they are trying to find the answer using as few clues as possible.

Play the three-by-three game a few times. Then graduate to the four-by-four game where there are 16 squares: four of each of four colors. This is a much better game. We don't recommend the five-by-five game.

The four-by-four game can be played in a number of ways. It is a good idea to discuss with the students how the pieces can be arranged. In fact, a good exercise for the students is to ask them to find all of the ways that four squares can be put together so that they are touching along at least one entire side.

Manipulatives will make the game and the associated thinking accessible to more students quickly. Give each group four squares of each color and have them draw a large four-by-four square on a piece of paper. The group manipulates the colored squares to try out different arrangements. Someone else in the group should have a four-by-four square written down to write in their conclusions.

The introductory game is played with the teacher making the solution then asking for a student to request a column or row. That one particular clue is posted and then discussed until it has been exhausted. Let students discuss possible conclusions in their groups first. Then have several students explain their group's reasoning to the class. Keep asking if anyone knows more squares than are shown. When no more squares can be deduced, let someone ask for another clue. Depending on the clue, this may be quick or it may take a few minutes.

The following is a sample game. There are four squares of each color: red, yellow, blue, and green. Each one will be abbreviated in the clues with the first letter.

In this game, the first clue asked for is the fourth column. This column is comprised of one yellow and three greens.

The colors are not necessarily given in order or out of order. This clue in particular would generate a fair amount of discussion as to where the yellow goes. At some point, a student should be able to deduce that the yellow must go at either the top or the bottom of the row because if it were placed in the second or third row there would not be enough greens to provide a contiguous figure.

The students are required to be able to prove which squares are a certain color, not just to provide possibilities.

As the students explore the possibilities on this square they will realize that whenever there are three squares available and two are a given color, the middle square must be that color.

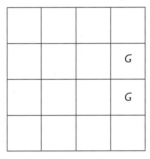

The next clue asked for was the second row. The students should be able to conclude that the middle square of the three squares remaining in the row is blue because otherwise the blues could not connect.

At this point the next clue the students asked for was the fourth row. Using this in conjunction with the fourth column, it was quickly evident that the last three of the fourth row were all yellow, and that the first one must be red.

				Y, 3G
				G
R, G, 2B		B		G
				G
R, 3Y	R	Y	Y	Y

That will also lead to filling the top square in the fourth column as green. As the students examine this set-up more, it's likely that they will realize that the red in the second row must appear in the first column as it cannot be in the third column and still connect to the red in the fourth row. That will also lead them to conclude that the square in between must be red in order for the reds to connect.

				Y, 3G
				G
R, G, 2B	R	B		G
	R			G
R, 3Y	R	Y	Y	Y

At this point the game becomes more difficult, but there are actually two more squares that can be proven. The first one is the remaining square for the second row. The next one is the first square in the second column. The proof of that is an indirect proof: By assuming in succession that the square in question is either red, yellow, or green, you find that it cannot be any of those because in each case those colors cannot connect to that square; thus the only possible remaining color is blue.

				Y, 3G
		B		G
R, G, 2B	R	B	B	G
	R			G
R, 3Y	R	Y	Y	Y

Choosing the next clue at this point has to be done carefully. Row 3 must contain the fourth yellow and could contain the fourth blue, green, or red. If it contains the missing blue and yellow, then asking for that clue will be inconclusive as to their exact location. The second column would also be inconclusive if it shows two blues and two yellows, as either of the two squares in column 3 could go to either blue or green. Asking for the clue for row 1 would tell us where the final red goes, but if the red is in that row, we will have the same problem with where the blue and the yellow are placed. So at this point, there is no guarantee that the next guess will end the game. At this point you can let each group decide on their own what to guess next, and walk around the room giving each group their own clue.

The next clue request in this game happened to be the second column.

The game basically ends now by filling in each of the colors in succession: the missing yellow, the missing green, and the missing blue.

	2B Y, R		Y, 3G
	B		G
R, G, 2B — R	B	B	G
R	R		G
R, 3Y — R	Y	Y	Y

The completed game is shown at right.

After you've played the game several times with the whole class, let students play the game in their groups. One person makes up the solution, and the other three solve it. The tendency for the students is to be too willing to make false conclusions. The teacher needs to set the tone by having each person who makes an assertion prove it step-by-step.

	2B Y, R		Y, 3G
B	B	G	G
R, G, 2B — R	B	B	G
R	R	Y	G
R, 3Y — R	Y	Y	Y

In another session, have students play the game in pairs in order to ensure that each student is an active participant. Suggest students play the game at home with friends and family.

The game can be developed a couple of steps further. The examples below can be written on the board or on an overhead projector with the instructions to "fill in as many squares as you can prove."

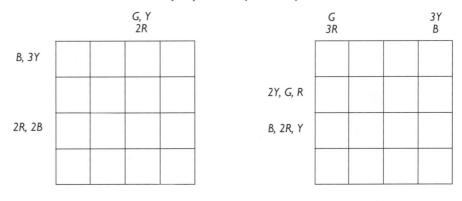

The problem on the left has two squares that cannot be proved, and the one on the right can be entirely proved.

Below is another variation:

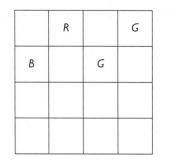

	R		G
B		G	

		R	
Y		B	
	G		

Fill in as many squares as you can prove are a given color.

The rainbow logic game develops step-by-step reasoning, small group interaction, the concept of proof by contradiction (indirect proof), and an atmosphere of questioning and substantiating.

See *Make it Simpler*, by Carol Meyer and Tom Sallee (Addison Wesley, 1985) for more information about Color Square.

The Digit-Place Game

A good group-building game is the Digit-Place Game. The game exists in several forms, including Fermi-Pico-Bagel, a letter version called Jotto, and a commercial version called Mastermind. This version appears in a number of sources, including *Make It Simpler,* by Carol Meyer and Tom Sallee (Addison Wesley, 1985).

The game is relatively simple to learn. One person chooses a three-digit number with each digit different. The others make guesses, and hints are provided by the person who knows the number. The hints relate how many of the digits are correct and how many digits are in the correct place. The hints do not include which digits are correct or in the right place.

As an example, let's use the number 487 as the correct number. The person running the game chooses a number and does not reveal it to anyone. In this chart, the "D" stands for "digit" and the "P" stands for "place."

Guess	D	P
541	1	0

The 4 is a correct digit, but it is not in the correct place. The person guessing has no way of knowing which digit is the correct one.

Guess	D	P
541	1	0
390	0	0

Now there are no digits correct, so none can be in the correct place.

Guess	D	P
541	1	0
390	0	0
267	1	1

The 7 is both a correct digit and in the correct place, hence a 1 is marked in both columns. The people playing do not know for which digit the tallies were made.

Guess	D	P
541	1	0
390	0	0
267	1	1
880	1	1

The 8 in the tens place is both correct and in the right place.

At this point, all digits have appeared at least once. The second guess has probably been the most helpful, because that indicated that all of those digits are not in the right answer. Since zero is one of those digits, when it re-appears in the fourth guess, we know it is not the one that supplied the mark in the digit and place columns. Therefore the 8 is definitely one of the numbers, and it is also in the first or second position.

In the first guess, one of the digits from 541 is correct. The tallies on the third guess indicate that one of the digits of 267 is also correct.

We will continue guessing, though we will not necessarily be demonstrating the most efficient method for reaching the number. That is left for the reader to discover!

Guess	D	P
541	1	0
390	0	0
267	1	1
880	1	1
856	1	0

None in the right place helps—the 8 must belong in the center position. Neither the 5 nor the 6 is correct as the 8 is known to be the digit that produced the tally for a correct digit.

Guess	D	P
541	1	0
390	0	0
267	1	1
880	1	1
856	1	0
481	2	2

The 8 produces one tally, the other must be produced by the 4 as we know that the one is not in the correct position from the clues for the first guess. Thus the number is known to be 48x at this point.

Guess	D	P
541	1	0
390	0	0
267	1	1
880	1	1
856	1	0
481	2	2
487	3	3

By using the third guess and clues, you can see that the 7 is the correct digit since the hint also indicates that the correct digit on this problem is in the correct position.

This game has a myriad of guessing strategies that will allow the students to get the number within a certain number of guesses. The game can also be modified to allow numbers that have two identical digits or even three identical digits (such as 232 and 777).

Play this game with your class a few times. After each guess, allow students a few minutes to discuss possible conclusions in their groups. Ask a few students to summarize conclusions reached so far. Have another student make a guess and repeat the process. After playing as a whole class for a while, you should have students play this in their groups. One person runs each game by determining the number and providing the digit-place clues. Have them rotate the person running the game. The students should next play it in pairs, to ensure full participation by all.

The game can also be done as paper and pencil exercises in which you provide a set number of guesses and clues, and the students must look through those hints to find the most useful ones in order to solve the problem.

The game can also be given as a homework assignment: "Play this game with somebody in your household ten times." Playing without a time limit may result in them playing for a long time and developing strategies at home.

The game can also be done where the students make ten guesses without getting any clues. The game director then provides clues for all ten guesses. The players must declare the correct number on the eleventh guess. This helps the students focus on guessing strategies instead of on the immediate task of determining the number.

You should actively encourage the students to look for guessing strategies and have the students verbalize these as they develop them. Verbalizing the strategy is important in helping students to develop precision in their mathematical communication.

One effective strategy is to write down the digits from one to ten. As you confirm that one number is valid, it gets circled. Cross off any number that you can eliminate from consideration.

Here are a couple of additional digit-place examples. Good luck finding the answers.

Guess	D	P		Guess	D	P
158	1	0		837	1	0
269	2	0		295	1	0
370	0	0		160	1	0
482	0	0		416	0	0
591	2	0		905	1	1
725	0	0		874	1	0
803	0	0		529	1	0
452	0	0		604	1	1
398	0	0		321	1	0
965	2	1		537	1	0

A SSESSMENT OVER the last few years has moved to become more holistic. Determining what students can do mathematically means looking beyond what students can compute to how well students reason and communicate. This change is driven partly by the availability of calculators and computers. At this point, those two tools can compute faster and more accurately than a human. But humans are better at reasoning. We must, therefore, no longer consider computation as the major focus of teaching mathematics. We must shift our focus toward teaching mathematical reasoning.

This book is designed to do just that—teach mathematical reasoning. An integral part of this is to move toward a view of assessment as part of course instruction.

One of the goals of this course is to develop the students' communication skills, both in general and in particular when dealing with mathematical topics. Another goal is to develop their ability to solve problems. The solution write-ups and the method of assessing the write-ups are designed to further both of these goals.

A solution write-up is like a take-home test. The student has access to resources, including classmates and class notes. The final product should be excellent. Your feedback to students' write-ups is necessary to produce the desired changes in attitude and development of skills.

Overall Grading for the Course

T HERE ARE AS MANY ways of assigning grades as there are teachers. However, in a new course such as this it may be helpful for us to mention how we assigned grades. We split the course's evaluation components into four main categories: Problem Sets B were worth 60% of the total grade; problems of the day accounted for 15%, presentations, 15%, and the final, 10%.

Methods for grading Problem Set B are described in detail later in this section. Problems of the day and presentations (and how to score them) were described in detail previously. And the final, along with discussion of how to grade it, is found at the end of the Teacher's Resources.

These are only suggestions. We do suggest not giving tests (because of the time limit in solving a number of problems quickly), although an occasional one problem quiz would not be out of line. This would have to be factored into the mix. You may also want to give long term projects of big problems and grade these also. You may also want to give some sort of group participation grade. Again, there are many ways of grading.

Grading Problem Set B

STARTING IN Chapter 3, each chapter ends with a Problem Set B. The students should have one week to do the five problems and write them up and turn them in. We suggest following the grading rubric provided here the first time you teach the course. You may want to modify it as necessary the second time you teach the course to fit your students' particular needs.

Problem solving is difficult to test in a class period. The issue of testing is constrained by the time allotted for the class and by the fact that in the real world those who solve problems in their work are not required to do it on their own. Some of the best problem solving takes place when you consult with the right people. Part of problem solving is distillation time. You often need to let problems stew in the back of your mind for a while before you can solve them. For these reasons, we advocate no tests. Instead we rely on the problem sets as "take-home" tests.

As the semester wears on, students may start to feel more pressure about getting Problem Sets B in on time. To alleviate some of this pressure in the second part of the course, we experimented with allowing some Problem Sets B to be turned in by groups of two or three students. Our policy is to require students to turn in their first six problem sets B by themselves. (If a student hadn't turned in one or more problem sets, they would have to wait until they had turned in six of their own before they qualified.) After that, they can turn in one problem set in a group for each one they turn in by themselves. So after they've turned in seven by themselves, they can do one in a group, then one by themselves, then one in a group, and so on. They can also save up several group credits by doing several in a row by themselves (again, after the first six) and then doing several in a group. They still each need to solve all the problems, but they save time on writing them up. I required the writeups to be fairly divided among the group (as fairly as you can divide 5 by 2 or 3). The group also had to document with a Venn diagram how they allocated their time. A Venn diagram for a group of three would show three intersecting circles representing the three people. In regions that didn't overlap, they would write the time (working alone) spent by the individuals represented by those regions. Time spent working in pairs or with all three group members would be written in the appropriate intersecting regions. Every student in a group received the same score for a group problem set. The students appreciated the flexibility offered by the group option and it did save them time.

We also allow the scores of one or two Problem Sets B to be dropped at the end of the semester. This helps out the student who is generally a good student but has a bad week or two during the semester. If students do better on the two dropped problem sets than their group does on the final, you can allow them to exchange their scores on these sets for the final exam score.

We have provided two versions of a grading rubric. They are our adaptations of the grading system described by Randall Charles in his book *Problem Solving Experiences in Mathematics* (Addison Wesley Publishing, 1986). The system assigns point values to different parts of the problem-solving process. Using this rubric helps make the assessment more objective; it also helps the teacher give valuable feedback to students in a way that is directed toward specific course goals and expectations. You should go over the rubric with your students. Consider copying the rubric and handing it out to your students.

Version One

Grade the papers with an ordered quintuple of numbers (2, 2, 2, 2, 2) for a total of 10 points per problem.

A. Trying the Problem
    0—Does not try the problem at all.
    1—Tries a little.
    2—Gives a good attempt.
B. Understanding the Problem
    0—Completely misinterprets the problem.
    1—Misinterprets part of the problem.
    2—Shows complete understanding of the problem.
C. Choosing and Implementing a Solution Strategy
    0—Makes no attempt to solve or uses a totally inappropriate strategy.
    1—Chooses a partly correct strategy based on interpreting part of the problem correctly, or chooses a correct strategy and implements it poorly.
    2—Chooses a correct strategy that could lead to a correct solution if used without error, and implements it with minor errors or no errors.
D. Getting the Answer
    0—Gets no answer, fails to state the answer, or gets a wrong answer based on an inappropriate solution strategy.
    1—Makes copying error or computational error, or gets partial answer to a problem with multiple answers, or labels answer incorrectly.
    2—Gets correct answer, states it, and labels it properly.

E. Explanation
   0—Makes no explanation or incoherent explanation.
   1—Gives an incomplete explanation, or the explanation is hard to follow.
   2—Gives a clear, coherent explanation.

Explanation of Version One

A. The first two points are for trying. This is one case where the student can ask "Doesn't trying count?" and you can answer, "Yes, for two points." The idea is to encourage students to put enough down on paper so that they can get the full two points for "trying."

B. The third and fourth points are for demonstrating an understanding of the problem. Understanding (or misunderstanding) is generally conveyed to the teacher through the student's work, including the written explanation of the solution. Ideally the student is placing before you a comprehensive map of how he or she solved the problem. This map should also show you exactly where he or she made turns, both right and wrong.

C. The next pair of points is for choosing and implementing a reasonable strategy. As you will see as you go through the book, there are many ways to solve many of these problems. Some problems may be more easily worked with one strategy as opposed to some other strategy. On some problems there may be more than one good choice of strategy.

The student must, however, also implement the strategy. For example, choosing a systematic list may be appropriate for a problem, yet if the student does not implement the strategy correctly (i.e., the list is not very systematic), then the results will not be correct. The student would obviously lose points in both the strategy and answer categories.

D. The seventh and eighth points are for stating the correct answer explicitly. Part of this is to make sure that the student gets the right answer. That is important. It is also important that the student state the correct answer, as sometimes the question asked may be different from the one the student answers. An answer that appears somewhere in the work but is not explicitly stated lacks the authority of being the definitive answer. With practice and guidance, students will quickly learn to state their answers explicitly.

E. The final pair of points is for the explanation. The students' explanations should be well thought out and well communicated "maps" of the reasoning they did solving the problem. Not every detail is needed—students do not need to provide you with a "stream-of-consciousness" novel—rather, the explanation is an organized, concise retelling of the thoughts, assumptions, and understandings students developed while they solved the problem. This exercise in writing out mathematical reasoning will be helpful practice for all kinds of writing that students will be asked to do in school and in their careers.

Version Two

Grade the papers with an ordered quintuple of numbers (2, 2, 2, 2, 2) for a total of 10 points per problem.

A. Understanding the Problem

0—Completely misinterprets the problem.

1—Misinterprets part of the problem.

2—Shows complete understanding of the problem.

B. Choosing a Solution Strategy

0—Does not give evidence of using a strategy or uses a totally inappropriate strategy.

1—Chooses a strategy that could possibly lead to a correct solution or chooses a strategy that will get them part way through the problem but fails to change strategies when appropriate.

2—Chooses a correct strategy that could lead to a correct solution if used without error.

C. Implementing the Strategy

0—Makes no attempt to solve, uses a totally inappropriate strategy, or uses a correct strategy totally incorrectly.

1—Implements a partly-correct strategy based on interpreting part of the problem correctly, or chooses a correct strategy and implements it poorly.

2—Implements a correct strategy with minor errors or no errors.

D. Getting the Answer

0—Gets no answer, fails to state the answer, or gets a wrong answer based on an inappropriate solution strategy.

1—Makes copying error or computational error, or gets partial answer to a problem with multiple answers, or labels answer incorrectly.

2—Gets correct answer, states it, and labels it properly.

E. Explanation

0—Makes no explanation or incoherent explanation.

1—Gives an incomplete explanation, or the explanation is hard to follow.

2—Gives a clear, coherent explanation.

Explanation of Version Two

As you can see, version two is basically the same as version one, but the "trying" points have been eliminated and the "strategy" points have been split into two categories. Comments on the changes follow.

B. Choosing a Solution Strategy

A student would get a 1 rather than a 2 if he or she picked a strategy that is unwieldy or cumbersome, but could lead to a correct solution. You have to be careful here, because a student may use a strategy that you had not thought of, even though it is a perfectly reasonable strategy.

C. Implementing the Strategy

Here the focus is on how well they are using whatever strategy they picked.

Examples of Scored Student Work

The next five pages are facsimiles of actual student work on the Golf Match problem found in Chapter 5, Problem Set B of the student text.

GOLF MATCH

Clark, Chris, Doug, and Diana are standing on the first tee of their favorite golf course about to begin a best-ball of partners match. (A best-ball match pits two golfers against the other two golfers.) They are standing in a square, with two partners standing next to each other on the cart path facing the other two partners standing next to each other on the grass. This standing arrangement is typical of the beginning of a golf match. They shake hands and then they throw a tee in the air and let it hit the ground. Whoever it points to will tee off first. Clark is standing diagonally opposite Diana. Chris is facing the person whose name begins with the same letter as the person who will tee off first. Partners tee off one after the other. Who will tee off second?

These solutions were scored according to the Version 2 system. You might want to score them first yourself before you read this explanation. You'll find that the scoring is inevitably subjective at times, but if you're consistent, students should understand why they get the scores they do.

Jason and Brandy, whose papers received 10's, clearly understood the problem, chose an appropriate strategy (drawing a diagram), carried it out correctly, and stated their answers succinctly and completely. Their explanations are also clear and complete, including explanation of both possible answers.

Brandy showed a little more of her reasoning by drawing the arrows showing Diana and Clark at diagonals and arrows showing people standing opposite one another. She also mentioned this information in her explanation. Jason explained the partnership relationships. Note that even if you find one of these "perfect" papers better than the other, it should still be possible to score a 10 with a less than perfect paper.

Don only gets a 1 for understanding. He does understand that Diana and Clark are diagonally opposite each other, and he also understands that Chris is facing the person whose name begins with the same letter as the person who will tee off first. However, he ignores the information in the problem that states partners tee off one after the other. In his explanation he mentions a person who will tee off first and then moves across to the other team for the second person to tee off. Because of this misunderstanding, he gets the wrong answer and thus gets 0 points for the answer. His strategy is appropriate, he carries it out well, and his explanation is good, so he gets full credit in those areas.

Carina draws a diagram showing Diana and Clark diagonal from each other. However, she makes an assumption that Chris cannot be facing Clark because their names start with the same letter. The problem doesn't say this, so she loses a point for understanding. She gets 2 points for choosing an appropriate strategy, but her diagram isn't very good, and it only accounts for one possibility, so she only gets 1 point for carrying out the strategy. She does get the right answer, but it's not completely supported—she didn't allow for both possibilities—so she only gets one point for her partial answer. She gets full credit for her clear explanation.

Halee's paper is a good example of why you want your students to explain their reasoning in a paragraph or two. It is also a good example of why you need to stress to students that when you say they must show their work, you don't mean scratch work. Halee understands the problem and does show diagrams allowing for both possibilities (if you can find them). She correctly reasons through both possibilities to indicate the partnerships and teeing off order. She also states her answer explicitly (though, despite the stars, it is hard to find at the top of the paper). Thus she gets points for everything except the missing explanation.

Thanks to Ken Johnson's students Jason Reynolds, Don Elias, Halee Epling, Carina Euyen, and Randy Whittle for contributing the work copied here.

47

Jason R
Problem Set B
Chapter 5
October 5, 1993

#1
Draw A Diagram

Clark
Chris
Doug
Diana

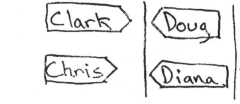

In this arrangement Chris is facing Diana. This means that Doug tees off first and his partner which is Diana tees off second.

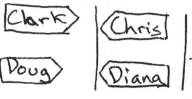

In this arrangement Chris is facing Clark. This means that Chris will tee off first, and his partner Diana will tee of second.

I drew a diagram for each of the possible arrangements and in both of them Diana tees off second.

zzzzz   10

41

Problem Set B
Chapter # 5

Brandy W
10-3-93

1. Golf Match

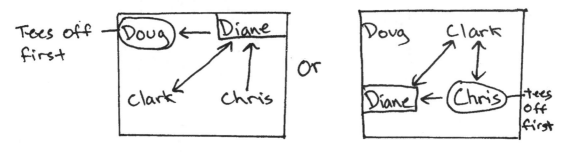

Diane is always second to tee
off. No matter who tees off first.
Diana is second.

In this instance, Clark
is diagonally across from
Diane and Chris is across
from the person who has
the same beginning letter
as the person who tees first.
Since Diane has the same
beginning letter in her name
as Doug, then Doug tees
off first and Diane second

𝟸𝟸𝟸𝟸𝟸

10

In this instance, Diane
is diagonally across from
Clark. Chris is directly
across from the person
who has the same
beginning letter in his
name as the person who
tees off 1st. Since Clark
is across from Chris,
Chris has the same letter
"C", therefore Chris
tees off 1st and Diane
tees off second.

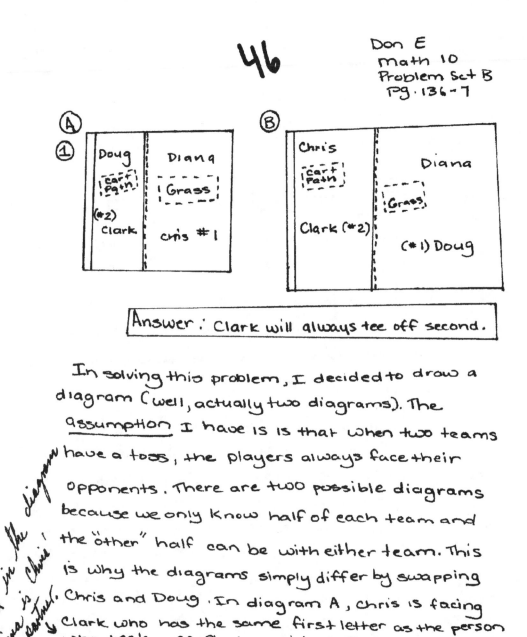

46

Don E
Math 10
Problem Set B
Pg. 136-7

Answer: Clark will always tee off second.

In solving this problem, I decided to draw a diagram (well, actually two diagrams). The <u>assumption</u> I have is is that when two teams have a toss, the players always face their opponents. There are two possible diagrams because we only know half of each team and the "other" half can be with either team. This is why the diagrams simply differ by swapping Chris and Doug. In diagram A, chris is facing Clark who has the same first letter as the person who tee's off first, which is Chris. Then clark would tee of second. In diagram B, Chris is facing Diana who has the same first letter as Doug who tees off first. Then moving across to the other team, Clark would once again tee-off second. Not to make this too confusing, but clark always tees off first for his own team.

But in the diagram Diana is Chris' partner.

The problem states partners tee off after one another

12202

7

37

Carina E
Oct 1, 1993

Ⅱ Golf Match

Clark } Doug

Chris } Diana

Doug will tee off first.

✱ Diana will tee off second.

Explainations: I drew a diagram for this problem showing Clark and Diana diagonal to each other. Which left me to figure out who Chris and Diana were teamed up with. From the clue that states that Chris is facing the person whose name starts with the same letter as the person who will start the game, I figured that Chris could not be facing Clark because that would mean that Chris would start first. So that means that Chris is standing opposite Diana. Chris is Clark's partner and Diana and Doug are partners. Therefore since Chris is facing Diana, Doug will start first. And since partners follow each other Diana will go second.

12112   7

(10/5 DUE)

WHO TEES OFF SECOND?

☆ DIANE tees 2nd ☆

Draw a diagram

Prob Set B pg 136-137 #1-5

Halee E.
16-5
PROBLEM
Set B
Chpt 5

1) Golf Match:

Names:
CLARK
CHRIS
DOUG
DIANA

2 golfers against two other golfers.

GRASS

KNOWN:
CLARK DIAGONAL TO DIANE
CHRIS FACES THE PERSON
whose 1st letter begins same as pers who tee's 1st

Many solutions to problem:?

1) Know that Clark ◦ Diane are always diagonal therefore they are never partners.
I made a list of the possible teams

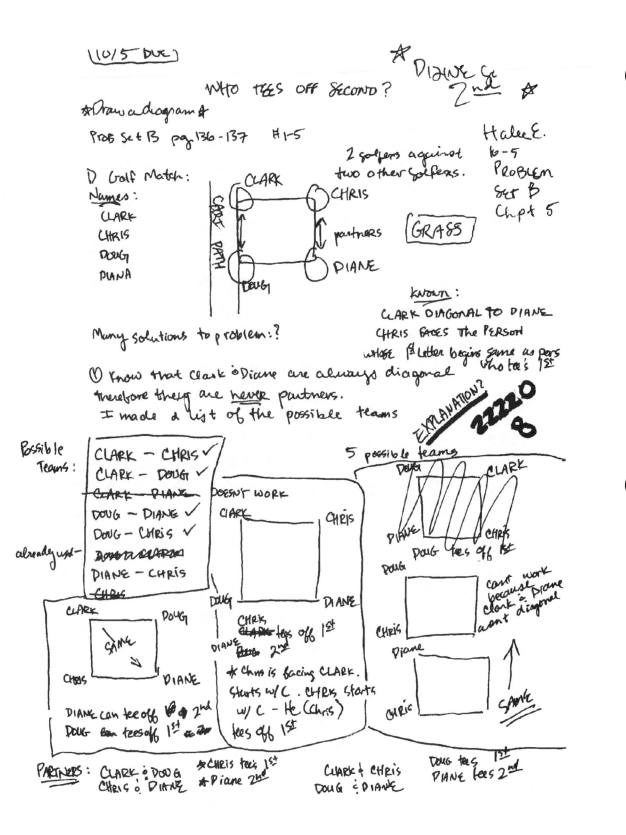

EXPLANATION? 2222.0 8

Possible Teams:

CLARK — CHRIS ✓
CLARK — DOUG ✓
~~CLARK — DIANE~~ DOESN'T WORK
DOUG — DIANE ✓
DOUG — CHRIS ✓
already used → ~~DOUG & CLARK~~
DIANE — CHRIS
~~CHRIS~~

5 possible teams

DOUG tees off 1st

can't work because Clark & Diane aren't diagonal

DIANE can tee off 1st & 2nd
DOUG can tees off 1st & 2nd

CHRIS, ~~CLARK~~ tees off 1st
DIANE tees 2nd

* Chris is facing CLARK.
Starts w/ C. CHRIS starts w/ C — He (Chris) tees off 1st

SAME

DIANE can tee off 1st & 2nd
DOUG can tees off 1st & 2nd

DOUG tees 1st
DIANE tees 2nd

PARTNERS: CLARK ◦ DOUG   *CHRIS tee's 1st
CHRIS ◦ DIANE   *Diane 2nd

CLARK & CHRIS
DOUG & DIANE

DOUG tees 1st
DIANE tees 2nd

34   TEACHING PROBLEM SOLVING

THE FIRST WEEK of the semester should be spent working on group dynamics and getting the students used to presenting solutions on the board. Helpful group dynamics activities include "The Color Square Game" and "The Digit-Place Game" described previously.

Also in the first week, introduce the Problem of the Day (POD). The Problem of the Day is one problem which you give at the end of class. The problems in Problem Set A at the back of each chapter are designed for this, but in the first week we suggest you use the problems from Chapter 0. The Problem of the Day was more fully explained in a previous section.

In the second week of class, you should start Chapter 1. A day-by-day description of the first two weeks follows.

Week 1

MONDAY

Introduce the course. We suggest you have the students fill out a three-by-five card with their name, address, phone number, and answers to some questions such as what their math background is, how they feel about math, whether they like puzzles and problem solving, how they feel about using groups, and things like that. Possibly have the students read the first page of Chapter 0. If you have time (we know there are a lot of other details to take care of on the first day), then put students in groups of four and do interviews as described in the Groups section. Give a problem of the day: We suggest the Soccer Game problem or the Elevator problem in Chapter 0. Also tell students to read Chapter 0.

TUESDAY

Begin the period with the presentation of the Problem of the Day. Encourage lots of people to present, as this will get them used to presenting. This should last about 20 to 30 minutes. If it goes longer, that's fine. Form groups of four. Tell them these groups will last for one or two weeks. Have students interview each other in pairs if they haven't already done so the day before. Play Color Square beginning with a three-by-three square and progressing to a four-by-four square with remaining time.

Choose another problem from Chapter 0 for the Problem of the Day.

WEDNESDAY

Again, start with the presentations. This will always be the first thing you do when there was a problem assigned the day before. Play Color Square some more.

Choose another POD from Chapter 0.

THURSDAY

Start with POD presentations, play Color Square or move on to Digit Place, and assign another POD from Chapter 0.

FRIDAY

Continue with more presentations. If students have had enough of Color Square and Digit Place, you may want to start Chapter 1: Draw a Diagram.

If you want to give a POD, give another one from Chapter 0. Don't feel as though you have to. You may want to assign Chapter 1 as reading.

Week 2

A possible week is shown below. This is only a suggestion. A lot of this depends on the time you have available for presentations and how long it takes students to do the problems you assign to the groups.

MONDAY

Discuss diagrams and where they are used. If you have assigned reading already, maybe use some of the Questions From the Reading. If you haven't assigned reading yet, demonstrate The Model Train and The Modern Basketball Association problems. Have students try Worm Journey and The Ups and Downs of Shopping (from Problem Set A) in groups.

Assign Floor Tiles (Problem Set A, number 4) for the Problem of the Day.

TUESDAY

Start with presentations.

In groups, have students do Follow the Bouncing Ball and Counting on Ninja Turtles (Problem Set A, numbers 3 and 5) in groups. If you have more time, have students work one of the problems from Problem Set A, Version 2.

Assign Race for the Problem of the Day (Problem Set A, number 7).

WEDNESDAY

Start with presentations.

Have students discuss Alien Invaders from the text, possibly using the Questions from the Reading. Discuss Pool Deck on the board or use the questions. Give students the Carissa's Table from Problem Set A, Version 2 to do in groups.

For the Problem of the Day, assign A Whole Lotta Shakin' Goin' On (Problem Set A, number 8) or Four Friends from Problem Set A, Version 2.

THURSDAY

Again, start with presentations.

Let groups work on Dangerous Maneuvers and Haywire (Problem Set A, numbers 6 and 9).

You could let those two problems carry over into Problems of the Day. The next day, instead of having the students present all of their reasoning (which is probably exactly the same for every student), you can have each person who wants to present draw their diagram on the board for whichever problem they want to do. Then ask them one question (like how would you get from Canine to Feline? Or how would you route a call from Cherlondia to Dalamatia?) and have them answer it with their diagram. You may also ask students to discuss in their groups or as a class which diagrams they thought were the most efficient.

FRIDAY

Start with presentations of Haywire and Dangerous Maneuvers as described above.

If everyone seems to be handling diagrams okay, then start Chapter 2: Make a Systematic List. If you think students need more work, then pull problems from Problem Set A, Version 2.

Week Three

The chart below offers suggestions for how to use problems from Chapter 2. The routine is more or less the same as described above.

	Demonstrate	Groups	POD	Reading
From Text:				
Loose Change	X			
Modern Basketball...	X	X		X
Penny's Dimes			X	X
Frisbin		X	X	X
Area and Perimeter				X
Which Books...	X			X
From Problem Set A:				
Cards and Comics			X	
Free Tickets		X	X	
It Sure is Tough...		X	X	
Storage Sheds			X	
Making Change		X		
Finished Product		X		
Kyle Craves Candy			X	

Week Four and Beyond

Chapter 3: Eliminate Possibilities, marks the appearance of the first Problem Set B. For a practice write-up, we use Nelson + Carson = Reward from Problem Set A. Assign this problem on Thursday or Friday and let students work on it in groups for a whole period, then ask them to write-up an explanation and turn it in the next day or on Monday of week five. Grade it on the ten-point scale before they turn in the first Problem Set B.

On Tuesday of week five (you will have started Chapter 4: Matrix Logic on Monday of week five) assign Problem Set B from Chapter 3, to be turned in the following Tuesday. We always give students one day each week, usually Thursday, to work on Problem Set B in class. On the day before that we do not give a Problem of the Day, so students have the whole period to work on their Problem Set B in their groups.

At this point in the course, you'll have a good sense of how to pace the class and use the text problems and problem sets. Typically you will follow the following schedule.

MONDAY

Presentation of POD
Introduce new strategy from Chapter X.
Do a sample problem.
Have students work a problem in groups.
Assign reading from Chapter X. No POD.

TUESDAY

Collect PSB from Chapter X – 2.
Assign PSB from Chapter X – 1.
Do some more problems in groups from Chapter X.
Assign POD from Chapter X and assign reading from Chapter X.

WEDNESDAY

Presentation of POD
Do some more problems from Chapter X.
Assign reading from Chapter X. No POD.

THURSDAY

Work on PSB from Chapter X – 1.
Assign POD and more reading from Chapter X.

FRIDAY

Presentation of POD
Do some more problems from Chapter X.
Assign POD and more reading from Chapter X.

TEACHER'S RESOURCES FOR CHAPTERS 1 THROUGH 17

draw a diagram

DRAWING A DIAGRAM is a central problem-solving skill. It is applied in many disciplines, both academic and vocational. Drawing a diagram is a form of organizing information. This is a strategy to use to organize your thoughts or to explain something to someone else. As the text mentions, "A picture is worth a thousand words," and even that may represent a serious undercount. Much information, such as this page of text, is presented in a linear, one-dimensional fashion. The reader is expected to start at the top left and read to the right on each line. If not for the edge of the page, the text could continue infinitely in a line. A diagram is different, however. The viewer can start anywhere and proceed in any direction within the diagram. This frees up the information from a linear presentation to a two-dimensional one. The extra dimension can convey relationships among pieces of information spatially.

Our sense of vision is extremely well-developed, both biologically and by training. We're called on more and more to interpret visual images: Newspapers feature graphic communication. Computers operate with interfaces that are primarily graphic. The question today is not whether our electronic gadgets should have graphical interfaces, but rather how those interfaces should be organized and presented.

There are times when diagrams serve as the main communication medium and other times when they play a supporting role. For example, in a newspaper article, there may be a diagram to show a parade route. The diagram could actually be the main communication, if the article is simply about the parade route. On the other hand, if the article talks about more than the parade route, the diagram plays a supporting role.

Organizing the information spatially allows the visual processing portion of your brain to become involved in problem solving.

Your students may resist drawing diagrams. In many cases, students' prior problem-solving experience is algorithm- or equation-based.

Emphasize, in these early chapters, that students need to write complete solutions with explanations. One of the emphases of this book is to develop mathematical communication skills. Students who write down their work and explanations will find it easier to recognize incorrect solutions and find where they went wrong.

A student who resists learning a strategy may miss a significant number of otherwise easy problems. Fortunately, the resulting cognitive dissonance should cause the student to re-examine his or her approach and make an adjustment. Written work can document to a student that his or her approach or attitude toward a strategy isn't working.

To motivate students to learn to draw diagrams, you may wish to point out that many people make their living in graphics. Graphic artists create images that convey information or feelings.

Notes on Text Problems

THE MODERN BASKETBALL ASSOCIATION

This is a rich problem that can be solved by a number of different strategies. At some point later on, you should ask students to find as many ways as they can for solving this problem. It will be discussed again in Chapter 2: Systematic Lists.

THE MODEL TRAIN

Students will tend to try to solve this problem in their heads because it appears so simple. They should be writing down their work on this for two reasons: to practice explaining their work and to be accountable for their processes and solutions.

FARMER BEN

This is another rich problem that can be solved in several different ways, and it appears again in Chapter 6: Guess and Check. You may wish to have students write an algebraic solution and then compare it line for line with the diagram.

Notes about Questions from the Reading

WHEN YOU READ a math book, it is necessary to stop and think about virtually everything you read. Very few people are used to this technique. The section Questions from the Reading is designed to help the students develop the technique. Questions from the Reading will only appear in the first three chapters of this Teacher's Resource Book. The pages have been formatted to be copied, but with the intent that the students do their work on another sheet of paper. The formatting is not correct for using the sheets as fill-in-the-blank worksheets.

You may wish to have the students work individually, in pairs, or as a group. You may also decide to do the questions **orally** in a whole class **discussion.**

Questions from the Reading

Instructions: On a separate piece of paper, answer each question with a full sentence or sentences. Each person working on this assignment is responsible for all parts of the assignment. Answer the questions in accordance with the textbook.

1. List a number of synonyms for "diagram."

2. List several places you have seen diagrams.

MODERN BASKETBALL ASSOCIATION

3. What does Rita's diagram consist of?

4. How many lines did Rita draw?

5. Why did she use a "3" in finding her answer?

6. List at least four things Rita did from start to finish.

7. Choose two major things Rita did and list them.

THE MODEL TRAIN

8. Who are the people who solved this problem (in the book)?

9. Next to each solver's name, give a brief (and distinctive) description of what each person did.

10. Draw a diagram of the solution that gave "25 seconds" as the answer. Describe what went wrong in this solution.

ALIEN INVADERS

11. Re-draw Jamie's diagram showing Gail more skilled than Mamie.

12. Re-draw Kurt's diagram showing Mamie more skilled than Gail.

13. This is another diagram (four concentric circles, the inside labeled "Ralph" and the outside labeled "Sam"). Describe one strength and one weakness of this circle diagram.

14. Rajesh did the problem in three parts. The diagrams below illustrate these parts, and one other illustrates part of someone else's approach. Identify whose approach corresponds to each diagram.

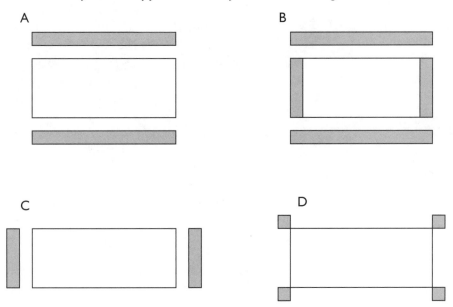

15. Draw a diagram with the corners attached to the width, and calculate the area of the deck using your diagram.

16. Explain why Hung's approach to this problem works. Draw a diagram that Hung may have used.

Answers to Questions from the Reading

1. *Drawing, picture, schematic, map, blueprint, graph, outline, plan, illustration, representation, sketch, chart. Many answers are possible.*

2. *Answers may and should vary.*

3. *Points to symbolize teams and lines connecting points to stand for a match-up.*

4. *21*

5. *She used a "3" because for each match-up, there were to be three games played.*

6. *Answers will probably vary.*

7. *This may be from number 6 above or a combination of items.*

8. *Dustin, Phong and Pete.*

9. *Dustin divided the track in thirds and got 10 seconds for each third for a total of 30 seconds.*

   Phong divided the track in sixths and got 5 seconds for each sixth for a total of 30 seconds.

   Pete also divided the track into sixths but failed to have the train go from the sixth to the first pole and thus got only 25 seconds.

10. *Answers will vary.*

11. *Gail should be taller than Mamie in this diagram.*

12. *Mamie should have a larger head than Gail in this diagram.*

13. *In this diagram, bigger size means more skilled. Strengths: Forces person to deal with the Mamie/Gail ambiguity, more people can be added on easily. Weaknesses: Cannot deal very well with the Mamie/Gail ambiguity.*

14. *Rajesh used diagrams A, C, and D. May used the diagram B.*

15.

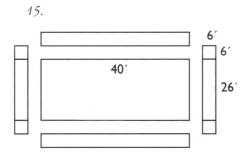

26 ft × 6 ft = 156 ft²
156 ft² × 2 = 312 ft²
40 ft × 6 ft = 240 ft²
240 ft² × 2 = 480 ft²
312 ft² + 480 ft² = 792 ft²

16. *Answers may vary. Hung's diagram would look something like this:*

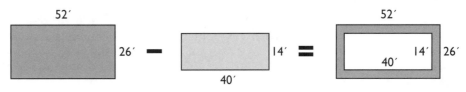

Text Problems

THE MODERN BASKETBALL ASSOCIATION

A new basketball league was formed in which each of the teams will play three games against each of the other teams. There are seven teams: the Antelopes, the Bears, the Cubs, the Dusters, the Eagles, the Foxes, and the Goats. How many games will be played in all?

THE MODEL TRAIN

Jenny's model train is set up on a circular track. There are six telephone poles evenly spaced around the track. It takes the engine of her train 10 seconds to go from the first pole to the third pole. How long would it take for the engine to go the entire distance around the track?

ALIEN INVADERS

Sam, Mamie, Ralph, and Gail are all skilled at the video game Alien Invaders. Gail scores consistently higher than Ralph. Sam is better than all of them, and Mamie is better than Ralph. Who is the better player, Gail or Mamie?

THE POOL DECK

Curly dug his own pool by hand with a shovel. He figured he needed a pool because digging it was hard work, and he could use it to cool off after working on it all day. He also planned a rectangular concrete deck around the pool that would be 6-feet wide at all points. The pool is rectangular and measures 14 feet by 40 feet. What is the area of the deck?

FARMER BEN

Farmer Ben has only ducks and cows. He can't remember how many of each he has, but he really doesn't need to remember. He does know that he has 22 animals, which is his age. He also remembers that those animals have a total of 56 legs, which is his father's age. Assuming that each animal is normal, how many of each does Farmer Ben have?

1. THE GIFT EXCHANGE

Eight relatives always give gifts to one another. They've been doing it now for five years. How many gifts have been given so far?

2. AIR WARBUCKS

There is a rumor that Daddy Warbucks is planning to start a new airline. He plans to serve six cities: San Francisco, Los Angeles, Dallas, Chicago, New York, and Miami. There will be direct flights between each pair of cities. How many different routes will this create?

3. COOKIE EXCHANGE

Nine people at a cookie exchange each brought a dozen cookies for each other person. How many cookies were brought to this exchange?

4. THE FINANCE COMMITTEE

Nine members of a finance committee could not get together to meet on an emergency basis. However, during the next three days, each member was able to talk to each other member on the telephone. What is the minimum number of phone calls needed to accomplish this?

5. THE MERRY-GO-ROUND

There are twelve horses on the merry-go-round evenly spaced on the outside perimeter. It took four seconds for the fourth one to reach Abe (starting when the first one was opposite him). How long will it take the merry-go-round to go around once?

6. FOUR FRIENDS

Allen, Lydia, Cindy, and Marcus are all friends. Marcus says he is older than Cindy, and he should know because he is her brother. Allen knows he's older than all of them, and Cindy is pretty sure that Lydia is younger than her. List the friends in order from oldest to youngest.

7. CARISSA'S TABLE

Carissa is building a new dining room table. The center of it is a rectangular section made from polished rocks. That section measures 36 inches by 64 inches. She is also going to place a wooden, eight-inch rectangular lip all the way around the perimeter. What is the area of the wooden part?

8. R-DOUBLE-7 RANCH

The "R-Double-7" Ranch has a new owner. The 30 animals, all ostriches and horses, are dismayed, as they have heard that he is both foolish and inexperienced. Not being quite sure what he was looking for, however, he checked on the health of his animals by inspecting all of their feet. There were 96 feet in all. How many ostriches are there on this ranch?

9. MALFUNCTIONING ROTOTILLER

The gearshift on Maxine's rototiller was malfunctioning. She found that it would travel forward four feet in one minute, but then shift into reverse and go back three feet before the shift would allow her to put it back in forward. The backwards part also took about a minute to complete. How long would it take her to till a 20-foot-long section of her garden with this rototiller?

10. RUNDOWN

We told Gavin not to run, but he did anyway. He took about 18 steps from second base, got caught in a rundown, took 7 steps back, then took 3 steps forward, 5 steps back, 11 steps forward, 4 steps back, and was tagged out half-way between second and third base. How many steps is it from second base to third base?

11. THE DOG WHO LIKES TO RUN

Annie the Dog loves to run. When we were walking home one day, she ran ahead of us, went all the way home, and then came back to meet us. She then ran back home again and came back to meet us. She did this three more times. Each time she came back, she met us at a point half-way from where she had left us. If she started running while we were about half a mile from home (let's say about 2400 feet), how far did she run total by the time she met us the fifth time?

12. TRAVELING ART SHOW

Ardith was in charge of making motel arrangements for the crew of a traveling art show. She had misplaced her list of cities, though, and needed to figure out how many more cities there were. She remembered that the eighth city was Phoenix and the seventeenth city was Pensacola, and that from Phoenix to Pensacola was one-third of the tour. How many cities are there on this tour?

13. GEORGETOWN RACE

There were five cars remaining in contention by the end of the Georgetown One-Hundred Mile Classic Car Race. The Dusenberg finished twelve seconds ahead of the Edsel. The Studebaker finished seven seconds behind the Model T Ford. The time from when the first finisher crossed the line to the last finisher was twenty-two seconds. The Pierce finished fourteen seconds after the Model T Ford. List the cars in order and the time between them from first to fifth places.

14. CLASSROOM CEILING

The classroom measures 24 feet by 36 feet. Each of the panels for the hung ceiling measures 1½ feet by 4 feet. How many panels will be required for the entire hung ceiling?

ARKANSAS CITIES

According to a map of Arkansas, there are a number of good roads connecting some of the towns south of Little Rock. The road between Malvern and Benton is 23 miles, and between Benton and Pine Bluff is 62 miles. The road between Malvern and Sheridan is 28 miles, and then from Sheridan to Pine Bluff is 22 miles. Arkadelphia is connected to two of these towns: It is 12 miles to Gurden and 21 miles to Sheridan. Fordyce has three roads to these towns: 45 miles to Pine Bluff, 39 miles to Sheridan, and 27 miles to Camden. The road from Gurden to Camden is 38 miles.

Unfortunately, the road from Fordyce to Sheridan is closed due to dangerous road conditions caused by the recent bad weather. Find the shortest route between each pair of towns:

From Malvern and Pine Bluff
From Camden and Pine Bluff
From Benton and Arkadelphia
From Fordyce to Malvern
From Benton to Camden

16. **WILDERNESS CAMP**

At a wilderness survival training camp, each person was to go out individually, set up camp, and survive for one week. Also, people got points by being able to pinpoint anybody else's camp on a map. You lost points if other people were able to find your camp. About three days into the exercise, Adrienne had come upon both Freda's and DuJannie's camps. Bart had found Eugenia's and Glenda's camps, and he and DuJannie both found each other's camp. DuJannie had also happened upon Hank's camp, while Hank and Eugenia had found each other's. Hank had also discovered Adrienne's. Carl detected Glenda's camp, and his camp was detected by Freda. Unfortunately, the base leaders needed to get in touch with Eugenia, as someone had crashed into her parked car. They found Carl. How could they get a message to Eugenia?

Suppose Hank decides to send a message out to the leaders the next day. How could he get it out by way of Carl (and, of course, without any more camps being discovered)?

Taking this another step, how could you get messages from

a. Freda to DuJannie?
b. Adrienne to Glenda?
c. Glenda to Hank?
d. DuJannie to Freda?
e. Bart to Carl?
f. Carl to Bart?

systematic lists

SYSTEMATIC LIST problems will give you some opportunity to assess students' learning from previous courses. Although a systematic list is relatively simple, watch for students who can do them well, as they have probably had prior experience. Usually you will find that people can make the list. The question is, how systematic is the list? Students may resist this strategy at first. They need guidance developing functional systems for their lists.

Systematic lists are a way of organizing information. The opposite, called "random flailing," does not help people function well. Organization makes things easier on the brain, as the brain organizes information as it stores it. Giving information a structure also allows the brain to view and interpret the information.

A systematic list can be made relatively quickly and efficiently. It can also be verified quickly by both the writer and the reader. Patterns will also emerge from the list. Patterns promote further insight and serve as verifiers when checking for accuracy. When a list is done systematically it becomes more of a learning tool.

For students using this book, communication must be a high priority. Part of the problem-solving process is to communicate the solution. In order to communicate it, you must understand it and record it in a form that is understandable.

Emphasize that students should work slowly and carefully. Careful work is especially important as students become evaluators of their own and their peers' work. Furthermore, concise solutions will be far easier to communicate than rambling solutions.

Students also need to realize that if something does not work well the first time they try it, they may need to try something else. Rather than continuing blindly down a dead end, the student may need to back out and find a better avenue. Starting over on a problem is a necessary skill. It is important to point out, though, that when someone starts over, they are doing it at an increased knowledge level—they have already learned what doesn't work in solving a particular problem.

Systematic lists show up in a number of places—so many that we may not think of them as systematic lists at first. The phone book is a prime example; it is an alphabetical listing of people and organizations. Its systematic nature makes it easy to use.

As the students progress through the book, you will find more and more problems that can be approached in a variety of ways. In order to encourage divergent thinking it is important to value alternative approaches, even if some are not as clear or efficient. On some problems, one method may not emerge as being the most efficient; instead, different methods will exhibit different strengths.

Notes on Text Problems

THE MODERN BASKETBALL ASSOCIATION

This rich problem reappears to be solved by a different method. The problem can be solved in a number of ways, including a number of different methods of making systematic lists.

PENNY'S DIMES

An important assumption in this problem rests on whether or not you can distinguish between the piles (and care that you can). The solution presented in the text assumes a case in which you do not distinguish.

WHICH BOOKS SHOULD YOU READ?

There may be other ways to solve this problem. Ask your students if they can find one.

Notes on Problem Set A

Fencing with Neighbors, Arcade, and Rudy's Shot Totals from Problem Set A, Version 2 will probably be more difficult for students. Kyle Craves Candy, from the student text, is similar. Demonstrate one of these in class and be aware that these may trip-up some students.

Questions from the Reading

LOOSE CHANGE

1. What are the possible coins that Leslie can have?

2. Why is the strategy called "systematic"?

3. Why did Brooke start off with two dimes?

4. Why did Brooke start with three nickels when she had only one dime?

5. What is Heather's system?

6. What is the difference between Heather's systematic list method and Brooke's method for organizing her list?

7. What does a systematic list have to do with organizing information?

THE MODERN BASKETBALL ASSOCIATION

8. How does John's solution compare to a systematic list?

9. Why is John's non-systematic list insufficient?

10. What does AB mean in Monica's list?

11. Why doesn't Monica include BA in her solution?

12. Why isn't GC in Monica's list?

13. Who can verify a systematic list?

14. List three ways you can tell that Monica completed her list correctly.

15. Suppose five teams play each other. How many games are there? Here is Samantha's list:

    PQ   SP   PT
    QS   QR   ST
    RS   TR   RQ

    What is wrong with her list?

PENNY'S DIMES

16. Explain what Randy's decision was about.

17. How does Randy's decision affect the way he solves the problem?

18. Why does Randy eliminate the solution 1, 15, 9?

19. Why does Randy have to start with a 3 in the second column when he puts a 3 in the first column?

20. What is the pattern established by starting with a 3 in the second column when he has 3 dimes in the first column?

21. What is another possible way to set up a systematic list for this problem?

22. Solve this problem again, but assume that you can tell the difference between the piles. Now how many ways can the dimes be arranged?

23. Chris solved the problem using a systematic list that was identical to Randy's list. Then Chris said, "I wanted to know how many ways there would be if you could tell the difference between the piles. So I multiplied 16 times 3 and got 48 ways." Discuss Chris's reasoning. Do you agree?

FRISBIN

24. Summarize Derrick's method of solving this problem.

25. What is the pattern in the 5-point column of Derrick's solution?

26. What process is the 10-point column subject to?

27. What process is the 5-point column subject to?

28. Summarize Julian's method of solving this problem.

29. In Julian's method, why doesn't he show:

    1st   2nd   3rd

    5   1   5

30. What system did Julian follow with Throw 1?

31. Why didn't Julian have to rearrange the throws in a different order?

32. What was Emily's system of organization?

AREA AND PERIMETER

33. What are the columns in Tuan's systematic list?

34. How did Tuan know he was done with his list?

35. What column did Tuan add to his chart?

36. Do you think it is possible to make a rectangle with an area of 120 cm² with a smaller perimeter if you don't have to use whole numbers? (If no, explain why not. If yes, estimate the length and width.)

37. At what point was TKM dropped from Li's list?

38. What two books are in the first three lines of Jim's solution?

39. Why isn't TKM checked in line 7 of Jim's solution?

40. Why is MND checked instead of HF in line 5 of Jim's solution?

41. Is David solving the same problem as Li and Jim?

42. What does David use to solve the problem?

43. What is a major challenge you may face as you work through the book?

Answers to Questions from the Reading

1. She can have pennies, nickels, and dimes.

2. It is a list that involves some type of system.

3. It is the most number of dimes Leslie could have.

4. It is the maximum number of nickels she could have and also have one dime.

5. Heather started with the most number of pennies and then filled in the nickels and dimes to make up the difference.

6. Brooke based it on the dimes and then worked down to no dimes, whereas Heather started with the number of pennies and used dimes and nickels to fill in the rest of the 25 cents.

7. It is organizing information in a chart.

THE MODERN BASKETBALL ASSOCIATION

8. It doesn't compare very well as his list is non-systematic.

9. There may be omissions or duplications, and it is difficult to verify either of those possibilities.

10. It stands for "Antelopes versus Bears."

11. It is already taken care of with AB.

12. It is already taken care of in the CG match-up. All of the G games were taken care of under previous letters.

13. A systematic list can be verified by either the person making the list or another person checking the solution.

14. Answers will vary.

15. She is missing PR and QT, and QR is repeated.

PENNY'S DIMES

16. Randy had to decide if 1, 11, 13 was the same as 1, 13, 11.

17. This makes a big difference in the total number of ways that the marbles can be arranged.

18. The solution 1, 15, 9 is a repeat of 1, 9, 15.

19. If he uses a 1, then he makes 3, 1, 21, which is a repeat.

20. Start both columns with the same odd number to avoid duplications.

21. You could start with 23 dimes in the first pile.

22. There would be 78 ways. This problem is much harder, and it helps to find a way to not write out the whole list. See the next question.

23. Chris's answer is incorrect. There would really be six ways to arrange each set of three. Example: if the numbers were 1, 3, 21, they could be arranged as 1, 3, 21; 1, 21, 3; 3, 1, 21; 3, 21, 1; 21, 1, 3; 21, 3, 1.

   That would give 16 × 6 = 96 ways. However, if there were a repeat in a pile, like 7, 7, 9, there would be only three ways to rearrange them: 7, 7, 9; 7, 9 ,7; 9, 7, 7.

   This happens with double 1's, 3's, 5's, 7's, 9's, and 11's. Each double contributes 3 less, and 6 × 3 = 18, which makes the total 96 – 18 = 78. This is the same answer you would get if you wrote them all out.

FRISBIN

24. He chose the maximum number of 10-point throws and then reduced the number of 10-point throws to 2, 1, and 0, filling in the rest with 5-point throws and 1-pointers.

25. It decreases by one from the highest number of 5-point throws that work with the current number of 10-point throws. (Answers may vary.)

26. It starts on the maximum and then decreases by one throw and stays at that level as long as possible.

27. It starts at its maximum for the given 10-point column then works downward.

28. Julian used the first column as the best throw, the second column as the next best throw, and the third column as the least best. He then worked out all possibilities.

29. He set up his chart to have better throws recorded on the left, and this avoided showing the same result twice.

30. He let it stay at 10 points as long as possible then decreased it when he had exhausted all of the possibilities at 10 points.

31. It would not have changed the total score (which is what the problem asked for).

32. She grouped them by three throws the same, then two throws the same and one different, and finally all three throws different.

33. *The columns are "width," "length," and "area".*

34 *He had reached 10 by 12, and the next possibility is 12 by 10: a duplication.*

35. *The perimeter column.*

36. *Yes, the perimeter is getting smaller as the length and width get closer. The smallest has the same width and length (a square) with sides equal to the square root of 120 (or ≈ 10.95).*

WHICH BOOKS SHOULD YOU READ?

37. *Li dropped TKM from her list once she had written all of the possibilities that included it.*

38. *The books are TKM and* All Quiet on the Western Front.

39. *He had exhausted all possibilities using TKM as one of the three books.*

40. *It was MND's turn.*

41. *David is solving a different problem—one concerned with the order in which the books are read.*

42. *He used a tree diagram.*

43. *Choosing an appropriate strategy is a major challenge you may face as you work through the book.*

Text Problems

LOOSE CHANGE

Leslie has 25 cents in her pocket but does not have a quarter. If you can tell her all possible combinations of coins she could have that sum to 25 cents, she will give you the 25 cents.

THE MODERN BASKETBALL ASSOCIATION

A new basketball league formed in which each of the teams would play three games against each other team. Initially, there were seven teams: the Antelopes, the Bears, the Cubs, the Dusters, the Eagles, the Foxes, and the Goats. How many games were played?

PENNY'S DIMES

Penny has 25 dimes. She likes to put them in 3 piles with an odd number of dimes in each pile. In how many ways could she do this?

FRISBIN

On a famous episode of Star Trek, Captain Kirk and the gang played a card game called Phisbin. This problem concerns a game called Frisbin. The object of the game is to throw 3 Frisbees at 3 bins that are set up on the ground about 20 feet away. If the Frisbee lands in the largest bin, 1 point is scored. If the Frisbee lands in the medium-sized bin, 5 points are scored. If the Frisbee lands in the smallest bin, 10 points are scored. Kirk McCoy is playing the game. If all 3 of his Frisbees land in bins, how many different total scores can he make?

AREA AND PERIMETER

A rectangle has an area of 120 square centimeters. Its length and width are whole numbers. What are the possibilities for the length and width? Which possibility gives the smallest perimeter?

WHICH BOOKS SHOULD YOU READ?

For an English assignment, you are to choose three of the following books to read: *To Kill a Mockingbird, All Quiet on the Western Front, The Stranger, Huckleberry Finn,* and *A Midsummer Night's Dream.* How many different sets of three books can you choose?

Problem Set A, Version 2

1. RIDE TICKETS

Marcy had $10.00 to spend at the state fair. She spent all of it on ride tickets. The rides cost either $.50, $1.00, or $1.25 each. What are the possible ways she spent her money?

2. LEARNING THE HARD WAY

Rhonda, Quincy, Steve, and Ted all went boating. Steve and Ted got into an argument. They stood up, then Rhonda and Quincy both stood up and told them to stop and sit down. One by one, each person fell off the boat. List the possible orders in which they could have fallen in.

3. RENTING A CAR

Axxel Car Rentals has two basic plans. One is to rent the car for $19 per day and then pay $.20 per mile. The second is to rent the car for $49 for the first day and then pay $29 for each subsequent day with unlimited mileage. Figaro expects to drive the car about 500 miles total, but he has no idea how many days he'll be needing it. (He might need it for two days, but he could see needing it for as many as 10 days, depending on the other people involved.) Make a systematic chart to help him decide which plan to use.

4. WAYLON'S CANDY

The corner convenience store sells candy in 20-cent, 30-cent, and 50-cent packages. List all the ways Waylon can spend exactly $3.00 on candy.

5. FENCING WITH NEIGHBORS

Seenonaybor's Fencing Company makes prefabricated fence units in 6, 8, 10, and 12-foot lengths. What combinations could be used to make exactly 30 feet of a straight fence?

6. ARCADE

Kerry challenges Pat at the arcade. They will each roll three balls and then total up their scores. Whoever has the highest score wins. The possible scores for the holes the balls can fall into are 50, 40, 30, or 25 points. What are the possible scores for three balls?

7. RUDY'S SHOT TOTALS

In the first quarter of a basketball game, Rudy had scored 8 points on a combination of 3-point shots, field goals (2 points each), and free throws (1 point each). What are the possible combinations of shots that could have scored his 8 points?

8. SKIING BIKERS

The bicycling club rented 3 vans to take people skiing. Each van could hold 7 people. As it turned out, 12 people could make the trip, but because of the amount of equipment they had to bring, they still needed all 3 vans. Peter, the leader, said, "I don't care who goes in what van, but obviously we need at least one driver in each one." In how many different ways can the 12 people be split up?

9. SUBJECT-VERB-OBJECT

A common structure for English sentences is "subject-verb-object." An example is "The horse pulled the cart." "Horse" is the subject, the verb is "pulled," and "cart" is the object. Here is a list of verbs and nouns. The nouns may be used as subjects or as objects.

Nouns:		**Verbs:**
alligator	bone	eat
dog	bird	scare
car	soda	drive
wrench		pour

How many different subject-verb-object sentences can be produced with the words in the above lists? For example, using "bone" as the subject, "eat" as the verb, and "dog" as the object, we can create the sentence: "The bone eats the dog." As you can see, the sentences may be ridiculous. The same noun cannot be used more than once in a given sentence.

Assume you were going to write out all of the possible sentences. Devise a method for dividing up the work among the members of your class.

3 eliminate possibilities

ELIMINATING POSSIBILITIES is a reversal of sorts. You are not looking for the right answer, rather you are looking for lots of wrong answers. As each wrong answer is eliminated, you get closer to the right answer(s).

Eliminating possibilities is useful in any sort of troubleshooting. Many times the problem is something that no one has thought of. So you eliminate whatever is not wrong, and whatever is left over must be the problem. This is one of the reasons the students need to write out complete lists of all possibilities. If a student's incomplete list doesn't include the correct answer, he or she may eliminate all the answers on the list and be left with the incorrect impression that the problem has no right answer.

Occasionally, possibilities must be made up in order to have something to eliminate. The last problem in the chapter (Who is Lying?) requires this. In the text, we refer to this as seeking contradictions. Seeking contradictions involves making up a possibility and then eliminating it (in order to show that its opposite is true). This sort of argument is similar to that used in an indirect proof.

Twenty questions is a good game for introducing the strategy of eliminate possibilities. One way to play the game is described in the text: Choose a number between 1 and 100 and have students ask yes or no questions to determine the number. Another more interesting way to play the game is to choose an item in the room. The item can be a specific piece of paper on the wall, a person, a piece of chalk, the clock, anything. The class again asks yes or no questions and tries to determine what the item is.

Solving conundrums is another good way to learn how to eliminate possibilities. Conundrums, also called stories with holes or two minute mysteries, are short stories that have some sort of secret. The leader states the story, then the class starts to ask yes or no questions to try to determine the mystery. Students who have heard the story before should not be allowed to play. (They'll still enjoy watching their classmates try to solve it.) The leader can also answer that a question is irrelevant and can ask the questioner to be more specific about the question.

Example: A man lives in a high rise apartment building. Every day when he goes to work, he gets in the elevator on the thirtieth floor where his apartment is, and rides down to the first floor and goes out of the building to work. When he comes home in the evening, most of the time he rides the elevator to the twelfth floor, gets out there, and walks up the stairs to the thirtieth floor. Occasionally, however, he rides the elevator all the way from the first floor to the thirtieth floor.

Possible questions and answers:

Q: Does he visit someone on the twelfth floor?

A: No.

Q: Does this have something to do with his job?

A: No.

Q: Is the elevator broken?

A: No.

Q: Is he trying to get some exercise?

A: No.

Q: Are there other people in the elevator?

A: Specify.

Q: Are there other people in the elevator when he gets out on the twelfth floor?

A: No.

Q: Are there other people in the elevator when he rides the elevator all the way to the thirtieth floor?

A: Yes.

Q: Does the mystery have something to do with the other people who may or may not ride the elevator?

A: Yes.

. . . and so on. The answer to this conundrum is that the man isn't tall enough to reach the button for the thirtieth floor. He can only ride there if someone else is in the elevator to push the button for him.

Here are some other famous conundrums and their answers. Many of these stories tend to be about death, but we tried not to list too many of those here. Conundrums are available in several books. (You might have seen some of these before in the *Discovering Geometry Teacher's Guide and Answer Key,* published by Key Curriculum Press, as well as in other places.) You can also make up your own conundrums from different or unusual newspaper stories.

Story: A man is afraid to go home because there is a man with a mask there.

Answer: The man is on third base in a baseball game and the man with the mask is the catcher.

Story: A man pushed his car past the hotel and smiled.

Answer: The man is playing Monopoly and he pushed his token (the car) past a hotel on Boardwalk that was not his.

Story: A man died with a hole in his suit.

Answer: The man was a skindiver (or astronaut) and his suit was punctured.

Story: A man walked into a bar. The bartender took out a gun and pointed it at the man. The man smiled, thanked the bartender, and left.

Answer: The man had the hiccups. Seeing the gun frightened the hiccups away.

Story: A man entered a large building, looked around, and then left. A few minutes later a policeman came in and arrested two people.

Answer: The building was a sports arena for a basketball game. The man's car had been stolen. In the car were two tickets to the basketball game that night. The man showed up to the sports arena and found two people sitting in his seats (wearing his clothes). The policeman came in and arrested the two men for car theft. (Contributed by Donna O'Neil from a newspaper story. This really happened.)

Story: A woman paid to enter a show, won two awards, and was embarrassed.

Answer: The woman paid to enter her dog in a dog show. The woman won the award for looking most like her dog, and her dog won for ugliest dog. (Contributed by Linda McDonald from a news story.)

Story: The firefighter immediately recognized the cause of the fire.

Answer: At the scene of a grass fire was a dead bird and a singed snake. The bird had been carrying the snake when it fell across two power lines. The bird and the snake were electrocuted, and the snake caught on fire. When the snake and the bird fell to the ground, the grass caught fire. (Contributed by Linda McDonald from a news story.)

Story: A man is found dead in a cabin on a hillside.

Answer: The man was found dead in an airplane cabin in an airplane that crashed on the hillside.

Story: (hard) A woman went into a restaurant at Fisherman's Wharf in San Francisco. She ordered Albatross Soup. When the soup came, the woman tasted it, smiled, and left the restaurant.

Answer: The woman had been shipwrecked on a desert island. Several people died of starvation. To survive, someone else in the group had made what he claimed to be albatross soup. The woman had the soup, but she never quite believed that it was albatross soup since she had never had it before. The woman was afraid that it was soup made from the humans who had died. When she tried the soup again in San Francisco, it tasted identical to the soup she had on the island, so she realized that she had not been a cannibal but had really eaten Albatross Soup. (Note: An albatross is a large sea bird that tends to follow ships.)

Story: A man and his young son were injured in a car accident. They were taken to the hospital. When the boy was wheeled into the operating room, the surgeon looked at him and said, "I can't operate on this boy, he is my son."

Answer: The surgeon is the boy's mother. (Note: This may not work as well in the 90's as it would have in the 50's. But maybe it will. How far have we come?)

Notes on Text Problems

THREE BROTHERS GO A-COURTIN'

This problem involves more than one strategy. Drawing a diagram works instead of making a list from which to eliminate possibilities. Problems whose complexity require more than one problem-solving strategy appear more often as you progress through the book. One strategy is applied to the problem in preparation for using another strategy.

PENNY'S DIMES (PART II)

It often helps to determine which clues are the most useful ones and start with those. For example, if one clue is that a number is even and another is that it is a multiple of 10, the latter clue is far more useful and, hence, is a better place to start.

In the problem write-up shown in the book, the students eliminated a lot of possibilities by not writing them down. They wrote down a list of the multiples of 5, thus eliminating numbers between 1 and 100 that are not multiples of 5.

Math students often think problems have only one answer. This is definitely not true but is an impression students can get from traditional math courses. Lately, more math curricula are becoming more integrated with other subjects. Math will be taught and used more as a thinking and analytical tool than as an isolated academic discipline. In this type of setting, "correct" answers become more difficult to ascertain. In this text, there will be more problems that have more than one correct solution.

LIFE ON THE FARM

The tendency for someone with an advanced math background might be to use simultaneous equations. It won't work, since there is more than one correct solution.

THE LETTER FROM COLLEGE

The students will need to be willing to reread sections of this problem write-up.

Again, the students need to make sure to write out all possibilities first. A key part of this problem is that you do not have an important piece of information (the product). It is, however, enough for you to know that Seymour was able to solve the problem using that information. Knowing that the hidden information helped solve the problem allows you to eliminate any possibility where that information would not be helpful.

Notes on Problem Set A

THE THREE SQUARES

This is another problem that will require more than one strategy. The students should be starting to accept a couple of things: (1) some problems will require more than one strategy to be solved efficiently, and (2) it is often a positive skill to start with one strategy and then decide to change to another one. Students should be showing signs of another goal of this course: They should be showing more persistence in solving problems.

Questions from the Reading

Instructions: Answer each question with a full sentence or sentences. Each person working on this assignment is responsible for all parts of the assignment. Answer the questions in accordance with the textbook.

TWENTY QUESTIONS

1. Why was asking "Is it 83?" a waste of time?

2. Why was the question "Is it > 50?" a good question?

3. Would "Is it < 50?" have been a good first question? Why or why not?

4. Could the number have been 100?

THREE BROTHERS

5. Why did Kim match up Andy's candy with Tooley's tickets in the diagram?

6. Why did Kim figure that Marty does not have Tooley's candy?

7. What conclusion does Kim draw from reasoning that Marty does not have Tooley's candy?

PENNY'S DIMES (PART II)

8. Why did James list the odd numbers?

9. Why does Marli think a list can be made more efficiently?

10. How does Marli want to do things more efficiently?

11. What clues does Troy think should be used?

12. Why does Troy favor using those clues?

13. Why did James cross off the 30 and the 40 (and some other numbers) on the list?

14. Why does Marli say that 15 needs to be crossed off?

15. What clue leads the students to eliminate 55 from consideration?

16. Why is 55 eliminated, but not 85?

17. How many correct answers are there?

18. Explain how, according to the text, this problem "mirrors life?"

19. How is it established that G = 1?

20. Why must the letter "O" equal 0?

21. What must be true about N and T?

22. What is true about A?

23. What is on Jack's first chart?

24. Why did Jack eliminate some numbers from his first chart?

25. How did Jack determine the values to use for M on this chart?

N:	2	3	4	6	7
T:	8	7	6	4	3
M:	7	6	5	3	2

26. Why did Jack eliminate the combination of N = 8 and T = 2?

27. Why does Jack say that there are "five families of solutions?"

28. How does Adrianne realize that O can't be 9?

29. What is Khue's reason that the O can't be 9?

30. What is the reason for concluding that M = 1?

31. Why can't S be less than 8?

32. How is it determined that S has to be 9 as opposed to 8?

33. Where does the statement "E is N − 1" come from?

34. How does "N + R = 10 + N − 1" give R = 9?

35. In order for R to equal 8, what must also take place?

36. How were the possible values for Y determined?

37. How were the possible values for N determined?

38. Why can't Y be 4?

    Use this chart from the text to answer the next questions:

	1	2	3	4
D:	6	7	7	5
E:	7	6	5	7
N:	8	7	6	8
Y:	3	3	2	2

39. Why were columns 1 and 4 eliminated?

40. Why was the second column eliminated?

DOWNTOWN DELI

41. Why does Seymour consider the Sausage and Meatball stores as his "prime" favorites?

42. How far is the Circle B from another landmark?

43. What problem-solving strategies did Richard use?

44. What was the first list Richard made? Why did he make it?

45. What was Richard's second step?

46. What strategy did Richard use in the second step?

47. What was Richard's third step?

48. Why did Richard put 45 and 49 on these rows?

FS #1	FS #2	CB
3	47	45
3	47	49

49. Why did Richard eliminate some possibilities based on numbers that appeared in the third column?

50. What did Gus remember?

51. What shortcut did Richard use in finding the last digit of the product?

52. What is the reasoning behind why Seymour can figure out the number even though Gus can only remember the last digit of the product?

53. What does the text list as a "key point" in Downtown Deli?

WHO IS LYING?

54. What is Danyell seeking? How does she plan to do it?

Answers to Questions from the Reading

TWENTY QUESTIONS

1. Asking "Is it 8?" is a waste of time since the previous question determined that the number was even.

2. The question "Is it > 50?" is a good question because it eliminated all of the numbers less than 50.

3. "Is it < 50?" would have been a good question as it would have eliminated half of the possibilities.

4. The number could have been 100. The game says we're looking for a number between 1 and 100 **inclusive**.

THREE BROTHERS

5. Kim matched up Andy's candy with Tooley's tickets in the diagram because each one had candy belonging to another and tickets belonging to the third.

6. Kim figured that Marty did not have Tooley's candy because she already knew that Andy had Tooley's candy.

7. Kim concludes that Marty must have had Andy's candy.

PENNY'S DIMES

8. James listed the odd numbers because the first clue said that when it was divided by 2, there was a remainder of 1.

9. Marli thinks making a list can be done more efficiently by using two clues at once. There will be fewer numbers to list.

10. Marli wants to use two clues at once to make the process more efficient.

11. Troy thinks clues 4 and 5 should be used.

12. Troy favors using those clues because there will be a shorter initial list.

13. James crossed off those numbers because they are even, and clue 1 indicates the number is odd.

14. Marli says that 15 needs to be crossed off because it is a multiple of 3, and the third clue indicates that the number is not a multiple of 3.

15. Clue 3 leads the students to eliminate 55.

16. Fifty-five is eliminated because it is one greater than a multiple of four (clue 3).

17. There are two correct answers to Penny's Dimes, Part II.

18. This problem mirrors life because there is no single certain correct answer.

LIFE ON THE FARM

19. It is established that $G = 1$ because when you add two numbers and carry, the highest you can carry is 1.

20. The letter O must be 0 because $O + A = A$, and there is no carrying from the previous column.

21. The sum of N and T must be 10.

22. The letter A can be any digit not used for any other letter.

23. Jack's first chart shows the possibilities for N and T.

24. Jack eliminated numbers that wouldn't work, such as 5 and 5 (two letters couldn't be the same digit) and 1, 9 since 1 was already known to be G.

25. Jack knew that T had to be one larger than M because of the ones column.

26. Jack eliminated the combination of $N = 8$ and $T = 2$ because it means that M would be 1, which is already the value for G.

27. Jack says that there are "five families of solutions" because there are five possibilities on his chart for N, T, and M; and A can be anything not yet used.

28. Adrianne realizes that O can't be 9 because both O and M would have to be 9 in order to have the necessary carry to the tens place.

29. Khue says that the only way GO can be 19 is if both T and N are 9, which is impossible.

THE LETTER FROM COLLEGE

30. The letter M must be 1 since it is the carried digit in the fifth column, which came from adding two four-digit numbers.

31. The letter S has to be 8 or 9 in order to be high enough to force a carry to the ten-thousands place.

32. The letter S has to be 9 as opposed to 8 because there is no carry from the hundreds place: $E + O$ can't carry since E has a maximum value of 7.

33. The statement "E is N – 1" is equivalent to E + 1 = N.

34. Subtracting N from both sides of N + R = 10 + N – 1 gives R = 9.

35. In order for R to equal 8 there must be a carry from the ones column.

36. The possible values for Y were determined by using the chart for D, E, and L.

37. The possible values for N were determined by adding 1 to E, since N has to be 1 more than E.

38. The letter Y can't be 4 because D + E must be 14, and that means giving one of them a value of 8 or 9. But those values are already committed to other letters.

39. Columns 1 and 4 were eliminated because N and R cannot both be 8.

40. The second column was eliminated because D and N both had the same value.

DOWNTOWN DELI

41. Seymour considers the Sausage and Meatball stores as his "prime" favorites because they are all on prime-numbered streets.

42. The Circle B is two blocks away from one of the Fast Stop stores.

43. Richard used a systematic list and eliminated possibilities.

44. Richard's first list is a list of pairs of odd numbers that add to 50. The Fast Stop stores are on streets that add to 50.

45. Richard's second step was to eliminate all of the pairs that were not both primes.

46. Richard eliminated possibilities in the second step.

47. Richard's third step was to add on the possible streets for the Circle B stores.

48. Richard didn't know on which side of the Fast Stop store the Circle B store would be located.

49. Richard eliminated all of the third numbers that were not prime.

50. Gus remembered the last digit of the product of the three streets.

51. Richard's shortcut was to only multiply last digits.

52. Seymour must be able to tell because the last digit of the product is unique to all of the remaining possibilities.

53. *A key point is the fact that you don't have all of the information that Seymour had. However, just knowing that by having the information Seymour can solve the problem gives you sufficient information to solve the problem.*

WHO IS LYING?

54. *Danyell is seeking a contradiction by assuming that today is Monday, then Tuesday, etc.*

Text Problems

THREE BROTHERS GO A-COURTIN'

Three brothers each arranged to spend an evening with women that none had ever met before. They each wanted to show off how suave and debonair they could be, so each formed a plan.

By coincidence, each brother decided to buy a box of candy at the same store, and each one bought tickets at the same computer ticket outlet.

Andy bought honey-based candies, as he wanted to show what a sweet guy he could bee. Tooley bought chews, as he wanted to show that he wouldn't accept just anybody—he was a choosy guy. Marty bought nuts without realizing the message it could send.

When it came time to leave, each brother grabbed a wrong candy box and ticket envelope. None of them took the candy or the tickets that belonged to him. Each took the tickets of one brother and the candy of the other. To make things short, Andy did not have Marty's candy, and you'll have to figure out the rest.

PENNY'S DIMES (PART II)

Penny's favorite coin is the dime, as we saw in the last chapter. Since we last saw Penny, she has spent some of her dimes and acquired some more, so she does not know how many she has now, although she knows it is less than 100. One day she was arranging them on her desk in different ways. She found that when she put them into piles of two, there was one left over. When she put them into piles of three, there was one left over, and the same thing happened when she put them into piles of four. She then tried putting them in piles of five and found that there were none left over. How many dimes does Penny have? (By the way, there is more than one correct answer.)

LIFE ON THE FARM

Emil and Olive lived on a farm with their father, Gordon. One day, Emil asked his father, "Dad, what happened to that cat we used to have?" Olive overheard this, and said, "Yeah, and we used to have a horse too."

Gordon replied, "That tomcat and that old nag were no use. I traded them for our new goat."

Emil said, "Hey, that sounds like a good cryptarithmetic problem. Come on Olive, let's go see if we can solve it."

Each letter stands for a different digit, 0 through 9. No two letters stand for the same digit.

TOM + NAG = GOAT

Determine which digit each letter represents.

THE LETTER FROM COLLEGE

The story goes that a young man away at college needed some extra cash. He sent his mother this plea. He wanted his mother to send the amount indicated by the sum.

SEND + MORE = MONEY

Just as before, each letter stands for one of the digits 0 through 9 and there is only one letter for any one digit. How much did the young man want? (You may assume that there is a decimal point between N and E, as the mother is probably not willing to send ten thousand or so dollars to her son on request.)

DOWNTOWN DELI

Seymour owns his own business. He puts together deli sandwiches, which he wraps to retain freshness and distributes to several convenience stores for resale. One of his favorites is the Sausage and Meatball combo, but it has a very low distribution. In fact, there are only three stores that take delivery of the Sausage and Meatball: two Fast Stop stores and one Circle B store. One morning, Seymour suffered an unfortunate accident. He slipped on the floor and banged his head. He seemed to be fine, except once he was out on his delivery route, he couldn't remember which streets the three Sausage and Meatball stores were on. The streets were numbered from 1st street up to 154th street. Fortunately, he remembered that the Fast Stop stores were on streets whose numbers added up to 50. He also remembered that the Circle B store was two streets away from one of the Fast Stop stores. And he also remembered that he considered the Sausage and Meatball combination to be his "prime" favorite, as all three stores were on prime-numbered streets. Unfortunately, that wasn't enough information. He called his friend Gus and, well, let's keep this short by saying Gus remembered Seymour having told him the product of the streets the stores were on, but Gus could only remember the last digit of the product. This proved to be enough for Seymour, who promptly double-parked, whipped out a pencil, made a systematic list, and eliminated possibilities to find the answer.

WHO IS LYING?

Jim tells lies on Fridays, Saturdays, and Sundays. He tells the truth on all other days. Freda tells lies on Tuesdays, Wednesdays, and Thursdays. She tells the truth on all other days. If they both said, "Yesterday I lied," then what day is it today?

1. SITTING IN THE PARK

Mary Ann didn't know if her eyes were playing tricks on her or what. When she first looked at the people in the park by the hill she was sitting on, it looked as if they were all in groups of twos. Those groups of two seemed to drift together to form groups of four, and then there were two people left over. Then the next time she looked, they appeared to be in groups of three, but there were the same two left over. As she double-checked, it seemed as though those groups of threes completely transformed themselves into groups of five, and this time there were four left over. There were less than a hundred people at the park. How many were there?

2. DANCING IN PE

Miss Von Thaden tried very hard to make sure that nobody was left out during the PE classes where they danced. She thought she had a correct head count, so she told them to pair up. This didn't work as there was one person left out. She then told them to get into groups of five, but this didn't work either as there was again one person left over. So she tried setting up groups of three, but unfortunately, there was one left over. Finally, she decided to try groups of four. Unfortunately, there was again one person left out. There are less than 80 students in the dance class. How many were present on that particular day?

3. A CUBE ROOT

The cube root of 68921 is an integer. Without using a calculator, determine what that integer is by eliminating possibilities.

TWO CRYPTARITHMS

The rules for each cryptarithmetic problem are the same as always: Each letter stands for one and only one digit.

4. LOVE LETTERS

```
    B  E  A
+   L  O  U
─────────────
 L  O  V  E
```

5. SHUTOUT

```
    S  O  C  C  E  R
+   G  O  A  L  I  E
──────────────────────
 N  O  S  C  O  R  E
```

The victor in a Monopoly game often depends on who has the most houses and hotels. You might say that the person with the most houses and hotels controls the game.

```
    H   O   U   S   E   S
 +  H   O   T   E   L   S
 ─────────────────────────
 C  O   N   T   R   O   L
```

Fill in the grid on the following page using each of the words below once only.

two	**three**	**four**	**five**	**six**
PE	pen	Band	Drama	French
		exam	Music	German
		Math		pencil
		test		sports

seven	**eight**	**nine**	**ten**	**eleven**
absence	homework	cafeteria	dissection	photography
Biology	language	classroom		
English	semester	detention		
History	textbook	counselor		
library	yearbook	principal		
Physics				
Spanish				

FRUITS AND VEGETABLES CRISSCROSS

Fill in the crisscross grid below using each of the following words once only.

Four	Five	Six	Seven
Kiwi	Apple	Banana	Apricot
Pear	Lemon	Orange	Kumquat
Plum	Peach	Potato	Pumpkin
		Tomato	

Eight	Nine	Ten	Eleven
Broccoli	Cranberry	Blackberry	Boysenberry
Cucumber	Greenbean	Strawberry	
Limabean	Raspberry		
Zucchini	Tangerine		

Fit all of these words into the grid.

Three	Four	Five	Six	Seven	Eight	Nine
bat	balk	bases	batter	bullpen	ballpark	sacrifice
era	ball	error	corner	catcher	baseball	
fly	bunt	homer	double	fielder	grounder	
hit	foul	pitch	relief	manager	hummbaby	
low	runs	popup	single	shutout	pitchout	
one	safe	score	strike	squeeze		
out		steal	triple			
rbi			umpire			
two						

Problem Set B, Version 2

1. LOG CUTTING

Selena cut a log into three pieces in 6 minutes. She then cut a similar log into five pieces. How long should the job have taken if she had worked at the same rate?

2. WEIRD WORDS

Write three-letter words according to this plan: The first letter must be B or C. The second letter must be a vowel, and the third letter must be chosen from T, V, or X. How many such words can be written? (These do not have to be English words, or real words of any other language, for that matter.)

3. GETTING AROUND TOWN

The state capitol in California is located in Sacramento. It's beautiful, but getting there is sometimes very tough. I actually needed to get to the corner of 12th and K streets from my location at the corner of 13th and N streets. Unfortunately, due to all the one-way streets, it was going to be very difficult. Sacramento has numbered streets that run north and south, and lettered streets running east and west. The numbers get larger as you drive east, and the letters get later in the alphabet as you drive south. The one-way and two-way streets are as follows.

Two-way: 6th, 11th, 13th, 14th, 17th
One-way: north to south: 7th, 9th, 12th, 15th
One-way: south to north: 8th, 10th, 16th
Two-way: M, O
One-way: west to east: J, N
One-way: east to west: I, L, P

K street is a pedestrian shopping mall with no cars allowed. (Cars can cross K street on numbered streets, but no cars can drive on K street.)

Now, this wouldn't be complicated except for the capitol. It takes up ten square blocks, with no streets going through it from 10th to 15th streets and L to N streets. (M street, 11th, 12th, 13th, and 14th streets are blocked by the capitol. 10th, 15th, L, and N all are continuous along the edges of Capitol Park.) And to top it all off, O street doesn't exist between 12th and 13th streets for some reason. How could I drive from 13th and N to 12th and K?

4. SLEEPY BABIES

The Simpson family gave birth to twins recently. In the twins' early months, they didn't do much except sleep and eat and sleep and smile and sleep. In fact, even when they were awake they did a lot of yawning. The twins' aunt was visiting one day when the father commented about their continuous yawns: baby + baby = yawns. The aunt said, "That sounds like a good problem."

```
      B    A    B    Y
  +   B    A    B    Y
  ─────────────────────
  Y    A    W    N    S
```

Each letter represents one of the digits from 0 to 9. No two letters can stand for the same digit. What sum does this problem represent?

5. VIDEO GAMES

My brother was playing some goofy video game at the arcade. He got 2 points for destroying a tank, 3 points for destroying a helicopter, 6 points for destroying a jet, and an extra point if the jet he blasted was equipped with atomic weapons. He scored 18 points before his quarter ran out. How many different ways could he have reached that score?

Problem Set B, Version 3

1. THE BIKE PATH AROUND THE LAWN

We have a 17-by-20-foot lawn. We want to pour cement for a sidewalk 3-feet wide around the lawn. To make the mold for the cement, we will need to buy some 2-by-4-inch lumber. How many feet of 2-by-4-inch lumber will we need just for the perimeter of the walk? (Consider both the inside and outside perimeter.)

2. FAST FOOD

Patty went to a hamburger joint. She considered the choices below. List all of the possibilities for Patty if she has one meat, a side dish, and a drink.

Meat: Hamburger, chicken nuggets, hot dog
Side dish: Fries, onion rings
Drink: Coffee, milk, soda, milkshake

3. A DARING CATFISH

A daring catfish went on a journey. He left his home early one morning and decided to explore the upper part of the river. Each day he swam about 5 miles upstream against the current, but as he tired and rested, he slipped back with the current about 2 miles each night. Eventually, he went just under 20 miles upstream to a fork in the river, and then swam downstream in the other branch of the river. Swimming downstream was easier, since he was able to swim at his regular speed and be carried along with the current. Then at night when he rested, the current carried him in the direction he wanted to go. He went 35 miles downstream from the fork in the river, and finally reached a lake. How long from the day he left home did it take him to get to the lake? (Assume night and day are each 12 hours long. Also assume that the current in both branches of the river is the same strength.)

4. FIND MY NUMBERS

From the clues below, figure out what five numbers I am thinking of.
1. All the numbers are odd.
2. All the numbers are two-digit numbers
3. The numbers add up to 97.
4. None of the numbers are the same.
5. The largest number is 25.
6. The second-largest number is 4 more than the third-largest number.

5. FOOTBALL SCORES

In how many different ways can the Denver Broncos score 21 points in a football game? Points are scored as follows: A safety scores 2 points, a field goal 3 points, a touchdown 6 points, and a point after touchdown (PAT) scores 1 point. (Note: A PAT cannot be scored unless a touchdown is scored first.)

Problem Set B, Version 4—Camping

1. TRAILERS

I was looking around the various campsites on a recent camping trip. I noticed that all the trailers present had the following characteristics.

Stripes: green, brown, yellow, or blue

windows: sliding, or jalousie

length: 18 ft, 24 ft, or 32 ft

Each trailer in the campsite was different, in some way, from every other trailer. Every possible different trailer was present. How many trailers were there?

2. TRAILER PAD

Each campsite featured a trailer driveway. The driveway measured 21 feet across by 42 feet back and was surrounded on 3 sides by a cement curb 6 inches wide and 8 inches tall. There was no curb on the front of the driveway so that you could drive in. What was the volume of the cement in the curb?

3. KITE CHASING

I was flying a kite during the trip, and my dumb dog was chasing the kite's shadow on the ground. He started out right next to me. He then took three steps ahead, two steps back, three side steps to his right, and two side-steps to his left. He executed this four–move sequence four times. Then he turned 180 degrees around. This time his sequence was three steps ahead, two back, two sidesteps to his right, and three sidesteps to his left. He also executed this sequence four times. Where did he end up?

4. FIELDING PRACTICE

I played baseball with my son on the camping trip. We invented a game called Fielding Practice. He got 10 points for catching a pop fly and making a good throw, 8 points for catching a pop fly and making a bad throw, 7 points for fielding a grounder and making a good throw, 5 points for fielding a grounder and making a bad throw, and 1 point for a good throw after making an error (on either a pop fly or a grounder). He scored 20 points in this game. In how many ways could he have scored 20 points?

5. SLEEPING IN THE TENT

After dinner we sat around trying to make up word arithmetic problems. My wife came up with this one. She told me that the sum of the unused digits is 16. Find the solution.

```
    T  E  N  T
 +  S  I  T  E
 ────────────
 S  L  E  E  P
```

4

matrix logic

L IKE THE STRATEGIES previously covered in the text (systematic lists, eliminating possibilities), matrix logic is a strategy with its roots in organizing information. It is also an extension of the eliminating possibilities strategy. In these problems, though, there is a specific answer or set of specific answers to be uncovered.

This strategy is a paper form of the game Clue. Students must work slowly and carefully, as estimation skills are thrown out the window in matrix logic. An error in matrix logic will not necessarily show up as an unreasonable answer at the end. This strategy is also extremely difficult to write about, as there are a number of steps and complex logical connections involved. For this reason, we advocate a notation that indicates from which clue each negation originates. This notation can help students check their work, explain their reasoning processes, and work together.

Matrix logic is typically used when setting up students' schedules in high schools. It is also often used (though not as uniformly) in setting up teacher's schedules. It can be used for distributing tasks to various people, some of whom can perform several tasks and others who are more specialized.

Notes on Text Problems and Problem Set A

COAST TO COAST

This problem hinges on using the methods of indirect proof. In the text, this method is referred to as "seeking contradictions."

CLASS SCHEDULES

This problem could be adapted for your particular school. Some elements of it may need to be simplified. It would be a high interest exercise for your students to set up the class scheduling matrix using the school's actual master schedule. They could then set up their own schedule and variations on it using matrix logic techniques.

Text Problems

1. FAVORITE SPORT

Ted, Ken, Allyson and Janie (two married couples) each have a favorite sport. The sports are running, swimming, biking, and golfing. Determine who likes which sport from the following clues.

1. Ted hates golf: He agrees with Mark Twain that golf is nothing but a good walk spoiled.
2. Ken can't run around the block, and neither can his wife.
3. Each woman's favorite sport is featured in a triathlon.
4. Allyson bought her husband a new bike for his birthday for use in his favorite sport.

2. OUTDOOR BARBEQUE

Tom, John, Fred, and Bill are friends whose occupations are (in no particular order) nurse, secretary, teacher, and pilot. They attended a church picnic recently, and each one brought his favorite meat (hamburger, chicken, steak, and hotdog's) to barbecue. From the clues below, determine each man's name, occupation, and favorite meat.

1. Tom is neither the nurse nor the teacher.
2. Fred and the pilot play golf together. The burger lover and the teacher hate golf.
3. Tom brought hot dogs.
4. Bill sat next to the burger fan and across from the steak lover.
5. The secretary hates golf.

3. COLLEGE APPLICATIONS

Four high school friends (one was named Cathy) were about to go to college. Their last names are Williams, Burbank, Collins, and Gunderson. Each enrolled in a different college (one was a state college). From the clues below, determine each person's full name and the college he or she attended.

1. No student's first name begins with the same letter as her or his last name. No one's first name ends with the same letter as the end of his or her last name.
2. Neither Hank nor Williams went to the community college.
3. Alan, Collins, and the student who went to the university all live on the same street. The other student lives two blocks away.
4. Gladys and Hank live next door to each other.
5. The private college accepted Hank's application, but he decided that he could not afford to go there.

4. COAST TO COAST

Four women live in different cities. One of the cities is San Francisco. Determine which city each woman lives in.

1. The women from Charleston and Gainesville, and Riana are not related.
2. Wendy and the woman from Provo are cousins.
3. Neither Phyllis nor Wendy is from the west coast.
4. Ann is from a coastal city.

Problem Set A, Version 2

1. THE HOBBYISTS

Elaine, Lisa, Brittney, and Consuelo each have hobbies (model railroading, building model airplanes, rocketry, raising tropical fish). Match each woman to her hobby using the clues below.

1. Lisa has never met the person who does rocketry.
2. Elaine is a pilot and ironically has a hobby that has nothing to do with aeronautics.
3. The rocketry hobbyist, the railroader, and Brittney are friends.
4. Lisa's hobby involves public transportation.

2. MIXED DOUBLES TENNIS

Amaya, Ostergard, Blue Cloud, and Katricz are the last names of Timothy, Diana, Mark, and Sherry. They are all playing in a mixed doubles tennis tournament. Two people are on each team. There is one man and one woman on each team. Determine the full name of each player using the clues below.

1. Mark is a better player than Ostergard.
2. Timothy is Diana's partner.
3. Sherry and Katricz are on the same team.
4. Amaya is known for his wicked serve.
5. Katricz is an opponent of Ostergard.
6. Blue Cloud is an opponent of Amaya.

3. SUMMER JOBS

Four friends are all working in summer jobs. Their names are LaTisha, Zack, Steve, and Michelle. The jobs they have found this summer include food server, lifeguard, construction worker, and bagger at a grocery store. Determine who is working which job by using the clues below.

1. The person doing the food serving job really likes his work.
2. Zack and the lifeguard have known each other for years.
3. Both Michelle and the lifeguard are outside most of the time, and the other two are inside most of the time.
4. Latisha and the person working construction met on their job last summer.
5. Neither Zack nor the food server worked last summer.

4. SPORTS IS ALL RELATIVE

Determine each person's favorite sport. (One person's name is Michael, and one sport was tennis.)

1. Two siblings had the same favorite sport.
2. Stefan liked a sport everyone else hated.
3. Ryan did not like bowling.
4. Bonnie was one of the two who liked basketball.
5. Ryan is Bonnie's cousin.

MATH DEPARTMENT MEETING

James: I've gathered the five of you here to discuss the class schedule for next semester. There are five classes left to staff: statistics, calculus, finite, algebra, and tech math.

Fara: I've been teaching algebra a lot recently. I want a break.

James: Okay, Cliff you've been teaching tech math every semester. Do you want it again?

Cliff: Yeah, it's okay, I'll take it.

James: Okay. What about finite? Who's interested?

Laurie: I am.

Fara: So am I.

(No one else said anything.)

James: Well, okay. Let's talk about calculus. Who is interested?

Fara: I am.

(Elaine and Maile said they were too.)

James: Well, can we agree on stats?

Maile: I don't want it.

Laurie: I've been doing it but I want a break.

James: Okay, well how about algebra?

Elaine: I've been teaching it and there are more things I want to try. Does anyone else want it?

James (after waiting a few seconds): Okay, you've got it Elaine.

(James made some notes and showed them to Fara.)

James: Is this okay, Fara? You've never taught it before . . .

Fara: Yeah, it's okay. I'll give it a try.

What classes did each person end up with?

6. **NEXT YEAR AT COLLEGE**

Akinte, Chuck, Jenny, and Norma are all going to college next year. Use these clues to find their full names and their respective colleges.

1. Akinte is not going to the University of Memphis or to Penn Valley, and the same is true of Van Hee.
2. Chuck applied to Penn Valley but decided to go elsewhere.
3. Penigar and the student going to Penn Valley are avid tennis players.
4. Norma, the person going to St. Mary's, and Penigar all want to major in biology.
5. Both Norma and Reynoso considered Penn Valley as their second choice.
6. Akinte and Oslowski both were summer counselors at Sierra Tech, even though neither one will go there during the regular year.

7. **LOOMIS DAY PARADE**

We didn't know who to root for to win "Best of Parade" in the Loomis Day Parade. We knew about half the people in the parade. We saw Stacy, Mort, Wayne, and Cloe, each participating in a different group. In fact, among them they finished first through fourth place as "Best of Parade," though not necessarily in that order. Match the names with the group or activity and the place each group was awarded.

1. Stacy's group placed higher than the dance company.
2. One of the band members had a bet with Wayne, but Wayne's group came in higher.
3. Cloe and Mort both used to belong to the baton twirlers' group but were too busy with their other activities to continue.
4. Mort's group placed higher than the horse rider but lower than the band.
5. Cloe, the trumpeter, and a member of the first-place group all go to Del Oro High School.

8. STUDENT ACHIEVEMENT AWARDS

The top students (Velma, Matt, Ginny, and Clyde) in four courses (English, Computers, Physics and Math) at Des Moines High were honored at a pre-graduation ceremony. Match each student's first name, last name, and course.

1. The girl who won in Computers was also a runner-up in English.
2. Sholseth moved to Des Moines eight months ago and couldn't get into the computer class because it was full.
3. Both Sholseth and Clyde were in the same math class with the top math student.
4. The top English student, the one named Kinsella, and Ginny have lived in Des Moines all their lives.
5. The boy who won the honors in math barely beat out Macomber. Both boys were runners-up in computers.
6. Perata knew she was close for math honors.

9. NOVEMBER ELECTIONS

Four political allies are running for different offices in the November elections: President, Governor, Assembly, and Senator. Their first names are Margurite, Darcie, Brent, and Amir. Their last names are Cusack, Tomfohrde, Wyckoff, and Hardy. Match up each person's full name to the office they are running for using the clues below.

1. Of Margurite and Tomfohrde, one is running for Senator and the other is running for Governor, though not necessarily in that order. Candidate Cusack did not enter either race.
2. Darcie has been helping the candidate for President campaign in her area.
3. Brent is not running for President and neither is Hardy.
4. Wyckoff and Darcie once opposed each other in a City Council primary race.
5. The candidate for Governor is neither Darcie nor Tomfohrde.
6. Marguerite has never run for office before.

Problem Set B, Version 2

1. PACIFIC RIM

Lois Onassis wishes to establish shipping routes around the Pacific Rim. She wants to set up freight services in the following eight ports: Los Angeles, Anchorage, Tokyo, Taipei (Taiwan), Manila (Philippines), Auckland (New Zealand), Valparaíso (Chile), and Lima (Peru). She wants a separate shipping route connecting each pair of ports. How many such routes does she need to establish?

2. PRIME JACKS

Five friends—Amy, Betty, Clarrise, Dawn, and Ellen—each have a certain number of jacks. Amy has the fewest, Betty the next fewest, and so on up to Ellen who has the most. Each girl has a different number of jacks and each number is a two-digit prime number ending in nine. The problem with having a prime number of jacks is that they cannot be arranged in piles with the same number of jacks in each pile. For example, if a girl had seven jacks, she could only put them into one pile of seven or seven piles of one. However, if she had eight jacks, she could arrange them in one pile of eight, two piles of four, four piles of two, or eight piles of one. For this reason, each of the girls occasionally likes to combine her jacks with one of the other girl's jacks to be able to separate them into piles with the same number of jacks in each pile. Which pair of girls can combine their jacks and be able to separate them into same-sized piles in the greatest number of different ways? Which pair combines for the least number of ways?

3. RELATIONSHIPS

Bob is Phil's father. Jack is Phil's only brother. Tina is Phil's sister-in-law. Phil is not married. Mary is Tina's mother-in-law. John is Jack's son. What relation is John to Mary? What relation is Tina to Bob?

4. TO TELL THE TRUTH

Four friends get together. One tells the truth all the time. One lies all the time. One tells the truth on odd-numbered days and lies on even-numbered days. One tells the truth on even-numbered days and lies on odd-numbered days. One day in May, they made the following statements.

Abe: I lied yesterday.
Bonnie: Today is the 12th.
Carol: Yesterday's date was even.
Doug: Carol's statement is true.

Which of the four friends tells the truth on even-numbered days and lies on odd-numbered days?

The news team at WOWM in Chicago is an outstanding group of individuals who have banded together to form an excellent broadcasting team. Four of the most outstanding are the anchor, sports reporter, director, and producer. Their names (in no particular order) are Alex, Chris, Pat, and Sam. The lengths of times they have been at the station are 5, 10, 15, and 20 years. From the clues below, determine each person's name, job, and years of service to the station.

1. Among the four are two women and two men. One man and one woman are on camera.
2. Alex (short for Alexandra) used to be on camera but 12 years ago switched to the off-camera job she currently holds.
3. Chris (short for Christopher) has been at the station longer than the anchor but not as long as Sam.
4. Pat (short for Patrick) has never worked behind the scenes.
5. Sam (short for Samantha) started at the station 10 years before the anchor. Her first job at WOWM was lighting technician.
6. The director has never held any other job.

Problem Set B, Version 3

1. DOOR IN AND DOOR OUT

An auditorium has 11 doors numbered 1 through 11. In how many ways is it possible to enter the auditorium through an odd-numbered door and leave through an even-numbered door?

2. JERRY'S AGE

Jerry got a phone call from a telephone solicitor who said he was taking a survey. First he asked how old Jerry was. Jerry gave the following clues.
"My age is between 30 and 69 inclusive."
The salesman asked if he was in his thirties.
"If I am not in my thirties, then my age is a multiple of four."
The salesman asked if he was in his forties.
"If I am not in my forties, then my age is a multiple of seven."
The salesman asked if he was in his fifties.
"If I am not in my fifties, then my age is not a multiple of five."
The salesman finally asked if he was in his sixties.
"If I am not in my sixties, then my age is not a multiple of eight."
How old is Jerry?

3. KLINGONS LIKE WORD ARITHMETIC TOO

When Captain Picard first visited the Klingon home world with Lieutenant Worf, they visited the home of Worf's brother, Kern. Kern was quite fond of word-arithmetic problems similar to the word-arithmetic problems Picard had done on Earth as a boy. Worf challenged Picard on a word-arithmetic problem provided by Kern. As is the custom in Earth problems, each letter stands for one of the digits 0 through 9, and no two letters stand for the same digit. You may not recognize the words, as they are Klingon. Find the sum represented by this problem.

```
    C   R   E   K   L   G
+   R   U   T   A   N   G
------------------------
    C   K   G   L   E   L   K
```

THE SHADOW KNOWS

John Henry was camping in a large, sparsely wooded area in southern Texas. One day he went for a walk. He packed some food and left at 8:00 a.m. on a cloudless, hot day. He walked for 2 miles with his shadow on his left. Then he walked for 5 miles with his shadow in front of him. Then he walked 3 miles with his shadow on his right. Then he walked 1 mile with his shadow behind him. By this time it was 11:00 a.m. He stopped in a nice meadow and had lunch. Then he fell asleep, as he was tired from walking. When he woke up, it was 1:00 p.m. He was a little disoriented from his nap as he set out to walk home. He figured he could reverse his previous distances and shadows and walk back to his camp. So he walked 1 mile with his shadow in front of him. Then he walked 3 miles with his shadow on his left. Then he walked 5 miles with his shadow behind him. Then he walked 2 miles with his shadow on his right. Unfortunately, he didn't arrive back at his camp. Give directions for him to get back to his camp by the shortest route.

5. **THE NEW FALL SEASON**

The program directors for WBC got together to discuss programming for the upcoming fall season. The result was four new shows: a comedy, a drama, a variety show, and a news program. The names of the shows were *Wall Street Blues, All in Favor, Murphy's Law,* and *Fifty-Fifty*. The shows were scheduled to air on Monday, Tuesday, Wednesday, and Thursday. From the clues below, determine the name, day, and type of each program.

1. Tuesday's show (which was not *Murphy's Law*) and the news program had been tried out during the previous spring.
2. *Fifty-Fifty* was not the variety show.
3. The drama (which was not *Fifty-Fifty*) and Monday's show (which was not *Wall Street Blues*) were produced by the same company.
4. *All in Favor* (which was not the drama) and Monday's show (which was not the news program) both featured a person named Bob.
5. Neither *Wall Street Blues* nor the drama would be on Thursday.

Problem Set B, Version 4

1. LUCKY SVEN

I went out shopping for a used car a few days ago. I stopped at Lucky Sven's Autorama. One car I liked was priced at $3,211, another was $2,311, and another was $4,111. I noticed that if you added up all of the digits, they added to 7. I talked to the owner (Sven), and he told me that every car was priced like that; the sum of the digits in the price was 7. Every car had a different price, and he never used a zero in the price. None of the cars cost more than $15,000 and none cost less than $1,000. How many different prices did Sven have available to him?

2. LETTER PUZZLE

In the puzzle below, each letter stands for a different digit from 0 to 9. The same letter stands for the same digit throughout the problem. What digit does each letter represent?

$$Y + W = D \qquad D - G = R \qquad W/Y = G \qquad C + M = C$$

$$H \times A = H \qquad Y + Y = W \qquad Y - G = A \qquad H \times G = L$$

3. TWO GUARDIANS

This problem was written by a student.

There are two guardians guarding two doors. One of the doors leads to certain death and the other doesn't. One guardian always tells the truth, and the other guardian always lies but you do not know which guardian is which. Each guardian made a statement.

Guardian 1: "The other guardian always lies."

Guardian 2: "The other guardian would say door number two leads to certain death."

Which door should you take?

4. RELATIVES

Denise was married to Ron. They had a daughter named Jeannine. Denise then married Scott and they had a son named Phillip. Scott had been previously married to Joan. They had a son named Tom. Ron then married Amy. They had a daughter named Nancy. Amy had been previously married to Bob. They had a son named Woody. Some of the kids are half-brothers or half-sisters and others are step-brothers or step-sisters. Other kids are not related at all. Determine all of the relationships among the kids.

Four high school friends, Wayne, Garth, Dana, and Mike (whose last names are Campbell, Algar, Carvey, and Myers) love to watch the movie *Wayne's World*. They each play one instrument in a four-piece rock band (guitar, bass, keyboard, and drums). From the clues below, determine each person's full name and what instrument each plays.

1. The friends think it very unusual that the two characters in the movie *Wayne's World* are named Wayne Campbell and Garth Algar, played by actors Mike Myers and Dana Carvey. However, none of the four friends has any of those full names.

2. Wayne and Carvey are seniors. Only one of them sings in the band.

3. Two of the three seniors and the keyboard player (who is a junior) are taking chemistry together. Mike (the other senior) is taking physics instead of chemistry.

4. Only two of the band members sing. One of them is a junior and the other is Myers.

5. The drummer phoned Algar to get the chemistry assignment and was surprised to find that Algar was not taking chemistry.

6. Neither the guitar player nor the drummer sing.

look for a pattern

LOOKING FOR PATTERNS is a central learning skill of mathematics. It is not just a learning skill, but it is also the central theme of mathematics study. Math is often called "the study of patterns." It is essential to be able to see and interpret patterns in order to enjoy the beauty of mathematics. This chapter looks at arithmetic, exponential, Fibonacci, and other types of patterns. It also develops looking for patterns as a problem-solving strategy. Looking for patterns will also be an integral part of the strategy described in Chapter 9: Solve an Easier Related Problem.

Looking for a pattern is another strategy based on organizing information. By organizing information, you will be able to extract more out of it.

It is important for students to take time to discuss patterns that may seem trivial to you. Many of these patterns are not trivial for students. And, as usual, it is important for students to write out their work, showing their thought processes.

Looking for patterns is an essential part of expanding thinking. Any type of research is based on discovering and describing patterns. In virtually any occupation, people are called upon to notice patterns. Auto mechanics may notice that certain makes of automobiles have trouble with injection systems. Or perhaps they notice early buildup of carbon inside cylinders on certain engines.

Real-life patterns don't have to be occupationally based. For example, you might notice someone keeps looking at you. That pattern may indicate a romantic interest, or possibly that you have twigs stuck in your hair. Effective parenting requires the ability to notice patterns—noticing that certain rewards work well with children and that certain stimuli exact negative behaviors from children. In softball, a batter who swings at pitches too far inside may find that the pitcher noticed that and will keep on pitching there.

Text Problems

SEQUENCES

Find the pattern and predict the next four terms. Then write a sentence explaining your pattern.

1. 1, 2, 4, ___, ___, ___, ___
2. 1, 3, 5, 7, ___, ___, ___, ___
3. 1, 6, 11, 16, ___, ___, ___, ___
4. 1, 4, 9, 16, ___, ___, ___, ___
5. 1, 3, 6, 10, ___, ___, ___, ___
6. 3, 6, 5, 10, 9, 18, 17, 34, ___, ___, ___, ___
7. 77, 49, 36, 18, ___ (the sequence ends there)

DODGER STADIUM

There is a joke among radio broadcasters about the number of people who start leaving Dodger Stadium in the seventh inning of baseball games. One evening, during a particularly boring baseball game in which the Dodgers were trailing by six runs after six innings, the fans began to leave at a record pace. After the first out in the top of the seventh inning, 100 fans left. After the second out, 150 fans left. After the third out, 200 fans left. The pattern continued in this way, with 50 more fans leaving after each out than had left after the previous out. The ridiculous thing was, the Dodgers tied up the game in the bottom of the ninth inning, and people still kept leaving early. The game lasted ten innings (the Dodgers lost anyway), and the pattern continued through the bottom of the tenth inning. How many fans left early?

TABLES OF VALUES

Determine the rule for each of the functions shown below. Then fill in the output for the inputs 5 and 895.

IN	OUT	IN	OUT	IN	OUT	IN	OUT
M	?	N	?	P	?	Q	?
0	5	0	0	0	-3	0	0
1	6	1	2	1	-1	1	-1
2	7	2	4	2	1	2	-2
3	8	3	6	3	3	3	-3
4	9	4	8	4	5	4	-4
5	?	5	?	5	?	5	?
895	?	895	?	895	?	895	?

Hint: if you can't figure out what the rule is, simply treat each problem as if it were a sequence written vertically. Note: These are four separate problems.

Jamie wanted to buy a rabbit. She had always liked the Easter bunny when she was a kid, so she decided to raise some bunnies of her own. She went to the store with the intention of buying one rabbit, but she ended up with two newborn rabbits, a male and a female. She named them Patrick and Susan. Well, rabbits being what they are (rabbits) it is fairly impossible to have just two rabbits for an extended period of time. She bought them on April 1, 1991, which happened to be the day after Easter that year. On June 1, she noticed that Patrick and Susan were now the proud parents of two newborn rabbits, again one male and one female. She named these new arrivals Thomas and Ursula.

On July 1, Patrick and Susan again gave birth to a male and female rabbit. She named these Vida and Wanda.

On August 1, Patrick and Susan again gave birth to a male and a female. And so did Thomas and Ursula. Jamie was running out of names, so she didn't bother giving them any.

On September 1, Patrick and Susan gave birth to a male and a female, and so did Thomas and Ursula, and so did Vida and Wanda. (Actually, Vida was no longer Vida and Thomas was no longer Thomas. Jamie was worried about maintaining a diverse genetic pool among her bunnies, so she traded the original Thomas and Vida to other breeders and named their replacements with the same names.)

Jamie also noticed a pattern. A pair of rabbits was born. Two months later they bred a pair of rabbits and continued to breed a pair of rabbits every month after that.

Jamie wondered, "If this keeps up, how many rabbits am I going to have on April 1 of 1992?"

FIBONACCI SEQUENCES

Find the next four values of each of these sequences.

1. 2, 2, 4, 6, 10, 16, 26, ___, ___, ___, ___
2. 1, 3, 4, 7, 11, 18, 29, ___, ___, ___, ___
3. 3, 1, 4, 5, 9, 14, ___, ___, ___, ___
4. 1, 2, 3, 6, 11, 20, 37, ___, ___, ___, ___
5. ___, ___, ___, ___, 16, 25, 41, 66, 107

MORE SEQUENCES

Find the next four terms of these sequences

1. 2, 3, 5, 9, 17, 33, ___, ___, ___, ___
2. 1, 5, 13, 29, 61, 125, ___, ___, ___, ___
3. 1, 4, 13, 40, 121, 364, ___, ___, ___, ___

Shawna liked to jog late at night. One night she noticed an unusual phenomenon: as she jogged, dogs would hear her and bark. After the first dog had barked for about 15 seconds, two other dogs would join in and bark. And then in about another 15 seconds, it seemed that each barking dog would "inspire" two more dogs to start barking. Of course, long after Shawna passed the first dog, it continued to bark, as dogs are inclined to do. After about 3 minutes, how many dogs were barking (as a result of Shawna passing the first dog)?

MILK LOVERS

Alysia and Melissa and Dante and Melody loved milk. They convinced their older brother, Mark, who did all of the shopping, to buy them each their own gallon of milk, because they liked it so much. They all put their names on their gallons. One day, they were all really thirsty and each took ten drinks according to a different system. Alysia started by drinking half of the milk in her container. Then she drank one-third of what was left. Then she drank one-fourth of what was left, then one-fifth, and so on.

Melissa started by drinking one-eleventh of her milk, then one-tenth of what was left, then one-ninth of what was left, and so on.

Dante started by drinking one-half of his milk, then two-thirds of what was left, then three-fourths of what was left, then four-fifths, and so on.

Melody started by drinking one-half of her milk, then one-half of what was left, then one-half of what was left, and so on.

After each had taken ten drinks, how much milk remained in each container?

1. SEQUENCE PATTERNS #2

Write the next three numbers in each sequence and explain your pattern.
- a. 5, 8, 11, 14, 17, ___, ___, ___
- b. -1, 1, 3, 5, 7, ___, ___, ___
- c. 2, 3, 5, 8, 12, ___, ___, ___
- d. 3, 2, 5, 7, 12, ___, ___, ___
- e. -1, 5, 4, 9, 13, ___, ___, ___
- f. 4, 5, 7, 10, 10, 15, 13, ___, ___, ___
- g. -2, -1, 1, 4, 8, ___, ___, ___
- h. 5, 7, 11, 19, 35, ___, ___, ___

2. SPREADSHEET #2

The chart below is a spreadsheet. The numbers in each column are reached by doing some operation on the numbers in the x and y columns. For example, Column D is the result of multiplying the number in the x column by 2, then subtracting the number in the y column. In row 1, $x = 1$ and $y = 3$. Multiplying 1 by 2 gives 2, then subtracting 3 gives the answer -1 that appears in the D column. Similarly, in row 2, $x = 4$. Multiplying 4 by 2 and subtracting 1 gives 7, which appears in the D column. The rules for some columns involve only one of the numbers x or y. The rules for other columns involve both x and y. Determine the rules that generate the numbers in the A, B, C, E, F, G, H and I columns.

x	y	A	B	C	D ($2x - y$)	E	F	G	H	I
1	3	2	2	9	-1	5	3	5	3	2
4	1	8	-3	3	7	8	-1	6	4	0
3	0	6	-3	0	6	7	-3	4	0	-3
5	-1	10	-6	-3	11	9	-5	5	-5	-10
2	3	4	1	9	1	6	3	6	6	4
4	2	8	-2	6	6	8	1	7	8	4
2	6	4	4	18	-2	6	9	9	12	10
-1	-2	-2	-1	-6	0	3	-7	-2	2	3
0	4	0	4	12	-4	4	5	5	0	0
3	2	6	-1	6	4	7	1	6	6	3
-2	5	-4	7	15	-9	2	7	4	-10	-8

3. FUNCTIONS

Determine the rule for each function. Then fill in the outputs for the other inputs shown.

IN	OUT		IN	OUT		IN	OUT
H	I		Q	R		W	X
0	0		0	4		0	-1
1	3		1	5		1	1
2	6		2	6		2	3
3	9		3	7		3	5
4	12		4	8		4	7
5			5			5	
145			318			77	

4. THE GREAT SALE

There was a great clearance sale going on at Tucker's Department Store. Asa called his friends Maggie, Spencer, and Pam right away starting at 9:00 a.m. Each of Asa's friends called three of their friends in the next half hour but did not call any more friends after those three. Each subsequent person who was informed about the sale then called three more during the next half hour. The pattern of friends calling friends continued until just before 3:00 that afternoon. How many people heard about the sale as a result of Asa and his friends?

5. MMM MACARONI AND CHEESE

Orie was too excited about his new toy to sit still. He came to the lunch table, ate ⅙ of his macaroni and cheese, then left to play with something, came back, ate ⅐ of what was left, ran and played, came back, ate ⅛ of what was left, and so on. After ten episodes of eating then playing, how much of his original macaroni and cheese was left?

6. BIRD AND BEEF

Paloma and Chuck opened a "bird and beef" stand, featuring hamburgers and gourmet squab filets. On the first day nobody came. On the second day, however, there were two customers. On the third day there were four customers and on the fourth day there were six customers. After 50 days, how many customers total will they have served if this pattern keeps up? (Note that after 3 days, they had served 6 total customers since $0 + 2 + 4 = 6$.)

7. MAILING LISTS

Millie was always buying things through the mail. At least sometimes Millie bought things through the mail. Well, actually, once she bought something through the mail as a present for her granddaughter from the *Fishing in the West* catalog. The order arrived in January, and so did five other catalogs, apparently spawned from the mailing list of the first one. If every new catalog sells its mailing list to five other companies, and it takes a month for the new company to deliver a catalog and sell the mailing list, how many total catalogs will she receive by the end of the year?

8. THE ANTS COME MARCHING IN

I left out some pizza last night, and I'm paying for my mistake this morning. When I got up I counted 50 ants. I followed their trail back and saw that more were coming. In fact, I noticed that there was a group of 10. Next came a group of 13. After that, a group of 16 marched in. Each group was bigger by 3 ants than the previous group. In fact, this continued through 13 more groups of ants. (I saw 16 groups of ants march in.) How many ants arrived in the last group?

9. PARTY TIME

A home supplies manufacturer sells their products through household parties. A skilled salesperson is able to develop three new parties for the next week out of each party held. Starting with two parties held the first week, how long will it take before this salesperson has held more than 300 parties?

10. YOUR OWN SEQUENCES

Generate your own sequences. Write out eight terms for each sequence.

a. Generate an arithmetic sequence based on adding or subtracting the same value each time.

b. Generate a geometric sequence based on multiplying or dividing by the same number each time.

c. Generate a Fibonacci sequence.

d. Generate a sequence based on an increasing difference each time (for example, add 1, then add 2, next add 3 . . .).

e. Generate a sequence in two steps (for example, multiply by 2, subtract 1, multiply by 2, subtract 1 . . .).

Problem Set B, Version 2

1. SOMETHING BUT THE TRUTH

The police were having a hard time with a case. They caught three people at the scene of a store robbery. According to all evidence, there had been only two perpetrators: one main burglar with an accomplice. Under questioning, the main burglar would obviously tell a lie, the innocent one would tell the truth, and the accomplice might lie or might tell the truth. From their statements below, determine which person was which.

Louise: I was the accomplice.
Manny: Rick is the main burglar.
Rick: Louise is the accomplice.

2. YALE RECORD CLUB

Yale Record Club made me an offer I couldn't refuse. For their cheap, low price I could buy millions of records, tapes, and compact discs (CDs) and save millions of dollars. Well, anyway, I joined. The first month I wanted (and bought) 3 CDs and the cost was $24.84. The second month I ordered 5 for a total $38.82. Did I mention that the cost covered the CDs and the shipping and handling? Anyway, for $31.83, I bought 4 CDs the next month. I paid $17.85 for 2 discs the next month. I looked through their catalog and picked out 38 more CDs that I wanted to buy sometime. If I buy all 38 at once, then I only pay the shipping and handling fee 1 time. On the other hand, if I buy them in smaller groups, well. . . . What I really need to know is, how much would it cost to buy all 38 CDs as one order?

3. TEN POSTS

Arranged in a straight line are 10 posts with 10 meters between consecutive posts. Mr. Jones must nail a sign on each of the posts. He wants to do as much walking as possible while doing this. He will only walk along the straight line of the posts. He is going to start at his home, which is 10 meters from the first post on the same line as the posts. He is carrying all 10 signs. What is the length of the longest possible walk that will allow him to nail a sign on each post and return home?

4. THE PET STORE CONTEST

The local pet store held a contest in which they drew 10 children's names as semi-finalists. (They gave each one a pet kitten—parental permission required.) They then held another drawing from among those 10 to determine who would win the top 2 prizes: a pair of homing pigeons or a cockatiel. The ages of the semi-finalists were 4, 5, 6, 7, 9, 10, 11, 13, 15, and 16. When the 2 winners' names were drawn, the older winner was a teenager. What is the probability that the younger winner's age is prime?

In the Broadway musical *How to Succeed in Business Without Really Trying*, a young man played by Robert Morse works his way up from window washer to vice president of a company without doing much work. This problem is based on that musical.

At the company picnic of the World Wide Widget Corporation (offices in Topeka, Kansas) five men got together. Their names were Gus, Woody, Ned, Dick, and Jake. They all lived in Topeka now, but had grown up in five other towns in Kansas: Wichita, Dodge City, Belleville, Concordia, and Lawrence. Their jobs with the company (in order, from lowest ranking to highest) were window washer, mailroom clerk, bookkeeper, manager, and vice president. Some people were hired at the absolute lowest position of window washer and worked their way up, while other people were hired at some higher level and worked their way up. In any case, a person worked at each level for one year and then moved up to the next level. (As you might expect, this company had lots of vice presidents.) From the clues below, determine each man's name, position with the company, and where he grew up. (Note: It is possible to play more than one game at the picnic.)

1. The man from Belleville worked in a position immediately higher than the man from Lawrence. They were each attending their first company picnic. Vice president Gus played softball with them.
2. Gus and Ned had played horseshoes with the man from Wichita at last year's picnic.
3. Jake played basketball with the window washer, who was attending his first picnic.
4. The man from Dodge City will be a vice president next year. He and Woody had eaten lunch together at last year's picnic.

Problem Set B, Version 3

1. BURBANK NEIGHBORS

There are exactly five houses that occupy the entire length of one block. In front of each house is a car belonging to the owner of the house. The five owners are Stanley, Neuerburg, Stump, Frick, and Wahhab. The colors of the cars are blue, green, maroon, red, and yellow. Determine who lives in which house, and which car each drives.

    1. The person who owns the fifth house owns the yellow car.

    2. The house Neuerburg owns has houses on either side of it.

    3. Stanley owns the maroon car.

    4. The person who owns the second house owns the red car.

    5. Wahhab owns the middle house.

    6. Stump does not own the yellow car.

    7. The person who owns the first house owns the green car.

2. KANGA AND ROO

Kanga and Roo decided to have a race. Kanga jumps 8 feet with every jump and made 1 jump every 4 seconds. Roo, on the other hand, jumps twice as fast (1 jump every 2 seconds) but only jumps 4 feet with each jump. The race course was 100 feet long, with the race being up and back. (So that's 200 feet total.) Who won and by how far?

3. BUCKS FOR CLUCKS

John loves game shows on TV—so much so that I promised I would go with him to a taping of *Bucks for Clucks* dressed as a farmer (John was dressed as a fox), and we would split whatever we earned down the middle. The costumes were apparently good enough, as we were chosen to "crack the golden egg." There were three huge fiberglass eggs on the stage, each painted gold and each with some sort of prize in it. (There is always one "turkey," a good prize, and a great prize. The real golden egg is the one that contains the great prize.) Each egg had a sign in front of it:

Egg 1: The turkey is in egg 2.

Egg 2: This egg is the golden egg.

Egg 3: The turkey is in egg 1.

As usual on this show, we knew that one of the signs was accurate and the other two were incorrect. (In the parlance of the show, the other two were "rotten.") Which egg should John and I choose in order to maximize our chances for getting the great prize?

4. DOG AND TREES

We had just moved into our new home in the country. I took my favorite howling dog, Spam, out so he could sniff around the yard. Well, dogs being territorial, he wasn't content just to sniff, but he, well, he, well he, putting it politely, he marked off his territory. I realize that dogs aren't that smart or we'd be the ones with collars around our necks. Anyway, there was a wind break at the edge of our property. Of course Spam had to make it part of his territory, so he went and marked each tree. There are only 12 trees in this straight line and they're all about 8 meters from the next one in the row. I'm sure that ol' Spam walked to and marked each and every tree. Furthermore, I'm sure that as he went from one tree to the next, he walked the greatest distance possible. I mean he didn't just go from one tree to the next, but he went to some other tree in the wind break so that he never marked the same tree twice and he walked, I'm sure, the longest total distance possible. How far did Spam walk from whatever tree he started at to whatever tree he ended at?

5. PRODUCT OF OUR TIMES

I think it was back in 1990, I wrote the date 3/30/90 and noticed that the month times the day gave the year. I noticed it again on October 9: 10/9/90. That made me wonder: How many times this does this occur during the decade of the 1990s?

Problem Set B, Version 4

1. NEW CAR OPTIONS

June wants to buy a new car. She visited her local new car dealer and found that he has cars with exterior colors of (in order from darkest to lightest) black, navy blue, burgundy, green, tan, and white. For the interior color she can order any of those colors, but the interior color must be the same as, or lighter than, the exterior color. However, there are no cars that combine green and burgundy or green and navy blue. Hood ornaments may be ordered on cars that have burgundy (either outside, inside, or both). Sun roofs may be ordered on cars with white or tan interior. Fancy hubcaps are available on cars with black or navy blue exterior. How many different styles of cars are available?

2. SHEET CAKE

Andrew's cake measures 18 inches by 20 inches. The cake sat on the table in front of Andrew with the 18-inch sides on the left and right. Andrew cut off pieces of the cake measuring 2 inches by 2 inches and served them to the guests at his party. His friends all like sugar, so he cut off side pieces, starting at the bottom right, and worked his way clockwise all the way around the cake. After he cut off the last side piece, he continued cutting and serving in a clockwise spiral starting from the bottom right. What was the original location of the last piece he served?

3. PLANET THREA

On the planet Threa, the days have 24 hours and there are 60 minutes per hour. The 12-hour locks go from 1 o'clock to 2 o'clock, and so on, up to 12 o'clock and then start again at 1 o'clock. The digital clocks are different than Earth's, however. The minutes come before the hours. So the time that reads 04:10 is actually 4 minutes after 10, a time which on Earth would appear as 10:04. A visitor from earth could get quite confused at certain times. On the other hand, the Threa time 21:06 would certainly not be confusing, since you would never see a time that looked that way on a 12-hour lock on Earth. What is the probability that an Earth visitor looking at the clock will see a time that could represent a valid time on Earth? (Assume all single digits have zeros in front of them.)

CAMP SACRAMENTO

At Camp Sacramento, there was a great playground. Five kids loved to play there: Lisa, Danny, Justin, Jacob, and Jamie. Their last names were Bland, Walker, and Horlick (there were two sets of siblings among the five). Each child had a favorite activity at the playground: slide, tire swing, monkey bars, rings, and a big rock. From the clues below, determine each person's full name and favorite activity.

1. At Camp Sacramento, there were three groups for the kids: the marmots for kids 10–12 years old, the chipmunks for 6–9 year olds, and the minnows for 3–5 year olds. None of the five children were minnows. Jacob and the younger Horlick were chipmunks. Lisa and the two Walkers were marmots.
2. Lisa didn't spend very much time in the playground, but when she did, she never went on the slide or the tire swing.
3. None of the marmots liked the rock. Danny didn't either.
4. Jaime was only 9, but she was a marmot anyway so she could be in the same group with her brother.
5. The elder Horlick and the two chipmunks didn't like the monkey bars. A girl liked the tire swing.

5. **PLAYING DETECTIVE**

Four suspects were assembled in the principal's office, having been accused of a devious crime: turning off the light switch during Mr. Buehler's social studies lecture. It was known that only one of the four turned off the switch. All four were friends, and the principal's secretary overhead them plotting before they were brought into the principal's office. They all agreed to tell the same number of false statements, although the secretary did not hear the agreed upon number. Their statements are below. Who turned off the light switch?

Joe: Frank didn't do it.

All of us always tell the truth.

I went to junior high with Felipe.

Felipe: I didn't do it.

Joe didn't go to junior high with me.

John didn't do it.

John: I didn't do it.

Felipe's best friend is Joe.

We all agreed to tell one false statement.

Frank: Joe did it.

Felipe's best friend is not Joe.

We all agreed to tell two false statements.

I didn't do it.

guess and check

GUESS AND CHECK is an effective, powerful problem-solving tool. It is a relatively newly articulated strategy, and as such faces a lot of obstacles. Many people who are trained in mathematics have a difficult time accepting guess and check as a valid problem-solving strategy that students should know. Although it is appearing in new editions of many textbooks, it's often presented as a sidelight—not an essential strategy for solving problems in the text. In time, guess and check will be more universally accepted, and the method(s) for teaching the strategy will be framed and refined.

Although we were generally taught in our own math classes not to guess, this strategy involves more than guessing. It is a strategy of guessing and then guessing again. Each guess is evaluated according to the conditions in the problem, and the results are recorded in an organized fashion. The next guess is not so much a guess as it is a "guesstimate." The strategy might be described as "guesstimate, compute, organize, evaluate, and refine." Each successive guess develops more information about the problem or develops more data about the solution.

In order for students to learn from their guesses, the guesses must not be random. It is essential to organize the guesses and computations in a chart. There is, however, no set formula for setting up the chart. In fact, part of the process that needs to be imparted to students is that a chart that doesn't seem to be doing the job needs to be scrapped. In general, it is better to have too many columns than too few, even if some of those columns contain information that remains constant through the whole problem.

Organizing the guesses and computations into a chart should allow students to see more things in the problem. It will help them understand the problem better. The inherent patterns in the problem will become more evident, and students can use these patterns to move toward the solution. Students may reach the answer through guess and check. Or they may learn enough about the problem to either start over or to abandon guess and check in favor of a different strategy such as algebra or working backward.

(Both of these strategies will be covered later in the text. Converting a guess and check chart into algebraic equations will also be covered.)

It's important for you to model refined guesses so that students learn to organize their guesses in a systematic way. Discuss what you learn about the problem as you go through it and how your guesses help you understand the problem better. Model writing out complete charts and "bracketing" (surrounding the solution with a high and low guess). Students tend to skip writing things down because of overconfidence, so you must be careful not to model overconfidence. They will also need to see how much more effective it generally is to start with smaller numbers instead of big numbers.

Many students will resist learning guess and check. This will especially be true of students with a good algebra background. Although we encourage divergent thinking as a central aspect of problem solving, this chapter is not the place for students to diverge. Some will use algebra as a way of avoiding learning this new strategy.

Guess and check is also a valuable tool in the real world. Even people who have mastered algebra find guess and check useful; the way guess and check mimics algebra helps them remember algebra they may have forgotten.

Guess and check needs lots of modeling and lots of practice. It is for this reason that Problem Set A contains a lot of problems. You can also use Problem Set A, Version 2, if your students need further practice.

One fun way to introduce guess and check is with The 2-4-6 Game, taught to us by Tom Sallee. The leader of the game thinks of a rule for three numbers which 2-4-6 always satisfies. Then the class asks if different series of three numbers satisfy the rule. The leader responds yes or no and the class tries to determine from these responses what the rule is.

Example:

2-4-6	yes		7-6-4	yes
2-5-6	no		6-7-4	no
2-3-6	no		6-4-0	no
2-4-7	no		6-4-2	yes
3-6-6	yes		8-5-5	yes
5-4-6	yes		8-5-7	no
4-2-6	yes		8-4-7	yes
800-4-6	yes		8-1-9	yes

In this example, the first two numbers together form a number that is a multiple of the third number. For example, 24 is a multiple of 6.

Notes on Text Problems

FARMER JONES

This is a rich problem that can be solved in a number of ways. Challenge students to find other ways to solve it.

Text Problems

1. SATURDAY AT THE "FIVE AND DIME" GARAGE SALE

Sandy held a garage sale during which she charged a dime for everything, but accepted a nickel if the buyer bargained well. At the end of the day she realized she had sold all twelve items and raked in a grand total of ninety-five cents. She only had dimes and nickels. How many of each did she have?

2. FARMER JONES

Farmer Jones raises ducks and cows. She tries not to clutter her mind with too many details, but she does think it's important to remember how many animals she has and how many feet those animals have. She thinks she remembers having 54 animals with 122 feet. How many of each type of animal does Farmer Jones have?

3. ALL AROUND THE PLAYING FIELD

The perimeter of a rectangular playing field is 504 yards. Its length is 6 yards shorter than twice its width. What is its area?

4. DAN'S NICKELS AND QUARTERS

Dan has twice as much money in nickels as he does in quarters. He has 33 coins in all (all nickels or quarters). How much money does he have?

5. FERDIE'S ROLLERCOASTER

Ferdie was excited. Tonight was the night of the big party, and Ferdie had been practicing his opening lines all week. However, as soon as Ferdie got to the party, 20 of the girls at the party left. There now remained two boys for each girl. This made Ferdie extremely bummed. A lot of the other boys got bummed too, so 20 of the boys left (probably to look for the 20 girls). There were now three girls for each boy. This made Ferdie happy. How many boys and girls were at the party when Ferdie got there?

6. ZEKE AND CLOE REVEAL THEIR AGES

Cloe is two years less than four times as old as Zeke. Cloe is also one year more than three times as old as Zeke. How old is each?

7. THE MONA AND LISA PAINTING PROBLEM

Working alone, Mona can paint a room in 4 hours. Working alone, Lisa could paint the same room in 3 hours. About how long should it take them to paint the room if they work together?

8. NEXT TRAIN EAST

A train leaves Roseville heading east at 6:00 a.m. at 40 miles per hour. Another eastbound train leaves at 7:00 a.m. on a parallel track at 50 miles per hour. What time will it be when the two trains are the same distance away from Roseville?

Problem Set A, Version 2

1. QUARTERS, DIMES, AND NICKELS

Jon has three times as many dimes as he does quarters. He has as many nickels as he has dimes and quarters combined. The total amount of money he has is $3.00. How many of each coin does he have?

2. CHANGE

Shadi has $4.60 in quarters, dimes, and nickels. She has three more dimes than nickels, and three more quarters than dimes. How many of each coin does she have?

3. ROCKS

Christopher has four more than twice as many rocks in his wagon as Gordon. If he gives Gordon six rocks, then he will have one more than Gordon. How many does each boy have in his wagon right now?

4. LONG JOURNEY

Maureen drove 50 miles per hour to her sister's house. The two of them drove from there to their mom's house. Maureen's sister, Leann, drives a tad faster than Maureen (at about 60 miles per hour). It took them a total of 4½ hours for Maureen to travel 255 miles from her house to her mom's house. How far does Maureen live from Leann?

Alternate question: How long did it take Maureen to drive to Leann's house?

5. HEALTH CLUB

Estela's current health club is raising their fees to $38 per month. Their membership fee is $160, which is a one-time-only charge. She is considering joining another club, but she'd have to pay a membership fee of $250 and then fees of $32 per month. How many months will it take before the new health club is the cheaper plan (in terms of total cost)?

6. T-SHIRTS

Blaise had a clerk use a mark-up of 25% on one line of T-shirts at his store. The selling price is $9.75. How much was the price of the shirt prior to being marked-up?

7. CENTRAL VIRGINIA COLLEGE

Central Virginia College has about 6 sophomores for every 7 freshmen. There are currently 1131 students in those 2 classes. How many more freshmen are there than sophomores?

8. MUTUAL FUNDS

As an investment principle, Hampton National Mutual Funds tries to keep a ratio of $9 blue-chip stocks to every $2 in high-risk stocks. If they currently have $95,700 invested in those categories of stocks, how much do they have invested in blue-chip stocks?

9. COMPACT DISKS

Keith wants to join Liberty Record club, which is offering new members a $20 membership fee and a cost of only $6.20 per compact disk. Patriot Music, on the other hand, charges no membership fee, and the cost of each compact disk is $8.10. Deanna wants to join Patriot Music Club. Keith and Deanna are married, so they don't need to join both. How many compact disks would they need to buy before Liberty would be cheaper?

10. STICKERS

Cici and Amatina have a lot of stickers. Cici had ⅓ as many as Amatina had, but then Amatina gave her six stickers, so now Cici has half as many as Amatina. How many stickers did each girl start with?

Problem Set B, Version 2

1. SPARE CHANGE

A cashier found that he was often asked to give change for a dollar to people who had made no purchases but wanted 20 cents for a telephone call. He started thinking one day about the number of ways he could make change. If he gave no more than four of any type of coin and made sure that the person received coins to make exactly 20 cents in order to make the phone call, in how many different ways could he give change for a dollar? (In other words, four quarters would not be allowed because the person would not have 20 cents for the phone call.)

2. THE MATH TEST

Violet was taking a test. On one problem she was given two positive whole numbers. The problem asked her to square the two numbers and add the squares together. Unfortunately, Violet misinterpreted the question. She mistakenly added the two numbers first and squared the result. Her answer was 60 more than the correct answer to the question. Find all possibilities for the original two numbers.

3. SKI TRIP

A group of friends decided to rent a house in Aspen, Colorado, for a week of skiing. They each had to chip in $70 for the week's lodging. If they had been able to convince 3 more people to go, the cost per person would have been reduced by $14. What was the rent for the week?

4. EXPENSIVE MISSILE

Some senators were sitting around discussing the latest defense department budget. Several of them asked the vice president how much the latest missile system cost the taxpayers. The vice president, who was known to be a clever sort, wouldn't tell them straight out, but instead gave them clues. Note, the first digit is on the left.

"The number is ten digits long (there are no decimal points) and each digit is different.

"The first, third, and fifth digits are powers of three.

"The first, second, third, fifth, and ninth digits are odd.

"The first, second, seventh, and ninth digits are prime.

"The sum of the seventh and ninth digits is the third digit.

"The first digit is not one, the second digit is not two, and so on with no digit occupying its numbered place, up to the tenth digit is not zero.

"No number is adjacent to a consecutive number. So one is not next to zero or two, two is not next to one or three, and so on."

How much did the missile system cost?

COLLEGE ROOMMATES

Helen and her three roommates live in a two-bedroom apartment at the University of Texas at El Paso. Each has a different major (one woman is majoring in chemistry). Coincidentally, each woman also has a different hair color (one is blonde). Determine each woman's full name, hair color, and major.

1. Joan, who isn't Ms. Bonds, doesn't have either of the two darker hair colors, and neither does Irene.
2. Glory doesn't share a room with Ms. Carlson or the accounting major.
3. Glory's major isn't physics.
4. The physics major has brown hair.
5. Ms. Daniels's hair is neither red nor black.
6. Ms. Bonds, whose first name is not Glory, is majoring in English.
7. Ms. Alder and Helen are both majoring in a science and often take classes together.

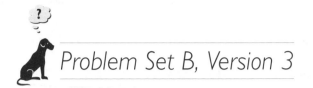

Problem Set B, Version 3

1. READY FOR "THE SHOW"

Carl is vain. He is so vain that he would probably think this is a problem about him. It's not, but let him think that anyway. Carl wants to be a major-league baseball player. Every day when he goes out in front to practice hitting on a T, he gets dressed up in one of his baseball outfits. He chooses a hat, socks, and shirt that all go well together. He has a blue hat, a red hat, and a black hat. He also has a green shirt, a yellow shirt, and a red shirt. Finally, Carl has baseball socks in each of the same colors that he has either shirts and hats, except black. He also has a pair of orange socks. He never wears more than two colors at a time. He also believes that blue and red together are "bush league" (they don't go together well), and red and green belong together only in the "off-season." He also refuses to wear yellow and black at the same time, as it makes him feel like a bumblebee. What is the probability that he wears something green?

2. BIKE RACE

The organizers of a long-distance bike race wanted to set up food and aid stations every 8 miles along the route. There would be no aid stations at the start and the finish. Each station would be staffed with one volunteer to give out food and dispense aid. Unfortunately, on the day of the race, three of the volunteers didn't show up. The organizers quickly determined that everything would work out if they put the aid stations every 10 miles apart instead of every 8 miles apart. How many volunteers showed up?

3. STORKE TOWER

The bell tower of the University of California at Santa Barbara chimes every hour at 10 minutes before the hour (to remind students that they should be getting to class) and also on the hour (to tell them that they are late). The tower chimes 24 hours a day, but it uses a 12-hour clock. (So, for example, it chimes 12 times at midnight and at noon.) Every time it chimes, it plays a 16-note tune, which is broken into 4 parts of 4 notes each. Each note lasts 1 second, and there is a 1-second pause at the end of each 4 notes. In addition to this, when it chimes on the hour, it also chimes out the time. So at 10 o'clock it would chime 10 times more after going through its 16-note tune. When it chimes for the hour, the chimes last 1 second, and there is a 1-second pause between chimes. There is a 3-second pause between the end of the 16-note tune and the beginning of the hour chimes. How much time every day does the bell tower spend chiming, including the pauses between chimes?

FAMILY OUTINGS

The Parker family plans four major outings every year. The outings take place on major holidays: President's Day in February, Memorial Day in May, Independence Day in July, and Labor Day in September. Each outing (one trip was to the county fair) is planned by one of the four Parker kids (one's name is Andy). During the outing the Parkers eat lunch (once they ate deli sandwiches). Determine which child planned which holiday's outing, where they went, and what kind of food they ate.

1. The trips, in chronological order, were: Erin's outing, the zoo trip, the time they ate hamburgers, and Phillip's outing.
2. They ate pizza after President's Day but before Jenny planned her outing.
3. The Parkers went to the museum on the Fourth of July (Independence Day).
4. They ate hot dogs at the amusement park, but not on Labor Day.

5. LUNCH MONEY

Cornelius and Sally are husband and wife. One day, they were discussing finances. Sally accused Cornelius of spending too much money on lunch.

Cornelius said, "But I really haven't spent that much money on lunch recently."

Sally replied, "Suppose you tell me how much you spent on lunch each of the last three days."

"Okay, but I will make you figure it out. Each day I spent a whole number of dollars. If you multiply the amounts I spent each day, the answer is 96."

Sally thought for a while and then said, "I need more information."

Cornelius answered, "The total amount I spent for the three days is the same amount as what you spent on golf last weekend."

Sally knew how much she spent for golf, but that still wasn't enough information for her to figure out the answer. She asked for another clue.

"Well, two of the meals cost less than $5."

That proved to be enough for Sally to figure out how much Cornelius spent on each meal. You figure it out too.

Problem Set B, Version 4

1. GRANDPA'S ATTIC

We always liked poking around Grandpa's attic whenever we had a family reunion. We found all sorts of neat stuff up there. Once we found a bunch of baseball cards, so Grandpa said "just divide 'em up among all the grandchildren." There were 5040 cards in all, so each of us got a lot of cards. But then we remembered that the Yakliches, who had five of the grandchildren, hadn't arrived yet. So each of those of us present had to give up 75 cards so that all the grandchildren would have the same number of cards. How many grandchildren does Grandpa have?

2. FROG CHORUS

Behind my house is a big field. Every winter, after a few rain storms, the field seems to attract lots of puddles, mud, and frogs. The frogs are quiet for the most part. However, when one starts croaking, they all do. This also serves to attract more frogs. And then they all seem to shut up at once. One night, there were 30 frogs present, and they all started croaking at 11 p.m. They all croak for a number of seconds equal to the number of frogs present. After that amount of time, 1 frog drops out at the beginning of every subsequent second. They all stop abruptly after the second in which they realize that only half of them are croaking. Two more frogs arrive every 20 minutes, and this starts the whole process over again with massive croaking. How many seconds of croaking took place from when I went to bed at 11:00 p.m. (and they started croaking) until I got up at 6:50 a.m.?

3. ROCK, SCISSORS, PAPER

Michael, Bonnie, and Stefan are playing rock, scissors, paper. It is a game for two players. The game has gotten sort of boring because Michael always chooses rock, Bonnie always chooses scissors, and Stefan always chooses paper. Thus when Michael plays against Bonnie, Michael wins (rock smashes scissors). When Bonnie plays Stefan, Bonnie wins (scissors cuts paper). And Stefan beats Michael when they play (paper covers rock). Suddenly, two of the participants exchange preferences, while the third participant remains the same. If Bonnie now plays Michael, who wins?

Lawrence and the three other Ayer children each have birthdays in a different month. One birthday is in August, another is in January. During the year 1993 all of the birthdays fell on a different day of the week (one was on a Saturday). The ages of the children at the beginning of 1993 were 7, 11, 14, 15. Determine the month and day of the week (in 1993) of each child's birthday and how old they each were at the beginning of 1993. Note: A week is considered to begin on Sunday and end on Saturday.

1. In 1992 two of the birthdays were on Tuesdays, but in 1993 none of the birthdays were on Tuesday, although one birthday was on a Wednesday.
2. The November birthday was not on a weekday in 1993.
3. Don and the person with the Monday birthday were the same age for more than two months during the year.
4. The person with the Thursday birthday was born four years earlier than Paul.
5. The July birthday came later in the week than Lucy's.

5. **POOR SCORE**

Bob and Bob played golf against each other in a tournament. Their score was kept by a marshall, but he had a difficult time because both players were named Bob. The scores the marshall recorded were the correct scores, but they may have been reversed. This is the way the marshall recorded their scores.

Hole	1	2	3	4	5	6	7	8	9	Tot
Par	4	4	5	3	5	4	3	4	4	36
Bob A	3	4	4	2	5	3	4	4	3	32
Bob B	4	4	7	4	3	4	3	5	6	40

When the match was over, the two Bobs glanced at the scorecard and complained.

Bob B said, "Wait a second, I only had one double bogey. And there is no way I lost by 8 shots: I had fewer total shots until after we played the fifth hole."

Bob A said, "I had the eagle, but I only had two birdies. I only won three holes."

Determine the correct hole-by-hole score for each player and their totals for the nine holes.

(Note: Eagle, birdie, bogey, and double bogey refer to scores made on one hole. An eagle is two under par for the hole. A birdie is one under par. A bogey is one over par. A double bogey is two over par.)

7

subproblems

S OLVING SUBPROBLEMS is a strategy based on dividing problems into smaller pieces. A subproblem is a mini-problem that must be solved before solving the original problem. Some problems break down into many subproblems. In order to attack the type of problem that breaks down into subproblems, it is often helpful to list the subproblems. This list of subproblems becomes a plan for solving the problem.

Solving subproblems is a lot like building a bicycle. It doesn't matter much whether you put on the front tire or the rear tire first. It also doesn't matter much if you put on the seats or handle bars before, after, or in the midst of putting the tires on. However, for the bicycle to be complete, each of the smaller steps must be completed. For many steps, the order is not necessarily important. For other steps, the order may be important. For example, you must put on the rear tire and the pedal crank before you put on the chain. The same is true in solving a problem with subproblems—some subproblems must be done before others; in other cases the order is irrelevant.

You or the students may also encounter situations where you can't do a problem immediately because you need more information. Breaking problems down into subproblems makes this much more readily apparent.

In the larger scheme of categories of strategies, solving subproblems is a strategy that requires you to change your focus. No longer are you looking at a large problem. Rather, you must delve into the interior of the problem in order to find the component parts (the subproblems).

Solving subproblems also has aspects of an organizational strategy, though you organize your approach rather than organizing information.

Solving subproblems is a useful strategy for real-life problem solving. Beyond tests that have a strong emphasis on subproblems (such as the SAT), much of human activity is complex enough that it can be viewed as subproblems. Manufacturing a bicycle is an example, and if you look beyond the manufacturing aspect, you see that there is also purchasing, training, and marketing to consider. The manufacturing stage is simply a subproblem of the larger problem of making, distributing, and selling bicycles.

Notes on Text Problems

LITTLE GREEN APPLES

Make sure the students understand the process of breaking down the larger problem. This problem was kept simple in order to help the students with understanding. Emphasize that they need to write down the subproblems. The writing process may seem slow and tedious to them, but it will pay off on many other problems. One of the first payoffs is the ease with which another person can verify the work that is laid out and organized. Another payoff is that students will be able to handle more complex problems, as a complex problem is simply a set of simple problems.

THE ELEVATOR

This is a very rich problem that can be solved in an astonishing number of ways. Challenge your students to find other ways to solve this and to share those methods with the class.

PAINT

This is a mixture problem of the type you may see in an algebra text. Notice, however, that algebra is not needed in order to solve it.

CHOCOLATE MILK

This is another typical algebra "mixture" problem. The text recommends using a combination of two strategies in order to solve it: subproblems and guess and check.

Text Problems

LITTLE GREEN APPLES

How many apples, each weighing 2 ounces, will be needed to balance three 2-pound weights?

WATERING THE LAWN

Three quarts of water are needed to water one square foot of lawn. How many gallons of water will be needed to water a lawn that measures 30 feet by 60 feet?

THE CAR BARGAIN

Paul went into the local new car lot to buy a car. He knew the kind of car he wanted, as his friend Barbara (often called Bar) Gain had bought the same car the day before. Barbara got a 30% discount on the car, which listed at $15,000. The salesperson offered Paul the $15,000 car at a 20% discount instead. When Paul protested, the salesperson offered an additional 10% off the 20% discounted price. This offer satisfied Paul and he bought the car, convinced he had paid the same price as Barbara. Had he?

THE ELEVATOR

The capacity of an elevator is either 20 children or 15 adults. If 12 children are currently on the elevator, how many adults can still get on?

PAINT

A mixture is 25% red paint, 30% yellow paint, and 45% water. If 4 quarts of red paint are added to 20 quarts of the mixture, what is the percentage of red paint in the new mixture?

CHOCOLATE MILK

Augustus is trying to make chocolate milk. So far he has made a 10% chocolate milk solution (this means that the solution is 10% chocolate and 90% milk). He has also made a 25% chocolate milk solution. Unfortunately, the 10% solution is too weak and the 25% solution is way too chocolaty. He has a whole lot of the 10% solution, but he only has 30 gallons of the 25% solution. How many gallons of 10% solution should he add to the 25% solution to make a mixture that is 15% chocolate? Augustus is sure it will be absolutely perfect.

Problem Set A, Version 2

Directions: Solve each problem by first listing all of the subproblems and then solving the subproblems to answer the question.

1. MAGNET SCHOOL

A magnet school program was set up to bring in students from all over the city. With the first 112 students, the magnet program had 50% from the south side of town, 12.5% from the north side, and 37.5% from the east side. If six more students from the north side and two more students from the west side enrolled in the program, what is the percentage of students from the north side of the city in the program now?

2. ORANGES

Oranges cost $.50 per pound. How many oranges, each weighing 4 ounces, can Wally buy with 5 quarters?

How much do 2 pounds of boysenberries cost if a 3-ounce basket of berries costs $.54?

3. BOYSENBERRIES

How much do 2 pounds of boysenberries cost if a 3-ounce basket of berries costs $.54?

4. STEREO SALE

Williams and Son Department Store was going out of business. At first they had all of the electronics marked 10% off. They then marked everything down an additional 25% from the last posted price. What is the current price of a stereo set that originally cost $189?

5. LIFE'S NECESSITIES

Jack and Tim have decided to run away, but they need proper sustenance. They have enough money to buy 30 doughnuts or 20 sodas. Jack told Tim that he thought they needed 18 doughnuts. How many sodas can they buy?

6. AN "A" IN MATH

Daniella wants an "A" in Math. So far, she has 598 out of 700 points possible. What percentage of the remaining 225 points must she earn in order to raise her average to exactly 90%?

7. SOIL AND SAND

Eight cubic yards of soil that is 50% sand had to be mixed with some soil that is about 10% sand to bring down the percentage of sand to 18%. From this action, how many cubic yards of soil with 18% were produced.

8.   ONE HUNDRED SIXTY-EIGHT INCHES OF STRING

One hundred sixty-eight inches of string were used to make these squares, which are all the same size. What is the total area of the 10 squares?

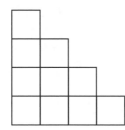

9.   JUAN'S CHURCH

Juan donates 10% of his salary to his church. He earns $3500 per month. He used to earn $3200, and he gave the same dollar amount. What percent of his income did he donate to the church when he earned $3,200?

10.   A LOT OF STUFF

A patch of grass measuring 6 feet by 6 feet requires two ounces of fertilizer. How many pounds should be used on a lawn that measures 30 feet by 75 feet?

11.   SHOOTING PERCENTAGE

Renee made 96 of 220 shots during the season up until tonight's basketball game. She figures she'll get about 20 shots tonight. What percent must she shoot tonight in order to raise her shooting percentage to exactly 45% for the season if she takes 20 shots? (Shooting percentage is determined by dividing the number of baskets by the number of shots taken.)

12.   CAMP STOVE

A camp stove uses up its gas in 195 minutes when it is on low. It uses about 7½ times as much gas when it is on high. The stove was on low for 30 minutes. How much time remains if the stove must be run on high for boiling water?

13.   ROAD RALLY

In a timed road rally, Sandy and Debbie know that the winner is the person who comes up with the correct time over the entire course. The correct time, of course, is given by what time it would take to drive the course at the posted speed limits. They drove 5.5 miles in a 55-mph zone (freeway), 5 miles in 25-mph zones, and 3.5 miles in a 35-mph zone. They now see that the rest of the course is all on a 40-mph street. So far it has taken them 22 minutes. There are 6 miles remaining, all on a long, country road. How fast do they need to drive in order to come up with the correct course time? (Don't worry about the stop signs and stop lights—there aren't any.)

Problem Set B, Version 2

1. USED CARS

While watching a commercial on late night TV, Bud noticed the following subtitles at the same time the announcer was saying something: "sochi na warak" was on at the same time as the man said "sale cars cheap." Bud was intrigued, so the next several times he saw the commercial, he wrote down the following subtitles and phrases:

"quandi bonki warak"   "big blue cars"
"quandi sochi"   "big sale"
"kandi sochi konaa"   "no sales people"
"warak na"   "cheap cars"
"bonki tayku ta"   "green and blue"
"konaa qualliak"   "no lemons"
"sochi na warak"   "sale cars cheap"
"wassa tayku"   "green money"

In whatever language this is, what is the meaning of the following sentence?

"qualliak na ta konaa tayku kandi."

2. THE NATURAL LOOK

A landscape architect worked on plans for the backyard of a client. She decided to use 15 trees and plant them in groups that were all different sizes in order to make the yard look "natural." The smallest group could have one tree in it, and there were at least two groups. With all possibilities considered equally probable, what is the probability that she included a group of two trees in her plans?

3. TYPESETTING

In the olden days, type was set by hand using lead pieces. The type had to be carefully put together. A printer wanted to print a list of whole numbers from 1 to 1000 in order to find the primes under 1000. If he only had 100 of each of the digits from 0 to 9, how many numbers could he set before he ran out of some digit?

4. A FAMILY MAN

Twelve years ago, a man was three times as old as his daughter. Nine years from now, the man will be twice as old as his son. Four years from now, the sum of the ages of the son and daughter will equal the age of the man. How old is each now?

I was sitting in a group of people arranged in a circle during a meeting. The meeting was rather boring, and I really wasn't paying attention to what was being said, so I began to count the people in the circle. I started with myself and went around the circle, counting by fours, then by fives, and so on, and looked at how many people were left over each time. The information is summarized in the chart below.

Counted By	Left Over
4	1
5	0
6	1
7	3
8	7
9	6
10	4
11	3

Somewhere in the middle of counting I realized that two people were missing. I didn't know when they left or if they left together. When I finished counting by elevens, I noticed that they were both back. But I don't know if they came back together or if possibly one or both of them came back and then left again. In any case, I still thought I had enough information to figure out how many people were in the circle at the beginning. Did I? Can you? To help you out a little bit, there was a sign posted by the fire marshall limiting the capacity of the room to 80 people. How many people were in the circle, when did each of the two people leave, and when did they each come back?

Problem Set B, Version 3

1. WHO'S ON THE BENCH?

During a really boring baseball game, I started counting the guys sitting on the home-team bench. When I counted by fives, there were two left over. Counting by twos, there was one left over; counting by threes, there were two left over; counting by fours, there were none left over. That last bit sort of surprised me. I knew there had been an odd number of players sitting on the bench because of the remainder from counting by two. But there was no remainder when I counted by four, which couldn't be correct. I sat there for a few minutes wondering what was going on. It suddenly dawned on me that the team had come in off the field. I looked up and saw two members of the home team out coaching the bases. There were two more guys (the batter and the guy on deck) who never made it into the dugout. Nine guys had been on the field, but I didn't know at what point in my counting that they came in. I counted the people sitting on the bench by sevens, and there was one left over. I knew there were fewer than 40 people on the team, including coaches. How many people were sitting on the bench when I started counting? At what point did the team come in from the outfield?

2. GAMUSE PLAYGROUND

A Gamuse playground is a sight to see and an engineering wonder. Each playground has 16 floors. Each floor is connected to another floor by various mechanical devices. Any even-numbered floor has an escalator up to the next even-numbered floor. Every odd-numbered floor has a slide down to the next odd-numbered floor. Several other floors (1, 2, 3, 5, 8, and 13) have an up-and-down "tube-chute" (they are like mail tubes in an office building) that will take you to another tube-chute floor above or below. How would somebody go from the eleventh floor of this playground to the twelfth floor?

3. SIERRA SLUGGERS

Five members of the Sierra Sluggers went out to get something to eat after the season. Each one discussed the others' hitting:

Larry: I had 18 more hits than Jack.

Mark: The total of us five was 708 hits.

KC: Larry's total was a prime number, and he was second of the five.

Jack: Chris was between Mark and KC in the number of hits.

Chris: Mark's total was a multiple of 6, and KC's was a multiple of 15. In fact, KC had 12 more hits than Mark.

Fortunately, each person's statement was accurate. Determine how many hits each player had during the season.

BICYCLE TRAINING

Sherwood is a bicyclist. He makes a daily ride of 40 miles at a constant speed. If he trains really hard he can increase his speed by 4 miles per hour, which would result in a half-hour decrease in time. Find his new speed.

PRIZE MONEY

The chamber of commerce in Pinehurst, North Carolina, decided to hold a professional golf tournament at the famous Pinehurst Country Club. They were able to get a TV contract from CBS. The TV revenue promises to be $4 million, and they figured they would sell 60,000 tickets at $8 apiece. The fund for prizes would be 20% of their total revenue (TV plus tickets) rounded to the nearest $10,000. The prizes are as follows. All prizes are rounded to the nearest dollar.

First prize—18% of the total prize money
Second prize—60% of first prize
Third prize—65% of second prize
Fourth prize—70% of third prize
Fifth prize—75% of fourth prize
Sixth prize—6% of the remaining prize money
Seventh prize—$900 less than sixth prize

Eighth prize—$900 less than seventh prize, and so on—with each subsequent prize $900 less than the previous prize. The final prize would be whatever was left over, even if it wasn't $900 less than the previous prize. Two golfers finished in a tie for tenth place, so they split the combined tenth and eleventh prizes. How much did each of them get?

Problem Set B, Version 4

1. MILEAGE SIGN

Recently I was driving down the freeway and spotted the following free-way sign with the distances to three upcoming cities.

Ahmanson 147 miles

Chandler 265 miles

Schubert 380 miles

I thought the sign was unusual because the distances to the three cities featured all different digits. In how many miles might I see another freeway sign with all different digits for the distances to these three cities?

2. A NEW VERSION OF SCRABBLE

My friends have changed the rules for Scrabble. In their rules, each letter has a positive whole number value. No two vowels have the same value. No two consonants have the same value. It is possible for a vowel and a consonant to have the same value. Scoring is done differently than in regular Scrabble. The points for the vowels are added up, as are the points for the consonants. These two numbers are multiplied together to give the word score. A list of words and their word scores is shown below. Determine the letter value of each letter and then determine the value for the word "problem-solving." (Note: Count this as one word and don't count the dash for anything.)

PLUM = 36	PLUME = 48	MELT = 15	MELBA = 51
ROME = 98	SAVE = 51	WEST = 20	WESTERN = 70
LAME = 18	PLANE = 39	VIPER = 150	PAPER = 66
PIPER = 110	OUT = 81	GREET = 40	

3. SLIDE

At the local playground three boys like to go down a very wide slide. After going down the slide, they turn around and walk back up the slide rather than walking around to climb the ladder. Fortunately, the slide is so wide that they are all able to do this independently without crashing into each other. Each boy slides down the slide in two seconds. It takes Daniel five seconds to climb back up the slide. It takes Jeremy six seconds to climb back up the slide. It takes Gary seven seconds to climb back up the slide. They all start together at the same time and slide down. How many seconds after starting will they all slide down together at the same time again?

4. THREE-DIMENSIONAL CHESS

The three-dimensional chessboard is four squares by four squares on each level and is four levels high. In a particular version of three-dimensional chess, the knight moves by going straight up or down two levels, then forward, backward, right, or left one square on the new level. It can also move straight up or down one level, and then two squares (in a straight line) forward, backward, left, or right on the new level. (It cannot stay on the same level for the entire move and act like the knight in regular two-dimensional chess.) How can a knight move from a corner square on the bottom level to get to the corner square directly above it on the next level?

5. LEAKY SINK

My old house had a leaky sink. I used to shave in this sink by filling up the sink with water and then shaving while the water slowly leaked out. The problem was that sometimes the water would completely run out before I was finished. I made some calculations. It took 30 seconds to fill up the sink completely when I turned on the tap. It took 3 minutes for the completely filled sink to leak out and be empty. It took me 2 minutes to shave. I figured that the sink had to be at least 5% full in order to have enough water to effectively shave. What is the minimum amount of time I should turn on the water to be sure I have enough water to finish shaving without having to add more? (Note: I turn off the water before I start to shave, and I start shaving immediately upon turning off the water.)

8

unit analysis

U NIT ANALYSIS IS a problem-solving strategy in which you deal carefully with the units of a problem. The basis of this strategy is simply multiplying by one. The key is to choose the correct form(s) of "one." The forms include fractions where the numerators and denominators are equivalent, though they appear different. The purpose is to cancel the unwanted units and leave units that answer the question.

Units are a necessary component of the problem and answer. When you solve any problem involving units you need to be careful to maintain the units throughout the problem until they cancel. An answer cannot be correct without the correct units.

Keeping the units in the problem organized will help lead to the correct answer. In the extreme, it is possible to work a problem (with no sense of what the problem is about) simply by using the units to move from problem to answer. This is not meant to be an endorsement of such shallow manipulation, but the application of this strategy can serve as a means for checking one's work. The units should be an integral part of the means for solving the problem and also an indicator of what ends (correct units) to work toward. Unit analysis will support other academic disciplines such as physics and chemistry.

Unit analysis is an organizing information strategy. The problems seem far less formidable when organized. By organizing the units, the problem should simply fall into place.

This chapter is written in three parts: Unit Conversions, Units in Ratios, and Compound Units.

Unit conversions is simply changing within the English and metric systems to other forms within the same system. In the English system we can change from feet to yards, or feet to inches, or even feet to miles. Conversions in the metric system are simpler: converting from meters to kilometers or perhaps from meters to centimeters. Unit conversions also involve converting from metric to English or vice versa.

Students should be taught to also analyze what types of units are presented in a problem—in other words, what is being measured (such as the standard measurements like length, mass, time, and volume).

In the section titled Units in Ratios, the examples are kept to simple, familiar ratios in order to develop the concept of unit ratios. For example, miles per hour is usually an easy concept for students to dissect.

When dealing with units in ratios, we have found that "miles per hour" is an extremely good example to start with. From there, we could proceed to the more abstract, though usually with some intermediate discussions. Another good example for students is 30 jellybeans for $1.50, as you start with jellybeans per dollar and you can change it into cents per jellybean and then into dollars per jellybean. The unit changes are easily done, and the results make sense to the students because of their prior experience. Miles per gallon and dollars per gallon also work well; and unusual ratios can be created easily, such as socks per person or bones per dog.

In the Compound Units section, again familiarity is a key. Though students are generally familiar with the concept of "square feet," their depth of understanding is often severely lacking. The discussion in the book starts with "inch-feet," and you may find it worthwhile to do some hands-on work with the students using "inch-feet." The students could cut out "inch-feet" from paper and use them to measure a region in the classroom.

The idea of "passenger-miles" is also within the grasp of most students since both units are so familiar. Compound units are extremely important in other disciplines, especially in physics. The design of this chapter is focused around making this strategy easily transferable to other academic disciplines.

Students also need to be conscious that solving subproblems is a major component of this strategy. It shows up quite naturally in a good number of these problems. In many problems, you will be unable to go directly to the desired units, so you must set up intermediary goals.

Though multiplying by one is fundamental to doing operations with fractions (since one is the identity element for multiplication), many students will not have a deep understanding of the unit analysis extension of this concept. The students may have trouble recognizing that "one" does not need to have identical numerators and denominators. They must merely be equivalent. It is important for students to be able to demonstrate the technique on simple problems and then work their way up to harder problems.

As usual, it is important to stress organizing work in order to make the solutions easier to check and easier for another person to verify. Furthermore, keeping the units organized arranges the rest of the problem. As part of the organization process, students need to be consciously thinking about what types of units (mass, volume, time, length) are involved in the problem and what types they want to go toward. Furthermore, students must also become accustomed to giving appropriate units in their solutions to problems. For example, 37 feet per second would be appropriate for describing the initial velocity of a projectile. On the other hand, it would be inappropriate, to describe the speed of a car near a school zone with these units.

When doing metric to English conversions, it is not necessary to develop a lot of different conversion ratios. We have found that simply using two is sufficient for the students to readily go back and forth between the measurement systems.

Linear Measure: 1 meter = 3.281 feet
Volume: 1 gallon = 3.79 liters

Finding the real-life connections with unit analysis is easy. Much of public policy is presented in terms of costs and benefits. One way to look at policy is to examine the cost-to-benefit ratio. For example, if it costs $35,000 per prisoner for one year of incarceration in a maximum security jail, is there some way to spend $35,000 prior to criminal acts in order to prevent them? Public schools are generally paid somewhere between $3000 and $5000 per year to educate each student. Can we identify potential criminals early and divert them into more positive channels?

These questions can be analyzed and discussed by students, as well as other governmental budget issues.

Another common use of unit analysis is as close as the grocery store shelf. Most stores have shelf tags giving the "unit price" of an item. Note that these are given in appropriate units: ounces per dollar, ounces per cent, pound per dollar, etc.

Another real-life instance that students may have experienced is in planning for large groups. In order to know how many hotdogs to buy for a company picnic of 200 adults and 350 children you can estimate the number per person, such as 1.8 hotdogs for each child and 1.3 hotdogs for each adult, and then use unit analysis to project the total number of hot dogs needed.

Notes on Text Problems

CONVERSION PRACTICE

Students need to practice setting up simple conversions and canceling the units before they attempt difficult problems. Many of these problems can be done by students without setting up the process of canceling the units. Emphasize that students need to practice this skill on easy problems or they will be lost on the hard problems.

You should discuss with the class that there is not a unique, correct way to set up units in ratios. Different purposes require different ratios.

There is an inherent assumption made in this problem that needs to be discussed: The pizzas are all assumed to have the same height. This is generally true of pizzas and is assumed here for the sake of simplicity. Perhaps a better way to compare pizzas would be to compare masses.

Text Problems

CONVERSION PRACTICE

Work these problems: You may use any English-to-English conversions that you want and any metric-to-metric conversions you want. However, the only English-to-metric conversions you may use are:
1 meter = 3.281 feet and 1 gallon = 3.79 liters

1. Change 12 feet to meters.
2. Change 6 meters to inches.
3. Change 5 gallons to liters.
4. Change 85 kilometers to miles.

TONI'S TRIP

Toni drove 90 miles in 2 hours and used 3 gallons of gas. You should realize there are three different types of measures here—miles, hours, and gallons—which measure distance, time, and volume respectively. How many ratios of measures are there, considering two at a time? After finding that, calculate all of the ratios you found. (Hint: There are fewer than 10 ratios.)

FASTBALL

Nolan Ryan has been clocked throwing a baseball 100 miles per hour. At that speed, how much time does the batter have to react? (How much time before the ball reaches the plate?) The pitcher's mound is 60 feet 6 inches from home plate.

PIZZA PRICES

Use the pizza parlor menu below to determine which cheese pizza is the best buy. All pizzas are round.

TYPE:	DIAMETER:	PRICE:
small	10 inches	$6.80
medium	12 inches	$8.50
large	14 inches	$12.60
giant	20 inches	$21.00

THE LONG COMMUTE

Gerónimo and three friends drove 208 miles. Their car got 35 miles per gallon during the trip. They drove at an average speed of 50 miles per hour and the gasoline for the trip cost them $8.02. Find each of the following:

1. Gallons of gas used
2. Hours
3. Average feet per second
4. Dollars per hour
5. Dollars per gallon
6. Dollars per passenger
7. Cents per mile
8. Total number of passenger-miles
9. Passenger-miles per gallon
10. Cents per passenger-mile

Janice,Stephanie, Rose, and Gina are going to be paid $84.70 for cleaning up Mr. Rogers' neighborhood. They each worked 5 hours, except Rose, who was 45 minutes late. How much should each one be paid?

Problem Set A, Version 2

1. MORE CONVERSIONS

Convert from metric to English or from English to metric as indicated. The only metric-to-English conversions you are allowed to use are the following:

1 meter = 3.281 feet, and 1 gallon = 3.79 liters

Of course, you may use any English-to-English conversions (such as 1 mile = 5280 feet) and any metric-to-metric conversions (such as 1 km = 1000 m).

a. 45 m to feet   b. 280 ft to m
c. 250 mi to km   d. 31 km to mi
e. 5 ft to cm   f. 24 cm to in.
g. 48 inches to mm   h. 50 mi/hr to m/sec
i. 3 gal to liters   j. 20 liters to quarts

2. WHAT'S UP, DOC?

A bag of carrots costs $1.75 and has 25 carrots in it. Since the bag is 5 lbs, find each of the following:
a. dollars/carrot
b. cents/carrot
c. ounces/carrot
d. carrots/lb

3. MASON'S TAXI SERVICE

Mason flew his plane 550 miles in 3 hours and 40 minutes. He used 9 gallons per hour, and the fuel cost him $1.85 per gallon. He took three passengers with him. Find each of the following:

a. gallons   b. miles/hours   c. ft/sec
d. $/hour   e. miles/gallon   f. $/passenger
g. cents/mile   h. total number of passenger-miles
i. passenger-miles/gallon   j. cents/passenger-mile

4. MARCEL'S TRIP

Marcel drove at a speed of 60 miles per hour over a distance of 420 miles, and the trip cost him and his 5 friends $16.24 in gasoline; they used 2 gal/hr. Find each of the following:

a. gallons   b. hours   c. ft/sec
d. $/hour   e. $/gallon   f. $/passenger
g. cents/mile   h. total number of passenger-miles
i. passenger-miles/gallon   j. cents/passenger mile

5. COMMUTER FLIGHT

An airplane is traveling 550 miles per hour. It is carrying 80 passengers. Answers the questions below:

    a. How many miles per minute?
    b. How many feet per second?
    c. How many passenger-miles on a 400 mile trip?
    d. How many passenger-miles per hour?
    e. How many passenger-miles per minute?

6. A SHOT IN THE DARK

A projectile is shot in space at 60 meters per second.

    a. Determine its speed in miles per hour.
    b. Determine its speed in kilometers per hour.

7. IT'S ABOUT TIME

Mrs. Ralls hired Cinnamon, Ricky, Jeannette, and Kari to clean her garage. They each worked 6¼ hours, except Jeannette, who started early and worked 7½ hours. They were paid a total of $126. Each worker will be paid at the same rate. How much should each person get?

8. AFTER THE DEADHEADS

Sassafras, Moonshine, Peace, Harmony, and Chynna were hired to clean up after a Grateful Dead concert. Moonshine started very late but worked the 3 hours until dawn. Sassafras put in 5⅔ hours, and Harmony worked as much as Sassafras but also got in an extra third of an hour. Peace had never worked before, but was hired to work 4 hours because somebody decided to give Peace a chance. Chynna worked 8 hours because she was isolated for the longest time and refused help from anybody else. The five were paid $128.80 total. If each person was paid the same hourly rate, how much did each person earn?

9. WHERE'S THE RUE?

Tova used to spend 40 minutes per day jogging and covered a distance equivalent to the distance from Rue de Vache to LaPointe 73 times during the year. The distance is 20 miles. What is her speed in miles per hour?

9B. WHERE'S THE VACHE?

Tova now spends 45 minutes per day and has sped up 1 mile per hour. How many times would she run a distance equivalent to the distance from Rue de Vache to LaPointe in a year?

10. MANUSCRIPT

A manuscript page generally has about 500 words on it. If you read a manuscript page in a minute and 24 seconds, what is

a. your reading rate in words per minute?

b. the number of pages read per hour?

11. EVENING EXERCISE

Sylvia walks 4 miles every evening. She is also a golfer. Since playing an average 18-hole golf course involves walking 6300 yards total, she wondered how many holes she walked the equivalent of every time she went for her evening walk. (By the way, don't worry about Sylvia. She hits the golf ball straight, so there's no walking from one side of the course to the other side when she plays golf.) What is the equivalent number of holes Sylvia walked each evening?

Unit Conversion Worksheet

Name: _____

Do each of these conversions using the "multiplying by one" method. Show your work.

Basic Unit Equivalents

1 mile = 5280 feet	1 yard = 3 feet	1 day = 24 hours
1 week = 7 days	1 minute = 60 seconds	1 hour = 60 seconds

1. 6852 inches to yards

2. 3 miles to inches

3. 51 yards to inches

4. 8,586,924 inches to miles

5. 3 weeks to hours

6. 3 days to minutes

7. 7,200,000 seconds to days

8. 2 weeks to minutes

Unit Analysis: Worksheet 2

Name: _____

Katrina drove 144 miles in 2 hours and 40 minutes. She used 5 gallons of gas that cost her $6.45. She took five other people with her on this trip. Find each of the following. (Be sure to show your work.)

a. miles per hour

b. miles per gallon

c. dollars per gallon

d. feet per second

e. dollars per hour

f. dollars per passenger

g. cents per minute

h. cents per mile

i. yards per second

j. passenger-miles per gallon

k. miles per dollar

l. gallons per hour

m. cents per passenger-miles

Unit Analysis Practice Quiz

Name: _____

You will be expected to know these:

I mi = 5280 feet
1 gallon = 4 quarts
100 centimeters = 1 meter
1000 meters = 1 kilometer

You will be provided these on the test:

1 meter = 3.281 feet
1 gallon = 3.79 liters

Javier drove 170 miles on 6.8 gallons of gas. It took him 3 hours and 20 minutes. Gas for his car costs $1.15 per gallon. Find each of the following and show your work.

1. miles per hour

2. miles per gallon

3. total fuel cost

4. dollars per hour

5. cents per mile

6. miles per minute

7. feet per second

8. gallons per hour

Veloxy traveled 500 miles on 15 gallons in 516 minutes. Show your work, including all conversions from the original data. Find the following:

9. miles per gallon

10. miles per hour

11. feet per second

Tyrone drove for 2½ hours, using 4 gallons of gas. He got 31.5 miles per gallon for a total fuel cost of $4.92. Find the following and show your work.

12. miles

13. dollars per gallon

14. miles per hour

15. feet per second

For a big party, Vida, Vera, and Von set up a baby-sitting center where all the parents could leave their kids. Vida was there for 4 hours, Vera was there for 2½ hours, and Von was there for 3¼ hours. They collected a total of $26.

16. How much should each sitter get paid?

Jerome, Hoppy, and Francien were going to Modesto together. Jerome and Hoppy drove from Sacramento and picked up Francien exactly halfway there. The distance for Jerome and Hoppy was 96 miles; they figure that the gas cost to where they picked up Francien was $10.20 total. Find the following and show your work.

17. total passenger-miles

18. cents per passenger-mile

19. What is each person's share of the gas cost?

Convert these units. Be sure to show your work.

20. 16.5 ft = _____ m

21. 5.6 km = _____ mi

22. 2 liters = _____ gal

23. 1 quart = _____ liters

24. 77.8 ft/sec = _____ m/sec

25. 32 mi/hr = _____ m/sec

Unit Analysis Test

Name: _____

Directions: Show all work because you may receive partial credit for wrong answers with correct work. Round off answers if necessary to two decimal places.

Useful Units: 1 m = 3.281 feet, 1 gallon = 3.79 liters

Convert these units. (6 points each)

1. 75.7 ft = _____ m

2. 6.4 km = _____ mi

3. 18.3 liters = _____ gallons

4. 18 quarts = _____ liters

5. 55 mi/hr = _____ m/sec

Allison, Ryan, and Janie helped a neighbor move some concrete out of a vacant lot. Allison worked for 5 hours, Ryan worked for 3½ hours, and Janie worked for 2¼ hours. The neighbor who owned the lot paid them $55.90 for their work. Find each of the following. (3 points each)

6. total labor-hours

7. dollars per labor-hour

8. Allison's share of the money

9. Ryan's share of the money

10. Janie's share of the money

Axelrod drove 396 miles on 14.4 gallons of gas. It took him 7 hours and 30 minutes. Gas for his car costs $.80 per gallon. Find the following. (6 points each)

11. miles per hour

12. total fuel cost

13. miles per gallon

14. feet per second

15. cents per mile

Zeke and 3 friends drove for 300 minutes, using 8 gallons of gas. They got 30.5 miles per gallon with a total fuel cost of $6.56. Find the following. (5 points each).

16. miles

17. dollars per gallon

18. miles per hour

19. passenger-miles per gallon

20. cents per passenger-mile

Problem Set B, Version 2

1. I CAN SEE FOR MILES AND MILES

Last week I drove to Los Angeles on Highway 5. There was one of those speedometer checks along the side of the road with posted signs one mile apart. I timed us on my wristwatch and found that it took us 4 minutes and 30 seconds to travel 4 miles. (We had the car set on cruise control, so we were traveling at a constant speed.) A while later we passed a sign that said "Bakersfield, 90 miles." How long did it take us to get to Bakersfield? Answer in hours, minutes, and seconds. (For example: 7 hours, 6 minutes, and 15 seconds.)

2. GENEROUS FRIENDS

Two friends went out for pizza and soda after work one day. They each ordered and drank one large soda and ate part of their pizza. They then decided they were still thirsty, so Molly went up to get another soda. Nancy didn't have any money, so she asked if she could share some of Molly's soda. Molly then poured half of her soda in Nancy's glass. Nancy protested, saying it was too much, and she poured one-third of the soda in her glass back into Molly's glass. Molly insisted that Nancy have some more, so she poured one-fourth of the soda in her glass back into Nancy's glass. Of course, Nancy would not take so much soda, so she poured one-fifth of the soda in her glass back into Molly's glass. This went on for quite a while, with each pouring increasing the denominator of the fraction by one. After 99 pourings, they decided to stop. At this point, how full was each glass of soda?

3. AN AGE OLD PROBLEM

When Lee was thrice as old as Kevin,
His sister Kate was twenty-seven.
When Kevin was half as old as Kate,
Then brother Lee was thirty-eight.
Their ages add to one forty three.
How old are Kevin, Kate, and Lee?

4. FILLING THE PLANTER BOX

A home builder put in a large planter box in the backyard. The planter box is 20 feet long, 3 feet back, and 2 feet high. The builder wants to fill the box with dirt. He is able to buy dirt in 3-pound bags. Dirt weighs 2 pounds per cubic foot. He has a wheelbarrow that will carry three bags of dirt at a time from his garage (where his truck with the dirt is) to the backyard. How many trips does he have to make with the wheelbarrow in order to fill up the planter box?

Find the two solutions to this cross number puzzle. All numbers are three-digit numbers, entered one digit per box. None of the three-digit numbers are the same. It is possible to have repeated digits in a number. There are no zeros in the puzzle.

Across:

1. The last two digits form a two-digit number that is a power of the first digit.
4. A square
5. A cube

Down:

1. A Fibonacci number
2. All digits are even.
3. A prime number

1	2	3
4		
5		

Note: The Fibonacci sequence (discussed in the patterns chapter) is the sequence 1, 1, 2, 3, 5, 8, 13, 21, …

Problem Set B, Version 3

1. DISCOUNT HARDWARE

A carpenter went to a discount hardware store to buy hammers, screwdrivers, and large nails. Hammers cost $10 each, screwdrivers cost $7 each, and large nails cost 50 cents each. The carpenter bought exactly 100 items and spent $150. How many of each did she buy?

2. LIFE SPAN

It has been estimated that a human heart is capable of beating 2.8 billion times in a lifetime. Assume this is true. If a person's average heart rate is 72 beats per minute, what is that person's life span? Express your answer in years and days. (For example: 5 years, 142 days.)

3. COIN COLLECTION

Daniel has a piggy bank full of coins. One day he counted them and said that he had an equal number of pennies, nickels, dimes, and quarters. His father handed him three coins. Daniel now had $7.22. What were the three coins that his father gave him?

4. THE GOAT PROBLEM

A goat is tethered to one corner of a 20-foot by 35-foot barn in the middle of a large, grassy field. The rope is 50 feet long. Over what area can the goat graze? (He can't go inside the barn, and there isn't any grass in there anyway.)

5. CROSS SUMS

Cross sums puzzles are very popular in crossword magazines. The rules are as follows. The numbers shown in the gray squares are the sums of the digits which you will fill into the empty spaces, one digit per space. A number above the diagonal is the sum of the digits in the empty spaces to the right. The number below the diagonal is the sum of the digits in the empty spaces below. Important rules: No zeros are used, and a digit cannot appear more than once in any digit combination. For example, if the sum of a two-digit combination is 6, then the two digits can be 15, 24, 42, or 51, but not 60 (no zeros allowed) or 33 (no repeated digits allowed).

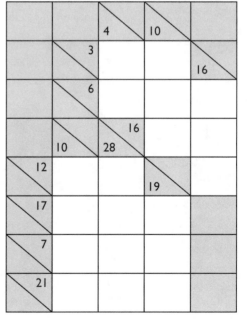

Problem Set B, Version 4

1. WEIRD WALLY'S WEIRD WINE

Weird Wine Company was owned by Weird Wally, who had a strange way of deciding in which years he produced new wine. He would produce a new wine in any year in which the sum of the digits in the year the wine is produced is equal to the sum of the digits in the year the wine is sold is equal to the age in years of the wine when it is sold. In what years in the 20th century did the company produce wine?

2. HOOVER LAKE FLOODS THE MOJAVE DESERT

The lake created by Hoover Dam on the Arizona–Nevada border has a capacity of 28,500,000 acre-feet. If the whole lake suddenly flooded the Mojave Desert (area 15,000 square miles), how deep would the water be? Assume the Mojave Desert is completely flat. (An acre-foot is the volume of water that would cover an area of 1 acre to a depth of 1 foot. An acre is 43,560 square feet.)

3. VCR

A VHS tape for a video cassette recorder can record 2 hours of programming at the SP speed, 4 hours of programming at the LP speed, and 6 hours of programming at the EP speed. The quality of the recording goes down as the time gets longer (the quality of SP is much better than the quality of LP, which is in turn better than the quality of EP).

Felicia has a VHS tape that has recorded the following shows:

Sesame Street—1 hour recorded at LP

Mr. Roger's Neighborhood—½ hour recorded at EP

Reading Rainbow—15 minutes recorded at SP speed

Pinnochio—40 minutes recorded at LP speed

Charlie Brown—10 minutes recorded at SP speed

Part 1: She wants to record *Rudolph the Red-Nosed Reindeer* (which is a one-hour show) on this tape without erasing any of the other shows. She would also like to have the highest quality recording possible, given the amount of tape she has left. On which speed should she set her VCR and how much time (at that speed) will she have left on the tape after recording this show?

Part 2: Suppose she wanted to optimize quality by recording as much of *Rudolph* as possible on SP and then switching to LP at just the right time to record the entire show and use up the whole tape. At what moment should she switch from SP to LP in order to do this?

SPRINKLERS

At each corner of a 16 ft by 16 ft square lawn there is a sprinkler that waters one quarter of a circle of 8-foot radius. In the center of the lawn, there is another sprinkler that waters a full circle of 8-foot radius. Part of the lawn is being watered by two sprinklers, and part of the lawn is being watered by only one sprinkler. What percent of the lawn is being watered by two sprinklers?

5. **CROSS NUMBER PUZZLE**

Ken Johnson's student, Erik Maness, wrote the next problem.

The puzzle below is a cross number puzzle, similar to crossword puzzles except that the entries are numbers. Enter one digit per square. The thick, heavy line is a separator.

Across
a. a prime number
c. the sum of the digits of *a* across

Down
a. square of the sum of the digits of *b* down
b. a prime number

a	**b**
	c

solve an easier related problem

I F A P R O B L E M I S hard to solve, why not just do an easier one? An easier related problem (ERP) needs to be (1) easier, (2) related, and (3) a problem. This strategy is a way of changing focus because instead of looking at the original problem, you look at a new problem that you make up (based on the original). This strategy also has elements of organizing information. Sometimes when using an ERP, you end up trying specific numbers and looking for a pattern.

Easier related problems are analogous to guess and check. In guess and check you try a number and see if it works. With ERPs you try a process and see if it works. There are a number of ways this can be done. All of these methods are demonstrated in the chapter in the text. Below is Tom Sallee's list of the various ways to make a problem simpler. The problems listed use these different methods and are from either the text or from Problem Set A.

1. Use a number instead of a variable. We used this in Averages, Square, and Hexagon.
2. Use a small or easier number in place of a more difficult one in order to develop the process for solving the problem. We used this in Simpletown Elections, Halloween Night, the math class discussion, TV Truck, Exponents, Averages, and Potatoes.
3. Do a specific, easier example and look for a pattern. We used this in From One to One Hundred, How Many Squares?, Fifty-Two Card Pickup, Last Digit, Diagonals, Sum of the First 5000 Numbers, and The 10,000-Day War.
4. Do a specific easier example and figure out an easier process that will work. We used this in Divisors and Reciprocals, and Odd and Even.
5. Change, fix, or get rid of some conditions. We used this in Good Luck Goats, Next Train East, Inscribed Square, Twenty-Five Man Roster, and Fifty-Two Card Pickup.
6. Eliminate unnecessary information. We used this in Simpletown Elections, Halloween Night, and Potatoes.

This strategy is very difficult to master. The key question to ask is "How can I make this problem easier?" Students must learn not only how to apply the strategy, but they must also learn to look for instances where it is appropriate. If a problem seems to be too hard or too confusing, they should look for an ERP. Sometimes you'll need more than one ERP to solve the original problem.

Sometimes irrelevant information is written into a problem. An ERP for such a problem would exclude the irrelevant information.

The idea of using a simpler problem in learning mathematics can be very powerful. Knowledge of some facts, such as ½ = .5, can allow a student to extend the concept to the general process of changing a fraction to a decimal. In order for an easier problem to work, the answer to the easier problem must be within your grasp.

Estimation also plays a role in ERPs but is different from the strategy. The purpose of an ERP is to allow you to determine the process needed to solve the problem. An estimate, on the other hand, can only be done when you know the process. It allows you to verify that you have successfully performed the process.

ERPs in real life can be extremely well hidden. The strategy is powerful enough that it extends a great distance outside the realm of mathematics. A nurse, Allyson, explained that she uses ERPs when she needs to stick an intravenous needle in a patient's forearm. Sometimes, usually due to advanced age or poor health, a patient has veins that are very difficult to stick. Allyson then looks at her own arm (she is in good health and is young—both factors are helpful in locating veins). She finds a good blood vessel and then searches for other physical landmarks around it on her arm. That is the easier problem. She then takes that knowledge back to the original (and difficult) problem of finding the blood vessel on the patient. She uses the corresponding physical landmarks on her patient to determine where to attempt to stick the needle.

Notes on Text Problems

SIMPLETOWN ELECTIONS

This is a case where organizing the information comes in very handy. You also need to use simplified numbers and to ignore the irrelevant information.

HALLOWEEN NIGHT

This is another example of ignoring some irrelevant information. It is also important to be able to estimate so that you have some idea of whether your answer is close.

HOW MANY SQUARES?

The process in this solution was to start with the easiest problem (a one by one square), do more easier problems, organize the data, and then develop a pattern.

DIVISORS AND RECIPROCALS

The process in this problem was to pick a small number so the divisors would be easy to add up. The prediction was then tested on another example. The same kind of pattern showed up again. Thus it was very likely, and it makes intuitive sense that this pattern would apply to the original problem.

GOOD LUCK GOATS

See "The Riddle of the Vanishing Camel," by Ian Stewart, *Scientific American,* June 1992, for a good article about this type of problem.

AVERAGES

The given averages and the number of quiz scores in this problem are difficult numbers. We used two types of easier related problems: (1) We replaced a variable with a number to see what was going on, and (2) we used easier numbers. Both of these substitutions made the problem much more manageable and gave us a plan of attack. From that point on, it was just a matter of applying the procedure learned on the easier problem to the hard problem.

INSCRIBED SQUARE

This problem can be made easier by eliminating one of the conditions. You will also need to draw lots of diagrams.

Notice that a lot of these problems can probably be done by programming a computer. Technology can therefore nullify cleverness to a certain extent. This does not mean that learning these strategies is a dead-end on Technology Avenue; rather, the thinking skills developed, the flexibility learned, and the specific strategies will be more important, as those are areas of mathematics that have yet to be conquered by computers.

Text Problems

FROM ONE TO ONE HUNDRED

What is the sum of the first hundred whole numbers?

SIMPLETOWN ELECTIONS

The clerk of Simpletown had the job of getting the materials ready for the next municipal election. There were 29 issues and candidates. In the last election, there were 28,311 registered voters, representing 18,954 households, and they voted at 14 polling places. She figures she needs about a proportionate amount of materials for this election. There are 34,892 people registered this time. How many polling places will be needed?

HALLOWEEN NIGHT

Last Halloween, each goblin was to scare exactly 3 people out of every 517 in the city. They were also supposed to find 47 newts (presumably for their eyeballs) for every 912 people in the city. And for hors d'oeuvres (for the All-Spooks party), they needed to bring in 19 wings of flies for every 33 people in the city. There were 1,414,512 people in the city that night, of whom 359,278 went to some kind of Halloween party. How many newts did the goblins need to find?

HOW MANY SQUARES?

How many squares are there on a checkerboard? (Hint: It is more than 64).

DIVISORS AND RECIPROCALS

The divisors of 360 add up to 1170. What is the sum of the reciprocals of the divisors of 360?

THE TEN-THOUSAND DAY WAR

If the Ten-Thousand-Day War started on a Wednesday, on which day of the week did it end?

EXPONENTS

Simplify each expression:

$m^{1/8} m^{5/13}$ $\qquad$ $(y^{1/3})^{6/7}$

GOOD LUCK GOATS

In ancient Kantanu, it was considered good luck to own goats. Barsanta owned some goats at the time of her death, and willed them to her children. To her first born, her favorite, she willed one-half of her goats. (The will was drawn up long before her death, and was written in general terms.) To her second born, who was not the favorite, she willed one-third of her goats. And last (and in the eyes of Barsanta, the least) she gave one-ninth of her goats to her third born (the "black sheep" among goat owners).

As it turned out, when Barsanta died she had 17 goats. Barring a Solomonic approach, how should the goats be divided?

AVERAGES

The average of a group of quiz scores is 31.8. There are k quiz scores in the group. The average of 10 of these quiz scores is 24.3. Find the average of the remaining quiz scores in terms of k.

NEXT TRAIN EAST

A train leaves Roseville heading east at 6:00 a.m. at 40 miles per hour. Another eastbound train leaves at 7:00 a.m. on a parallel track at 50 miles per hour. What time will it be when the two trains are the same distance away from Roseville?

INSCRIBED SQUARE

Given any triangle, draw a square inside of it so that all four vertices of the square are on the triangle. Two of the vertices of the square should be on one side of the triangle, and the other two sides of the triangle should each have one vertex of the square.

Make the problem easier by eliminating one of the conditions. You need to draw lots of diagrams.

Problem Set A, Version 2

1. LAST DIGIT AGAIN

What is the last digit in the product of $(3^1)(3^2)(3^3)(3^4) \ldots (3^{398})(3^{399})(3^{400})$

2. DIAGONALS OF A POLYGON

A certain convex polygon has 14 sides. How many diagonals can be drawn?

3. SUM NUMBERS - LOTSA NUMBERS

Find the sum of the first 8000 multiples of 3.

4. AIR FARE

Marlene is responsible for making sure that enough packaged meals are put on several flights for her company. She needs to get 86 meals on flight 914, which is leaving at 10:23 from gate 27 at Metro airport. They usually fly a 747 on that route, though sometimes they use a 737 when there are less than 92 passengers ticketed. She also needs to make sure that she gets 134 meals, including 9 vegetarian meals, loaded on flight 797, which leaves at 12:13. The flight takes 4 hours and 22 minutes. She and the other 28 employees of ACME Airmeals have a total of 19 flights that they are responsible for. What is the difference in the departure times for the two flights mentioned?

5. SEASON TICKET PLANS

The Carolina Shores baseball team considered offering a unique season ticket plan. You could choose anywhere from 1 game to 42 games (all are home games). How many different ticket plans does this really mean they have? (How many different combinations of home games are there?)

6. ONCE A YANKEES FAN, ALWAYS A YANKEES FAN

My younger sister Gianna is a Yankees fan: always has been, and the way I see it, always will be. When she was about two and I was just a little older, she used to to tell me who her favorite players were. She'd pick up the stack of Yankee trading cards and show me her favorite player. Sometimes it was Mickey Mantle. Sometimes it was Roger Maris. Sometimes she had two or three favorites, like Joe Pepitone, Tony Kubek, and Clete Boyer. Once she went through the whole stack, saying, "This is my favorite, this is my favorite—all 25 of them!" In how many different ways can Gianna select from 1 to 25 of her favorite players out of the stack of 25 baseball cards?

7. CLASSIC MUSTANGS

None of us really got along as friends, but we shared several things in common. We had some joint business dealings and a love of old Mustangs. We only liked the ones from 1964½ through the 1968 model year. When we found out that the collection of Mustangs from the Sparks Auto Museum was going to be auctioned off, we put our minds and our money together. Instead of bidding against each other, we decided to bid as a group on each Mustang available. We set a maximum price we would bid, and, quite frankly, none of us had any favorites; we loved them all equally. We also agreed to divide "our take" as follows: half to Travis because he was usually the big money on our projects, ¼ to Sandra as she was usually the brains that got things done, and I was to get a ⅙ share. In the end we were the winning bidders on 11 Mustangs. How many Mustangs do each of us get?

8. VIVE LA DIFFERENCE!

Find the difference between the sum of the first 500 multiples of 3 and the sum of the first 500 odd numbers.

9. RICARDO & MARITZA

Ricardo kept saving pennies. Every day he saved the same number of pennies as the day's date (e.g., 12 pennies on March 12). Maritza did something different. She saved five cents on the first day of the month. She then saved five cents more each day than she had the previous day. At the end of March, who had saved more money, and how much more money was it?

10. BUSINESS CARDS

Frank opened up a cafe. On the first day, he had no customers. On the second day, however, he had five customers. On the third day, there were 10 customers, and on the fourth day there were 15 customers. He also ran a lunch giveaway, whereby if you left a business card, he would enter it in a drawing for a free lunch. On the first day no one left a card (since there were no customers) on the second day, three people left cards and each following day three more people left business cards than on the previous day. If this pattern continues for a full year (365 days), what is the difference between the total number of customers he would have and the total number of business cards?

Problem Set B, Version 2

1. COVERING THE PATIO

Mr. Smith needs to nail some fiberglass pieces to a wooden frame to cover the patio on the back of his house. The patio measures 30 feet by 20 feet and each fiberglass piece measures 2 feet by 6 feet. (The panels are actually slightly bigger to allow for overlapping.) He needs to nail each panel to a wooden frame (which is the same size as the patio), placing the nails along each of the four edges of the fiberglass. The nails will be spaced 1 foot apart. How many nails does he need to put all of the fiberglass in place? (Note: A nail can be driven into several pieces of overlapping fiberglass.)

2. LIKE A WILDFIRE

The firefighters were frustrated with their efforts at basic fire-prevention training. It seemed that no matter how many fire-safety meetings they set up, hardly anybody ever paid attention. They devised a plan. They decided that each of them (there were eight volunteer firefighters) would teach two other people the fire-safety basics. At that point, the teacher retires but each student would then teach two others. Those people, in turn, would teach two others. The whole thing would be mandated by the city council, and each person would have a month to fulfill his or her teaching requirement. The firefighters taught the first group of people in the first month. Under this plan, how many people would know the fire-safety basics after 10 months of this program?

3. SUM OF TEN

If you add the digits in a number, how many numbers between 0 and 10,000 will have a sum of 10? (For example, 334 is one such number because 3 + 3 + 4 = 10.)

4. LAPPING JOGGERS

Jan can run around a quarter mile track in 90 seconds. Silvia can run around the same track in 72 seconds. They started running in the same direction from the same place at the same time. The two women agreed to stop when Silvia caught up to Jan for the third time (lapping her twice, then catching up to her again). How far did each one run?

5. THE PHOON BROTHERS

The Phoon brothers—Buff, Ty, and Kung—drove from Lane County, Oregon, to Disneyland, a total of 1020 miles. They picked up Helen Highwater in Visalia, which is 340 miles from Disneyland. Their car got 30 miles per gallon. Gas cost $1.15 per gallon. How much should each pay? Note: There are at least two different ways to do this, and the answers come out quite different. Be prepared to defend your argument.

Problem Set B, Version 3

1. PYRAMID SCHEME

Alan and his two buddies decided to run a pyramid investment scheme. The plan was simple. They told investors that if they paid in $1000, in one week the investors would receive $1500. On their part, the investors had to also bring in two more people into the pyramid that week. The new people would need to pay in $1000 and bring in two new people the next week. Alan and his buddies each started by bringing in two people as their first set of investors. All went well for the first 12 sets of investors, but then it all fell apart and Alan and his buddies were arrested. How many people (other than the three buddies) had invested by the time the pyramid was flattened? (Note: Pyramid schemes are illegal and perpetrators are dealt with severely by the courts.)

2. LOSING TIME

When I reset my clocks for daylight savings time, I took care to make sure that each one had exactly the same time on it. A week later, however, I noticed that the clock on the VCR was 14 minutes slow. I didn't have time to reset it, and as I drove out, I noticed that my car clock was 7 minutes fast. (My watch is extremely expensive and extremely accurate.) I decided not to reset them, but I finally got sick of it and changed them when the car clock was exactly an hour ahead of my VCR clock. I initially set the clocks to daylight savings time on a Sunday. How many days later, and on what day of the week, did I reset them?

3. DRIVE ME WILDE

The Wilde cousins—Fawn, Kat, and Wolfgang—decided to drive to Disneyworld, a 630-mile drive from their home. One hundred ten miles into the drive they picked up their cousin, Duckie. In Florida, about 115 miles from their destination, they picked up another cousin, Mildred. (If you're wondering about her name, it's different because she's not from the Wilde side.) Their car got 35 miles per gallon and gas cost them $1.13 per gallon. They all agreed to share the gas costs. How much should each pay? (Warning: There are two valid ways to compute the shared costs—be prepared to defend your answer.)

SOCCER LEAGUE

In the Great Falls, Minnesota soccer league, there were six teams: Allosaurus, Brontosaurus, Cetiosaurus, Dimetrodon, Hypsilophodon, and Triceratops. (The kids in the soccer league were really fond of dinosaurs.) Each team played each other team twice. At the end of the season the sports editor of the Great Falls Gazette was looking over her notes from the season before publishing the results in the paper. Her son played on Brontosaurus and her niece played on Dimetrodon. She remembered that no team tied more than one game. She also had written down the number of play-off points that five of the teams had acquired. (A play-off point is awarded as follows: 2 points for a win, 1 point for a tie, 0 points for a loss.) Help her determine the final standings. She also wanted to know who tied whom and how her son's team did in the two games against her niece's team.

PLAY-OFFS				
TEAM	WINS	LOSSES	TIES	PLAY-OFF POINTS
Allosaurus				3
Brontosaurus				10
Cetiosaurus				20
Dimetrodon				11
Hypsilophodon				
Triceratops				1

5. **RUNNING ERRANDS**

Willy has ten errands to run. However, he has his three kids with him, who are all really young. With all of the waiting in stores, getting in and out of car seats, naps, diapers, potty breaks, whining, crying, etc., Willy sticks to a rule of thumb: no more than three errands at a time before going home. How many different sets of three errands can he arrange?

Problem Set B, Version 4—Gary's Van

1. TWO VEHICLES

Gary has two cars: his fairly new van and his old clunker station wagon. The wagon currently has 16 times as many miles on it as the van had when the wagon had 3 times as many miles as the van has now. Between now and then, each vehicle has driven the exact same number of miles. The wagon has not yet driven 100,000 miles. All mileage amounts are in thousands. How many miles has the van driven now?

2. DIGITAL CLOCK

In Gary's van, the digital clock is messed up. One or two of the lines in each digit are always shorting out, although not necessarily the same lines in each digit and not the same lines all the time. One day, Gary drove over to his friend Jeff's house. When Gary got into the van, the clock read the time shown below left. When he got to Jeff's house, a drive of no more than a half hour, the clock read the time shown below right. What time was it when he got to Jeff's house?

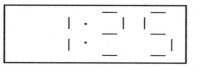 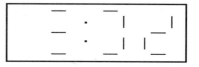

3. WATCH YOUR SPEED

Gary had to buy a watch because the clock in his van was so messed up. Unfortunately, he bought a used watch and it didn't work too well. He compared it to his good clocks in his house and found that his watch was fast: When his watch showed one minute had passed, it had really only been 57 seconds. One day, Gary was taking a trip to Monterey. He suspected that the speedometer in his van was off, but he wasn't sure by how much. He found one of those mileage checks on the freeway. He drove 5 miles (according to the mileage signs, which you may assume are accurate) in 5 minutes and 30 seconds according to his watch. He kept his speedometer on 53 miles per hour the whole time. If the speed limit is 65 miles per hour, what is the fastest he can drive according to his speedometer and avoid breaking the law? (Note: His speedometer reads 0 miles per hour when he is stopped.)

On Gary's trip to Monterey he found himself in the midst of 100 cars, driving on what seemed to be an endless two lane highway (one lane in each direction). The cars were all closely bunched because they were traveling in reverse order of their desired speeds. In other words, the person who was in the lead car wanted to travel the slowest and thus had the huge line of cars behind him. The person following the lead car wanted to go faster than the lead car but slower than everyone else. The person following the first two cars wanted to go faster than the first two cars, but slower than everyone else. This pattern continued, with each person wanting to go faster than everyone in front of them but slower than everyone behind them. The drivers all decided that they wanted to pass everyone in front of them and be passed by everyone behind them so that the entire order of 100 cars would be reversed.

If more than one passing can take place at the same time, what is the fewest number of passing periods that must occur for all the cars to end up in the desired order?

Note: only two cars can be involved in each passing (the passer and the passee) but multiple passings can occur simultaneously. For example, car 2 could pass car 1 at the same time that car 4 passes car 3, at the same time that car 52 passes car 51, and so on. All of that would only count as one passing period.

Lori was walking down the street on her way to the grocery store. As she got to a crosswalk she noticed a van coming from her left, passing under a railroad overpass just as she started to cross the street. As she finished crossing the street, the van reached the crosswalk behind her. (It was Gary, coming home from Monterey.) She turned left when she reached the sidewalk. It took her 15 seconds to cross the street and 2 minutes and 20 seconds to reach the overpass. She walks 3 miles per hour. How fast was the van going? (Assume it was traveling at a constant speed.)

40 physical representations

" **I** F A PICTURE IS worth a thousand words, then a model is worth a million." Physical representations is an umbrella term that encompasses strategies that could be considered separately. It includes using manipulatives, making models, and acting out problems. It is sometimes difficult to determine where each of these strategies ends and another begins.

There are also elements of guess and check involved in physical representations. Much of solving a problem with manipulatives involves making the incorrect guesses and adjusting subsequent guesses. An advantage of the manipulatives in doing guess and check is that it is possible to do the guessing, checking, and revising very quickly. Using manipulatives also differs from guess and check in that a record is not usually kept of the incorrect guesses with manipulatives, whereas in paper and pencil guess and check, the record is an integral element of the strategy.

The different variations of physical representations have distinguishing characteristics. Models, for example, generally need to have some critical elements made to scale and need to function in the same manner as in the items they represent. That is not necessarily true of a manipulative, which might have no scaled elements. A manipulative is generally set up to deal with spatial relationships and may or may not be a realistic rendition of the item it represents.

Models can physically represent a number of mathematical concepts, including magnitude, scale, quantity, directional movement, positional relationship, static relationship, number, number combinations, relative size, or orientation. Any useful model represents at least one key element. Models in many cases are extensions of diagrams.

While much of the power of modern mathematics comes from abstraction, we risk overlooking real-world connections when we rely too heavily on abstract methods for solving problems. As we learn more and more abstract methods, we may even lose our capacity for using models and manipulatives in problem solving. Fortunately, current trends in mathematics education towards real-world applications should prevent teachers and students from losing their touch with physical representations.

Using models and manipulatives can be especially helpful for students who are kinesthetic learners. It gives other students the opportunity to develop skills they might not otherwise have developed.

When you teach this section, there are a number of things you should recognize. Many of us did not have strong role models for instruction with manipulatives. We are further disadvantaged in that many of our students will enter our classes with similarly scant experience. Things that may seem obvious to us may need to be emphasized to students.

Students may also enter the class with a negative mindset against manipulatives. They may develop this attitude from their lack of facility and familiarity with the strategy, or they may learn it directly from teachers or people at home with the same attitude. ("We didn't do it that way, and I learned this just fine.")

Finally, people sometimes avoid manipulatives because of the time it takes to set them up.

You will need to spend time emphasizing the benefits of physical representations, such as how they allow you to check guesses easily. Point out how the problems in the text are more easily solved with manipulatives. Students may also be motivated by how physical representations connect with other disciplines. There are numerous real-life applications of physical representations you can relate to your students. Some examples include mechanical or civil engineering projects, planning processes (the volleyball examples in the text are from real recreational league situations), and logistical operations (such as a "war room"). The article, reprinted in the text, about the Hubble telescope is a good example of a real-life application of manipulatives.

A manipulative approach should not be used for its own sake. There should be an underlying purpose: making the problem easier, approaching through another learning modality, bringing out key elements, teaching the use of manipulatives directly, and so on.

You will find that your students' spatial visualization skills are improved by using models. They will gain concrete experience in more math concepts and will practice transferring that experience to pencil and paper. Depending on the students' prior abilities, spatial visualization may need to be approached more formally with some students than with others.

When students act out a problem, they should arrive at a solution once the acting is done. As the solution unfolds, each person involved should be actively checking the problem constraints. Students will need to review the constraints after they reach a solution in order to verify it. Any recording should wait until after the solution is reached and verified.

Act It Out day

Spend an entire class period practicing the act it out strategy, using the problems in Section 1 of the student text. Divide the class into groups and assign each group a problem to do. Make sure each group has the right number of students for each problem. Every student in the group needs to take an active role in solving the problem. Let the groups have 15 to 20 minutes of rehearsal. Encourage them to get up and move around the room or even go outside if that is possible at your school. Suggest (if they don't think of it themselves) that they use signs to label the actors (horse, dog, goose, coyote, etc.) and that they use something to represent inanimate objects in the problem (boat, money, figurine, etc). After rehearsal, have the entire class sit down to be the audience and have each group come up to the front of the room and act out their solution to their problem.

The following problems require the number of people indicated. You can have an extra person in a group to act as a director or narrator if you want. You probably have more problems than you need. You could use one as the problem of the day and skip some others.

Jackals and Coyotes: 6 people

Horse Trader: 3 people

Three Adults and Two Kids: 5 people (easy)

The Dog, the Goose, and the Corn: 4 people (easy)

Hoop Ritual: 10 people (Note: You could have a group with many fewer people than this to rehearse, then have them get volunteers from the audience for the performance. Or don't assign this problem at first and leave it for people who finish early on other problems.)

Switching Jackals and Coyotes: 6 people

The Hotel Bill: 5 people

Persis' Gift Shop: 4 people

Buckingham Palace: 4 people

Using Manipulatives

The day after act it out day, put your class in their groups and have them do the two versions of Jackals and Coyotes over again using manipulatives. Little pieces of paper marked J and C work well, as do centimeter cubes, pennies and nickels, and various other things. Then have students work in their groups on the problems in Problem Set A-2 using manipulatives. The first problem in that set, Two Jackals Lose Their License, is very tough. Students should all have done the first two Jackals and Coyotes problems first, before they tackle this one.

Notes on Text Problems—Section 2: Manipulatives

In Section 1: Act It Out, the physical representation was having people act as other animals and/or inanimate objects. Each person presumably moved herself or himself and had a degree of self-direction.

With models and manipulatives, most of the direction will reside in fewer hands and minds. The direction will not be in the hands of the problem-objects; instead, students act as problem directors.

Students should probably wait to record their work until after they've found a complete solution. Seek the students' creativity in finding ways to record the process.

FOUR CONTIGUOUS STAMPS

Problems of this type abound in any sport. They can be found in arranging batting orders; positioning soccer players; and demonstrating plays in football, soccer, and basketball.

THE VOLLEYBALL TEAM

Orientation is important. Some students will have difficulty devising a systematic approach to this.

MEXICAN RESTAURANT

Initially, the manipulatives are important because each one contains an element of the problem. Their position is also important. Their shape and orientation become more important as you tape the positionally-related pieces together.

Notes on Problem Set A-1

THREE MEN AND TWO BOYS

Possibly do the solution using a length of 10 color rods as the boat, length of 8 as each man, and length of 5 as each boy. This approximates one man fitting, two boys fitting, but not one of each. Pounds are converted to length if you work this out in this manner.

Notes on Text Problems—Section 3: Conversions

The first six problems consist of three problems that are restated as manipulative problems. You can duplicate each problem with its manipulatives counterpart on paper of the same color, different from the other problems. Have students work one set of three problems and compare with another group that did the other set of three problems. Even side by side, many will fail to recognize the correspondence between the problems.

Notes on Problem Set A-3

TRAINS FROM SALT LAKE CITY

Try using color rods on this problem.

VAT'S THE PROBLEM?

This problem tends to be counter-intuitive for most people. Try using ten pieces of red paper as the red liquid and ten pieces of black paper as the black liquid. "Pour" from one by moving any number of the red pieces to the black. Return the same number of pieces—either all red, all black, or mixed colors—to the first "vat," so each vat has ten pieces in it. No matter what, the number of reds in the black will equal the number of blacks in the red. Alternative manipulatives for this problem include a deck of cards (use ten black cards and ten red cards) or coins (use dimes for red and pennies for black).

Text Problems

THE JACKALS AND THE COYOTES

Three jackals and three coyotes are on a trek across the Mokalani Plateau when they come to a river filled with carnivorous fish. There is a rowboat in sight, and the party decides to use it. (Both species are known for their cleverness, regardless of how much this problem exceeds reasonableness.) However, the boat is too small for any more than two of the group at a time. So they must traverse the river in successive crossings. There is one hitch, though. The jackals must not outnumber the coyotes at any time, in any place. If it happens, for example, that there are two jackals on the western bank, and only one coyote, then this problem is reduced to simple subtraction and gluttony. (The jackals will overpower, kill, and eat the coyotes.) It's okay to have an equal number of each, and it is also okay to have more coyotes than jackals in a given place. Neither situation poses a danger to the coyotes, and the coyotes do not pose a threat to the jackals. So, the trick here is to use the one small rowboat, a lot of sweat, and a little brainpower to assure the coyotes' survival while both groups cross the river.

THE HORSE TRADER

Once upon a time, there was a horse-trader. One day, the horse trader bought a horse for $60. Just after noon, the horse trader sold that same horse back to the original owner for $70. He then bought it back again just before 5:00 for $80. By midnight, he managed to sell the horse back to the original owner for $90. How much money did the horse trader make or lose on this horse?

FOUR CONTIGUOUS STAMPS

In how many ways can four stamps be attached together? Be sure to pay attention to the thrust of this chapter. Take care to record each configuration.

LETTER CUBE

Build this cube to see what letter is opposite the letter T. Pay attention to the orientation of the letters as well.

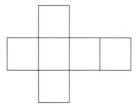

Draw this figure on a piece of paper (graph paper works well), cut it out, and fold it to make a cube. Then write the letters on it.

THE VOLLEYBALL TEAM

The volleyball team has six players: Betty, Martha, Karen, Walt, Guy, and Steve. Put them in their positions by using the clues to get the best rotation. (From the net, there are three players in the front row and three in the back row. The server is in the back left corner.)

1. The players must alternate by gender.
2. Betty is the team's best server; she should start in the serving position.
3. Guy and Karen are the team's setters. They must be opposite each other at all times.
4. Walt and Martha communicate well—it helps to put them next to each other.
5. Steve is an effective server. He needs to be positioned so he will rotate into the serving position quickly.

Note: A volleyball court has six players. They rotate in a clockwise manner. (See the diagram below.)

```
┌──────── BACKLINE ────────┐
│                          │
│  Srvr 1    Srvr 6   Srvr 5 │
│                          │
│  Srvr 2    Srvr 3   Srvr 4 │
│                          │
└──────────── NET ─────────┘
```

Players are considered opposite if there are three positions between them. So server 1 is opposite server 4, server 2 is opposite server 5, and server 3 is opposite server 6.

NUMBER PUZZLE

Use the digits 0, 1, 2, 3, 4, 5, 6, 7, 8, 9, once each to fill in the blanks in this puzzle:

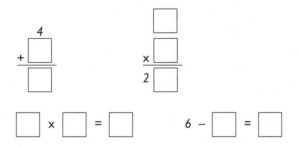

Work this problem by cutting up little pieces of paper and labeling them with the numbers 0 through 9. Then manipulate them around in the puzzle until you find a way that works. There is more than one possible solution.

FOOTBALL SCORES

How many ways are there to score 20 points in a football game? Use color rods to solve this problem.

MEXICAN RESTAURANT

Four friends (one is named Janie) went out to dinner at a Mexican restaurant. The hostess seated them in a booth. Each ordered a different meat (one ordered pork) and each ordered a different kind of Mexican dish (one was a tostada). Use the clues below to determine what dish each person ordered, the kind of meat it contained, and where each person was sitting.

1. The person who ordered mahi-mahi sat next to Ted and across from the person who ordered a burrito.
2. Ken sat diagonally across from the person who ate the fajita and across from the person who ordered beef.
3. The person who ordered a chimichanga sat across from the person who ordered chicken and next to Allyson.

(For those unfamiliar with California-Mexican cuisine, burritos, fajitas, chimichangas, and tostadas are flour tortillas with various fillings such as mahi-mahi, pork, beef, and chicken.)

A LITTLE RUSTY

Use manipulatives to balance this chemistry equation.

$Fe + O_2 \rightarrow Fe_2O_3$

(Fe is iron, O_2 is oxygen gas, and Fe_2O_3 is rust.)

MALCOLM'S HONDAS

Malcolm used to brag that he had 11 Hondas at his estate; all were either motorcycles or cars. In all, his vehicles had 36 wheels. How many of each did he have?

A DRIVE TO THE LAKE

My grandfather told me about the time he, his sister, and his cousins drove to the lake from his cousins' house. They took separate cars. My grandfather and his sister drove 30 miles per hour. His cousins left two hours later and drove 40 miles per hour. Both cars arrived at the lake at about the same time. What was the approximate distance from his cousins' house to the lake?

Problem Set A, Version 2

Instructions: Solve each problem by acting it out or using manipulatives.

1. HANUM'S ISLAND

Hanum and her friends went to play on an island about ¼ mile offshore at the lake. They have a sailboat, but the sailboat is very small and can only take about 220 pounds at a time. Hanum weighs 120 pounds, Sara weighs 100 pounds, Eliza weighs 95 pounds, Carmen weighs 110 pounds, and Les weighs 140 pounds. How many trips will it take to get Hanum and her friends off the island? (Consider a trip to be one way between the island and the mainland.)

2. MAGIC TRIANGLE #2

To do this Magic Triangle, you must use the digits one through six, once each. Tear up little pieces of paper and write the digits one through six on them. Place one digit in each square to give each side of this triangle a sum of 12.

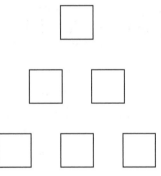

3 ROOKIE PURCHASE

Max paid only $1500 for a rookie Willie Mays card worth $1800. He later sold it for $2000, but the buyer came back and showed him that it was actually a fake. Max gave the customer back his money. Who lost how much on this?

4. LAWN CHAIR AND BARBEQUE

Sammie bought a lawn chair and a barbeque grill at his neighbor's garage sale for $20. He then sold the lawn chair to Wilma for $9. He sold the barbeque grill to Marc for $12. Marc later sold the grill to Wilma for $14, who then sold both items back to Sammie for $22. How much money did each person make or lose on the grill and the lawn chair?

5. STAMPS

How many ways are there to make 29 cents in stamps if the stamps all cost 8, 5, or 2 cents each?

Use color rods to solve this problem.

6. FIVE TILES

Belinda decided to do her own bathroom tiles. As part of her plan, she decided to use pentominoes (five squares that touch along at least one complete side). How many different pentominoes are there? (One is shown below. Reflections and rotations should not be considered different.)

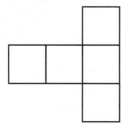

7. LETTER CUBE

Build this cube to see what letter belongs on the blank face. Pay attention to the orientation of the letters as well.

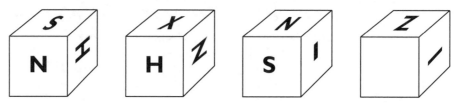

Draw a figure like the figure below on graph paper and cut it out in order to assist with this problem. (Cut on the solid lines, fold on the dotted lines.)

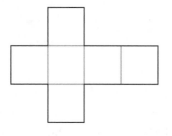

8. SIX AND FOUR

What is the minimum number of 90-degree rotations needed to bring this standard pair of dice to the point where each die has the six in front and the four on top?

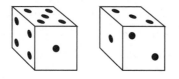

9. A HEART IN THE RIGHT PLACE

There is a heart to the right of a diamond. There is a diamond to the left of a diamond. There is a heart to the left of a diamond. The sum of the card values is 11. One of the card values alone is greater than the sum of the other two card values. The cards are arranged from least to greatest in order from left to right. There are no aces. What are the cards?

10. TWO DICE

Two dice are placed side by side. From the front, the dice show a sum of nine. On top, the dice show a sum of four. The sum of the right and left ends is six. How are the dice positioned?

11. JUST A PEW KIDS

Dad and four kids are sitting in a church pew. Barbara wants to sit away from Sonny because he squirms so much during the service. Sonny doesn't want to sit by his sister Tara. The youngest, Krista, needs to sit by Dad and Dad likes to sit by the aisle so he can take Krista out when she gets antsy without making much of a disturbance. How should they sit in five consecutive seats in church?

12. LONG TABLE

Five people are sitting at a long table in a cafeteria. No one is sitting at the end of the table. Each person is either sitting immediately next to another person or directly across from another person. How many seating arrangements are possible?

13. MAGIC SQUARE

The sum of rows in a magic square is 15. The sum of each diagonal is 15. The sum of each column is also 15. Use the digits 0, 2, 3, 4, 5, 6, 7, 8, and 10 and find the proper location of each. (There is more than one correct solution.)

14. CARDS IN TWO ROWS

Three cards were placed face up in a row. Three more cards were placed on top of them, also face up, but you could still see the bottom row cards. There was a King on an Ace. The Queens were not in the same row. The Jack was to the left of an Ace. One of the aces was to the right of a Queen, and the other was to the left of a Queen. The Jack was under one Queen and to the left of another. The King was to the left of an Ace. No two cards of the same rank were in the same stack. Any cards to the left or right of one another have to be in the same row. How were the cards arranged?

15. BLUEGRASS AT DINNER

At a musician's conference, several friends got together for some dinner before the evening performance. As fate would have it, there were three different bluegrass groups represented. Each group consisted of a guitarist, a banjo player, and a fiddler (violinist). Determine who is in what group. (By the way, fiddles have four strings, banjos have five, and these guitars have six.)

1. Irving and Ben play banjo.
2. Kathleen and Sue are in the same group.
3. George and Ben haven't seen each other since the last conference.
4. Kris and Irving are in the same group.
5. Emily's instrument has fewer strings than both Ben's and Kris's. Kathleen's instrument has more than four strings, and Sue's instrument has fewer than six.
6. Kris and Lucille play the same instrument.
7. Marty, who plays banjo, always feels inspired listening to Lucille's group.

Who plays the violin in Marty's group? Who plays banjo in Emily's group? What instrument does George play, and who else is in his group?

Suppose you had two figures, each comprising three squares as shown below.

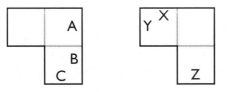

In Figure 1, *A* and *Y* were placed next to each other. The figure does not form a cube when folded.

In Figure 2, *A* and *X* were placed next to each other. The figure does form a cube when folded.

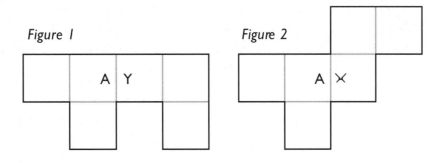

1. Can a cube be folded by attaching *A* to *Z*?
2. By attaching *B* to *Y*?
3. By attaching *C* to *X*?

1. DUELING PINS

Three married couples who are friends of one another decided to have a bowling competition. The first game featured the Sanchezes against the Wojics. The second game matched up the Wojics and the Carsons. The Carsons bowled against the Sanchezes in the third game. It was hard to tell who was pushing the competition more, the women (Lani, Fawnda, and Rhonda) or the men (Mark, Hank, and Bill). The winner was declared on the basis of the total score for the two games. From these clues determine the names of each couple and the scores of each game. Clues 1 to 5 refer to single games. Clue 6 refers to the whole match.

1. Hank and his wife lost to Fawnda and her husband.
2. Lani and her husband beat the Sanchezes.
3. The Carsons won one match, 258 to 217.
4. Rhonda and her husband lost to the Wojics, 243 to 290.
5. Bill and his wife lost one match, 211 to 281.
6. Lani and her husband came in second in the competition with a total of 507 pins. The winning couple had 524 pins.

2. STOPLIGHTS

On San Francisco's 19th Avenue, the stoplights are all timed. There is a stoplight on every corner, and they stay green for 1 minute, yellow for 5 seconds, and red for 1 minute. The intersections are 200 yards apart. The lights are timed so that each light turns green 10 seconds after the previous one. You are stopped at a stoplight. When the light turns green, it takes you 7 seconds and 50 yards to reach a speed of 30 miles per hour. From then on, you travel a constant 30 miles per hour. How many stoplights will you be able to drive through before you have to stop for a red light? Assume you will go through a yellow light if it has only been yellow for 2 seconds when you reach it, but you will stop if it has been yellow for more than 2 seconds when you reach it.

3. TICKET PRICES

Four theaters are on the same street in Miami. One day the four theater owners were discussing their ticket prices. The movie tickets were cheapest, followed by the community theater tickets, the dinner theater tickets, and the symphony tickets. They noticed that if three of the ticket prices were averaged and then added to the ticket price of the fourth theater, the numbers 25, 27, 31, and 39 would result, depending on which price you left out of the average. What are the ticket prices?

4. CAPICUA NUMBERS

Your Spanish cousin is in town for a week. She tells you about "capicua" numbers: numbers that read the same forward or backward. (In English they are called "palindromes.") For example, 55 and 94549 are capicua numbers. It is considered good luck to get one for your ticket number on the Madrid subway. How many capicua numbers are there between 1 and 100,000?

5. A FAST(?) SPACESHIP

Light travels at a rate of approximately 186,000 miles per second. The North Star is approximately 460 light-years away from Earth. (A light-year is the distance light travels in one year.) How many years would it take a spaceship traveling at 1 billion miles per hour to reach the North Star?

Problem Set B, Version 3

1. ODD-ODD NUMBERS

Odd-odd numbers are numbers that not only end in an odd digit: all of their digits are odd. For example, 3515, 73, 1, and 97757931 are all odd-odd numbers, while 3576, 64428, and 997553121 are not. How many odd-odd numbers are there between 1 and 1,000,000?

2. THE BRIDGE TOURNAMENT

Three married couples named Friedrich, Muir, and Hatfield decided to have an informal three-way bridge tournament. Each couple played each of the other couples once in a series of four-game matches. The third couple would watch TV while the other two couples were playing bridge. It turned out that each couple won one match and lost one, and so the winner was declared to be the couple who won the most points altogether. The women's names were Anne, Mary, and Jean. Their husbands were Randy, Jim, and Dave. Using the clues below, determine the full names of the couples and figure out their order of finish in the tournament. Each clue refers to a single match.

1. The Hatfields lost to Anne and her husband, 320 to 410.
2. Jean and her husband beat the Muirs.
3. Randy and his wife lost, 80 to 280.
4. Dave and his wife beat the Friedrichs.
5. Jim and his wife lost to Mary and her husband, 400 to 560.

3. DISCOUNT TICKETS

Kelly and her adult friends made plans to go to the amusement park. She looked in the paper and saw that at the regular ticket price it was going to cost her $204 to buy enough tickets for herself and all her friends. She started calling her friends and found out that none of them could go. So she changed her plans to a family-oriented day. She invited half as many adults as she had earlier planned and a bunch of her teenage and pre-teen cousins. With all these adults, teens, and children, she needed 15 more tickets than she had originally planned for her adult friends. Surprisingly, it was still going to cost her $204 at regular prices. The next day she went to the park to buy the tickets. It turned out that they were having a sale, with all tickets 20% off, so she actually spent less than $204. There were three kinds of tickets: adult, teen, and child. For the price of an adult ticket she was able to buy a teen ticket and a child ticket. Teen tickets were $4.00 on sale, and she bought five of them. How many children's tickets did Kelly buy?

4. DRIVING ON THE FREEWAY

In my driver's education class last week, my teacher was talking about driving on the freeway. He said that you should stay 1 car length behind the car in front of you for every 10 miles per hour that you drive. (So if you were driving 60 miles per hour, you should be 6 car lengths behind.) I went home and told my dad, and he said that his driver education teacher told him that he should stay 2 seconds behind the car in front of him. Assuming that a car length is 20 feet and you are traveling 60 miles per hour, how many car lengths behind should you stay, using dad's 2-second rule?

5. CAKE RECIPE

A recipe for Four Egg Cake in *The Joy of Cooking* calls for the ingredients listed below and is supposed to be baked in three 9-inch-diameter, round cake pans. Unfortunately, you only have three 10-inch, round cake pans. You want to make your cake about the same height as it would have been in a 9-inch cake pan. Determine the amounts needed for each ingredient. Hint: Do the eggs first.

Ingredients
2⅔ cups cake flour
2¼ teaspoons baking powder
1 cup butter
2 cups sugar
4 eggs
1 cup milk

Problem Set B, Version 4

1. BATTING AVERAGE

I went on vacation recently. When I left, my favorite baseball player had 138 hits in 423 at bats for a batting average of .326. He had played in 110 games so far. I was gone for 12 days, and the team played a game every day. When I came back he was batting .320. What was his probable batting average for the games that I missed? (Assume he played in every game.)

2. PYRAMIDS

The eight cheerleaders from Hangum High liked to do various acrobatic stunts in which they would climb on each others shoulders to form pyramids. However, to prevent injury they had agreed that no person would stand on the shoulders of someone who weighed less than themselves. Three of their favorite pyramid schemes are shown below. Note: The far right shows vertical pyramids of one person on another's back. In scheme 1 it shows Kelly on Barbara's back. In scheme 3 it shows Debbie on Barbara's back, with Barbara on Carmella's back.

Scheme 1
			Lori				
Carmella		Diane				Kelly
Kate		Lisa		Debbie		Barbara

Scheme 2
| | Diane | | | Lori | | Lisa |
| Carmella | Barbara | | Debbie | Kelly | | Kate |

Scheme 3
						Debbie
	Lori	Kelly				Barbara
Lisa	Kate	Diane				Carmella

Rank the girls in order from lightest to heaviest.

3. STEP ON A CRACK AND BREAK YOUR BACK

Stan is out taking a long walk. He always finds it interesting to see how many sidewalk cracks he stepped on. The cracks are 5¼ feet apart. The cracks are very thin. His stride is 2¾ feet long (measured from heel to heel or toe to toe). His feet are 12 inches long. Assume his foot has to overlap a crack by at least an inch in order for him to count it. If he starts his walk with both heels just barely past a crack, what fraction of the cracks will he step on during his walk?

4. START YOUR ENGINES

Thursday night is classic car night at Jasper's Hamburgers. Every night about 150 classic cars are on display, there's oldie music, and people eat hamburgers and french fries. It's a lot of fun. The restaurateurs decided to sponsor several vehicles at a regional car show but had trouble deciding which cars to choose. So Marsha (the restaurant owner) devised a plan: She told everyone to turn on their headlights. Marsha then counted off every other car (the second car, the fourth, the sixth, and so on). The owners of those cars had to turn off their headlights. Marsha then counted every third car (the third, sixth, ninth and so on) and told the car owners that had their headlights on to turn them off. Those that had their headlights off had to turn them on. She continued in this fashion, counting by each subsequent number (next by fours, then by fives, then sixes) until she had finished counting by 153's. (There were 153 cars, and counting by 153's didn't take very long.) Each time she counted off cars, the cars she pointed to switched from lights on to lights off, or vice versa. Which cars still had their headlights on when Marsha was done?

5. RODGERS AND HAMMERSTEIN

At our house, we love movie musicals written by Richard Rodgers and Oscar Hammerstein. We own five of their most famous movie soundtracks on compact disc (CD): *Oklahoma* (1955), *Carousel* (early 1956), *The King and I* (late 1956), *South Pacific* (1958), and *The Sound of Music* (1964). I like to listen to them all in one afternoon, and I like to listen to them in chronological order. Fortunately, I own a five CD carousel which will play discs 1 through 5 continuously. Unfortunately, the discs were put in the machine by my son, who didn't understand my preference for playing them in chronological order. The current order is: disc 1, *South Pacific*; disc 2, *The King and I*; disc 3, *The Sound of Music*; disc 4, *Oklahoma*; disc 5, *Carousel*. I need them to start with *Oklahoma* in the disc 1 spot all the way through *The Sound of Music* in the disc 5 spot. In order to switch the discs, I start at disc 1, take that disc (which is *South Pacific*) out, press "disc skip" whatever number of times is necessary to move to the disc I want to exchange, then exchange that disc for the one in my hand, and so on. (I can only hold one disc in my hand at a time.) The carousel rotates from disc 1 to disc 2, 3, 4, and 5, and then returns to disc 1. How can I get the discs in the right order and press "disc skip" the fewest number of times?

work backwards

ORKING BACKWARDS is analogous to the process used in solving algebraic equations. If you think of an algebraic expression as a variable with a bunch of operations performed on it, you can think of solving an equation as working backwards to isolate the variable you started with. Working backwards is a commonly used strategy in real-life problem solving, too. Budgets are often made by working backwards from how much money is available. Scheduling is often performed by starting with the question, "when does it need to be done?" Then by working backwards through the project you can determine when different tasks need to be started. An accident investigator must work back from the end result to see what transpired.

Working backwards is a way of changing focus. While most problem solutions describe a result of a number of actions or operations, the solution to a problem solved by working backwards usually describes a state that existed *before* the action of the problem occurred. You must start by focusing on the end state of the problem and work backwards from there.

Students can write their own problems that can be solved by working backwards. Cookies are a good problem subject. Suggest students choose a number of cookies and then describe what happens until they reach some number of cookies left. Students can trade problems to practice solving them.

When teaching this strategy, you will need to emphasize two things: doing the opposite operation and doing these operations in reverse order. Students will likely find doing operations on fractions in reverse the most difficult concept. For example, $\frac{1}{5}$ of 100 is 20, so if someone ate $\frac{1}{5}$ of the jelly beans, there would only be 80 left. However, you need to recognize that the 80 is $\frac{4}{5}$ of the original number. To get back to 100, you need to multiply by $\frac{5}{4}$, or add $\frac{1}{4}$ (not $\frac{1}{5}$) of 80. Diagrams and pictures of fractional pieces will help with this. Here's an example of using diagrams to work the fractions backwards.

"Barry ate ⅗ of Willie's cookies. Willie had eight left."

Draw a diagram with five parts in it (to show the "before" state). The eight remaining cookies are the ⅖ left, so they are put in two of the boxes.

Fill in the other boxes with the same number. Each fifth represents 4 cookies; hence all 5 fifths make 20 cookies.

Point out to students that solutions found by working backwards can be checked just like solutions to equations: Start with your answer at the beginning of the problem, perform all the actions working forward, and see if you arrive at the expected result.

Text Problems

POOR CHOICES

Half of the ballet company stayed up late watching tractor pulls on TV, the night before their debut in Carnegie Hall. Excuse me, make that half of the company plus one more. There were 13 tired dancers in all, so how many dancers were in the company?

THE STOLEN PIGEONS

Bad Bargle snuck into Homer's pigeon loft one day. He took half of the pigeons. He decided that wasn't bad enough, so he took one more and left. Later, Homer opened the door of the loft in order to exercise his prize possessions. Half of the remaining flock flew out, leaving six inside the pen. How many pigeons did Homer have before Bad Bargle did his dirty deed?

DAD'S WALLET

On Wednesday, Dad got paid. Thursday morning my brother took half the money to go open a checking account (because he was always short of money). On Friday, I needed some for a date, so I took half of what remained. Sis came along next, and took half of the remaining money. Dad then went to gas up the car and used half of the rest of his money, and wondered where it all went so fast. He only had $5 left. How much money did he start with in his wallet?

Don't forget to reverse the actions and reverse the order.

THE MAGIC TRICK

Start with a number between 1 and 10.
Multiply the number by 4.
Add 6 to the number you have now.
Divide by 2.
Subtract 5.
Tell me the number you ended with and I'll tell you the number you started with.

Two students, Glenda and Sonia, played this game. Sonia started with a number, did the arithmetic, and told Glenda that she had ended with 12. Glenda then figured out what number Sonia started with. What number did Sonia start with?

A RICH ESTATE

Mr. Phil T. Rich left half of his estate to his wife, $30,000 to his daughter, half of what was left to his butler, half of what remained for the care of his goldfish, and the remaining $8,000 to charity. What was the value of the estate?

Three friends, returning from the movie Friday the 13th Part 65, stopped to eat at a restaurant. After dinner, they paid their bill and noticed a bowl of mints at the front counter. Sean took ⅓ of the mints, but returned four because he had a momentary pang of guilt. Faizah then took ¼ of what was left but returned three for similar reasons. Eugene then took half of the remainder but threw two that looked like they had been slobbered on back into the bowl. (He felt no pangs of guilt—he just didn't want slobbered-on mints). The bowl had only 17 mints left when the raid was over. How many mints were originally in the bowl?

Problem Set A, Version 2

1. MARY'S CAR LOT

Mary decided to focus on selling luxury cars and needed to sell off one line of sports cars: the LaMancinis. She held a clearance sale. The first week of the sale, she and her associates sold half the LaMancinis. The second week, they again sold half the remaining sports cars on the lot and one more. Mary and the other three sales representatives then each chose one of the remaining sports cars to keep, and there were none left over. How many LaMancini sports cars were on the lot at the start of the sale?

2. ORANGE YOU HUNGRY?

Leslie set up a fruit stand in order to sell some of her crop of oranges. The first person who came by bought ⅓ of her oranges. The second person bought four. The third person then bought ¼ of the remaining oranges. Leslie took the last 15 oranges home and made orange juice. How many oranges did Leslie have at the beginning?

3. TURNPIKE

Maury was driving down the turnpike. Every time he got to a tollbooth, he had to pay $1. He went through one tollbooth and then stopped at a restaurant. He spent half of his money on dinner and then continued. A while later, he went through another tollbooth and then stopped to buy some snacks for $2. He then passed through another tollbooth, spent half of his money on a soda, and then spent his last dollar on a tollbooth, just before turning off at his exit. How much money did Maury have when he started on the freeway?

4. THE MONOPOLY GAME

In the last two times around the board, Wendell thought he was a goner. First, he had to pay half of his money in rent to somebody. He then had to pay $25 because of a "Chance" card. After that he landed on another property where he had to pay ⅗ of his remaining money in rent. Fortunately, on his next turn he passed "Go" and collected $200. However, he landed on a property that whacked him for half of his money. Next he got a "Chance" card and landed in jail. After he paid $50 to get out, the poor guy only had $70 cash left—no property, no nothing. How much did he have at the beginning of this narrative?

5. BROWN THUMB

I can't believe how bad my brother is at growing things. He bought a whole bunch of plants at the nursery the other day. Right away, five died. Then our dog dug up $\frac{2}{9}$ of them. Out of the remaining plants, half of them died pretty soon afterward. Then a rabbit came and ate half of what was left and half a plant more. Rudy only had three plants left then. How many did he buy at the nursery?

6. JELLY BEAN RABBITS

My sister and I used to have a great time playing with jelly beans. First we would make "rabbit families" with them on the living room floor. Then we would pretend they were rabbits and we were hawks. So we would swoop down and eat them up. One time in particular, Lilly got the first shot: She ate $\frac{1}{5}$ of the jelly beans. I went next, and I ate $\frac{1}{6}$ of the ones on the floor. Lilly then let out a shriek and ate 2/5 of the remaining beans. I then ate $\frac{2}{3}$ of the ones left. After Lilly ate half of the remaining jelly beans, there were two yellow ones left, which we shared. How many jelly beans did each of us eat?

7. WINNING GOLDFISH

Triva went to the arcade at the state fair to win some goldfish. She already had some at home, but she wanted more. Right away, Triva won enough goldfish to double her stock. However, her mom made her give four to her cousin. She put her new ones in the fish tank with the others, but by the next morning, half of her goldfish had died. Triva's friend Keisha gave her six more. Unfortunately, the next morning two-thirds of her goldfish had died. Triva was left with two goldfish after having given one to a neighbor. How many goldfish did Triva start with?

8. PRETTY FISHY

Triva took the fishbowls she bought cheaply to the flea market. In the first hour, she sold one-third of them and a third more. In the second hour, she sold half of them, and a half more. In her third hour there, she sold one-third of them and a third of one more. The next hour, she sold half of them and half of one more. Finally, she sold the last two and went home. How many fishbowls did Triva sell?

9. LOST HIS MARBLES

Livingston is a marble freak and loves to play at school. During the first break he doubled the number of marbles he had. During the second break he lost four marbles (no big deal). During the third break, he increased his stock of marbles by $\frac{1}{3}$. During lunch, however, he lost half of his marbles. After school, Livingston played again and tripled what he had. He went home with 72 marbles. How many did he start with? (Thanks to David Lee, a former student of Ken Johnson's, for contributing this problem.)

Problem Set B, Version 2

1. CHICKEN EGGS

If a chicken and a half lays an egg and a half in a day and a half, how many eggs will be laid by 6 chickens in 12 days?

2. HEARTBEATS

It has been speculated that the fewer times your heart beats every minute, the healthier you are, and a longer life span will result. Joanne and Ken compared their heart rates. Joanne had been exercising regularly for at least a year. Her heart rate during the 45 minutes each day that she exercised was 150 heartbeats per minute. But her heart rate dropped down to 60 heartbeats per minute for the rest of the day. Ken didn't exercise at all and had a day-long average heart rate of 72 beats per minute. During the last non-leap year, whose heart beat more times and how many more times did it beat?

3. PENNIES IN THE SAND

I hate taking my little brother, Carl, to the park. All he does is find ways to cause trouble. For example, the other day he took a bunch of pennies to the park. He promptly lost ⅖ of them and cried. I stopped swinging and helped him look for them. He managed to let three more fall out of his pocket while we were looking. When I tried to grab them before they sank in the sand, he threw a temper tantrum and lost another third of the pennies he had left. I gave him 10 pennies from my pocket to try to stop him from crying, but that didn't help. He then got mad and started throwing them. He threw away ¾ of his remaining pennies and ended up with 7. We looked for them some more but found a lot of cigarette butts and no pennies. How much money did my brother lose at the park? I don't know, but I would have gladly paid him that much not to go to the park. Find out how much Carl lost at the park.

4. JOGGING

I was walking down the street one day, and a jogger passed me. I was curious to know whether I could figure out how fast the jogger was running, so I started paying attention to where the jogger was. When she passed a light pole a little ways in front of me, I began to count seconds. It took me 9 seconds to get to the pole. When I reached the pole, I looked up to see that she was just passing a fire hydrant. I again counted seconds until I reached the fire hydrant, and it took me 11 seconds. When I reached the fire hydrant, she was passing a parking meter. It took me 14 seconds to reach the parking meter. I knew that I walked 2 paces in 1 second, and my pace was 1 yard long. Approximately how fast, in miles per hour, was the jogger moving?

Sam Action had a tough task. He was a scoutmaster and had to get a group of boy scouts back to their campsite after a long hike. A number of these boys would whine and complain if they were left with some of the other boys unless Sam himself was present. The whining and complaining had something to do with which soccer team the boys played on and can be summarized as follows. Any of the six Rattlers would complain if left with any of the four Thunder. Either of the two Dragons would complain if left with the Eagle. Any of the Thunder would complain if left with the Eagle or one or both Dragons. Sam had to be present among any of the complainers to prevent complaining. All went well until they reached Rat-Tongue Ravine with the rickety bridge over it. Sam estimated that the bridge could safely handle only five people at a time, though he figured that it should be able to handle six people for three trips. He had been on the bridge before and knew it well. Sam needed to guide each group across to avoid capsizing the bridge, so he planned to cross the bridge with each group. He had to devise a way to get everyone across without any complaining. How did Sam arrange crossing the ravine, and how many trips did it take?

Problem Set B, Version 3

1. HOT DOG

If 30 hot dogs can feed a family of five for three meals, how many hot dogs would be needed to feed just the three kids for eight meals? (Assume that adults and kids eat the same amount.)

2. FRATERNITY OUTING

The fraternity brothers at Phi Phi Pho Phum had arranged an outing with some other fraternities. They planned to attend a pie-eating contest together. There were five members of Phi Phi Pho Phum, four members of Eta Pi, three members of Nu Kappa, two members of Beta Zeta Theta, and one member from Tau Rho. They all met in front of the library to drive over to the contest. Unfortunately, they only had one vehicle: an old, beat-up Volkswagen bug. They figured it would hold six people plus the driver, who was John Vernon, dean of the fraternity council. The giant Phi Phi Pho Phum members were exceptions to this formula. Each of them took as much room in the car as two members of any other fraternity. To further complicate matters, many of the fraternities were enemies and would play malicious practical jokes on some of the others, even if outnumbered. The enemies are as follows: The Tau Rho member would be quite eager to play a trick on anyone else from any of the other fraternities. Any of the Nu Kappa members would gladly play tricks on any of the Eta Pi members. Any of the Phi Phi Pho Phum members would gladly make fun of any of the Beta Zeta Theta members. No tricks would be played in the car while Vernon was present, and no tricks would be played when all 15 members were together at the original gathering or at the pie contest. How did Vernon arrange the transportation so that no member played a trick on anyone else?

3. WHICH CAR SHOULD THEY TAKE?

The Jones family has two cars, a small compact car and a large van. They can never decide which car to take when they go to visit the kids' grandmother. The kids like to take the van because it is much bigger and there is room to move around inside the van. The father likes to take the compact because he hates driving the van and the compact gets much better gas mileage. One day, they decided to find out how much they would save if they took the compact and whether it was worth the extra hassle. The compact gets 30 miles per gallon, and the van gets 20 miles per gallon. The kids' grandmother lives 2½ hours away when they drive 60 miles per hour. Gas costs $.85 per gallon. How much more does it cost them to take the van?

4. HOT DOGS AGAIN

My mother told us kids that if we wanted to go on this camping trip, we had to plan the meals. No problem. We planned to have hot dogs. That's not all, of course. We also took along mustard, relish, catsup, and buns. We figured we had it made. However, after setting up the tent, we didn't take care to make sure that the food was safe. Raccoons got into it and ate ⅓ of the hot dogs. After discovering the loss, our family had six hot dogs with our eggs for breakfast. When we went out sightseeing, we just left the hot dogs on the table and returned to find that jays had eaten another ¼ of our remaining supply. Despite the tragedy, we persisted in enjoying the camping trip. We went to the store and bought 12 more hot dogs and added that to our supply. Then some of our camping neighbors had a strong hunkering for normal food and "borrowed" ⅖ of the remaining hot dogs. At our dinner that night, we ate 10 more hot dogs. That evening, bears got another ¾ of the last part of our supply, and in the morning we all shared the remaining two hot dogs. How many hot dogs did we start with?

5. LOST IN GRIDLOCK

Jack Holentyre was fed up with gridlock. He was stuck in some heavy traffic in the San Fernando Valley and abandoned his car (it was a piece of junk anyway). The unfortunate thing is that he left most of his navigating brains in his car. (The car knew how to get home; Jack didn't.) So Jack decided to "hoof it." He started out walking north. He walked one block north then turned right and walked another block. Then he turned right again and walked another two blocks. He turned right again and walked two more blocks. By now he had decided on a pattern: Jack would keep increasing his distance after every two directions. (He had already walked one block north and then one block east. Then he increased his distance and walked two blocks south and two blocks west.) Next he would walk "three and three," as in three blocks north and three blocks east. Then "four and four," and so on. He figured if he kept turning and kept changing his distance, eventually he'd get close to his house and recognize something. After he had walked 75 blocks in this fashion, he recognized his friend's house. He knew how to get home from there. He then walked six blocks north and two blocks east to his own house. Unfortunately, Jack left the envelope he needed to mail (with the car payment) back in his car. Help Jack out by giving him directions back to his car by a direct route.

Problem Set B, Version 4

1. LOST CARDS

My sister has really bad luck. She started a baseball card collection last year, but unfortunately, she can't seem to keep track of all of her cards. Recently she had a really bad string of luck. She took all of her cards with her on the bus to school. On the way there, some bully sixth graders stole ¼ of her cards. Then she dropped six cards in the gutter when she got off the bus. She went to class and lost ⅔ of her remaining cards during show and tell. Then she gave three cards to her best friend. The teacher was really interested in baseball, so she gave ⅗ of her remaining cards to the teacher. When she went to recess, she found eight cards on the playground. Then at lunch, she accidentally threw half of her remaining cards away in her lunch bag. When she came home, she only had ten cards left. How many cards did she have when she left for school?

2. FENCE PAINTING

Three painters can paint six fences (all the same size) in three hours. How many fences can seven painters paint in five hours?

3. JOHN AND MARCIA

In this city all of the streets that run north and south have lettered names (A, B, C, etc.), and all of the streets that run east-west have numbered names (1st, 2nd, 3rd, etc.). As you drive east, the letters get later in the alphabet. As you drive south, the numbers get bigger. John lives at the corner of A and 1st. His girlfriend Marcia lives at the corner of E and 8th. John enjoys riding his bike to Marcia's house. However, he likes to go a different way every day. If he only rides east and south, how many different routes can he take from his house to Marcia's house?

4. WALKING

I was walking down the street following someone. He was at a pole as I passed a parking meter. It took me 14 seconds to get to the pole. When I reached the pole, he was at a fire hydrant. It took me 11 seconds to get to the hydrant. If I walk 3 miles per hour, how far will I have to walk from the parking meter to the point where I pass him?

The long-awaited marriage of Amanda Smith and Kevin Jones had finally taken place. But trouble was brewing at the reception. A horse and buggy had been hired to take the most-honored guests and some members of the wedding party from the church to the reception. The following people needed to be transported in this buggy, which held at most four people: the bride and groom, Amanda Smith and Kevin Jones; Phil and Jerri Smith, parents of the bride; Len Smith, brother of Phil; Walter Lewis, brother of Jerri; Lincoln and Jill Jones, parents of the groom; J.R. Jones, brother of Lincoln; J.R.'s wife Mina; and Brian Jones, son of Mina and J.R. Unfortunately, the following restrictions were placed on the transportation: Jerri must go on every trip, as she is the mother of the bride and hostess of the wedding. Married couples must always remain together (this restriction does not include Jerri and Phil, as they are divorced). Len must always be with Phil, as Phil is the only one who will laugh at Len's jokes. Brian cannot be left at the same location as Amanda, as sparks tend to fly when they get together. Brian can't be left with Walter either, as Brian tends to talk about the Miami Dolphins and Walter hates the Dolphins. Jill cannot be left with J.R., as they used to be married, but Jill divorced J.R. and married his brother, Lincoln. How can the transportation to the reception be arranged in the fewest number of trips? (Note: Restrictions do not apply to the very beginning and the very end of the problem. They do apply at all other stages of the problem, however.)

12. venn diagrams

VENN DIAGRAMS allow you to organize information spatially. In particular, they make classification schemes easier, especially complex classifications that cannot be well-represented linearly, such as in a list.

Make sure students understand the three basic relationships of Venn diagrams. The first is the disjoint relationship, depicted with two non-overlapping loops. The objects represented by one loop have nothing to do with the objects represented by the other. The word "no" often appears in descriptions of disjoint relationships, as in the statement "No lawn mowers are roses."

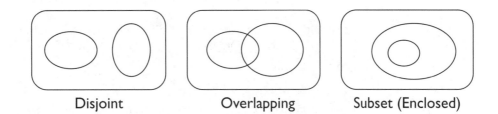

| Disjoint | Overlapping | Subset (Enclosed) |

In overlapping loops, the overlap represents objects with characteristics common to two sets of objects. The word "some" often describes overlapping relationships like "Some math students are chemistry students." Finally, when one loop encloses another entirely, the inner loop represents a subset of the objects represented by the outer loop. Inner loops possess all the characteristics represented by any subsequent outer loop. For example, "All roses are flowers" states that roses are a subset of flowers and possess all the characteristics of flowers.

The universal set, usually drawn as a rectangle, describes the most inclusive set among those under consideration. Animals would be a universal set encompassing household pets, cats, and dogs.

It is important to lay some ground rules for students. There are a number of things you can say about categories of animals, such as "No bears are lawn mowers." Some students may propose a pet bear whose name is "Lawn mower." Emphasize that we are using the principal, common understanding of these words.

Negations, that is, attributes objects don't possess, are key and should be made clear. Many times we label the different zones in Venn diagrams and then describe the things represented by those zones.

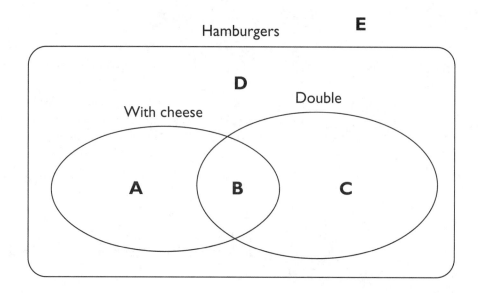

It is helpful to have students give the most specific characterization possible for each zone. The list should include attributes the objects in that region do and don't have.

> A—Hamburger, with cheese, not double
> B—Hamburger, with cheese, double (a double cheeseburger)
> C—Hamburger, double, no cheese
> D—Hamburger, no cheese, not double
> E—Not a hamburger

You can prepare students for Venn diagrams by having them classify themselves in a Venn diagram on the board. Draw a Venn diagram on the board like the following diagram. As students enter, they write their initials in the appropriate region. Make it clear to students that they can only initial in one place. Venn diagrams are often extremely intuitive, so students can understand the concepts, relying on their previous experience.

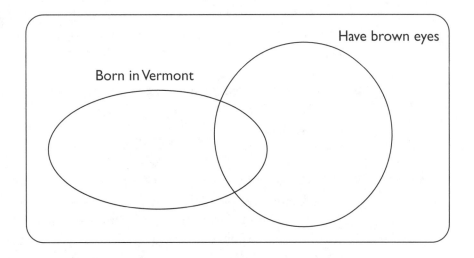

Here are other examples of good Venn diagrams to use on the board:

1. Four concentric circles labeled with the country, state or province, county, and city your school is in. Ask students to initial the region that describes where they were born.
2. Three intersecting circles labeled with three sports. Ask which sport or sports students like to play or watch.
3. Three intersecting circles labeled with popular TV shows. Ask which show or shows students like to watch.

Students may have trouble counting correctly. The diagram below represents ten flowers. Six of the ten are roses. Four of the ten flowers are not roses. Students need to be careful that when they write a number in a region, the number represents only objects in that region and not objects in subregions. (In this example, the four flowers obviously does not include the six roses.)

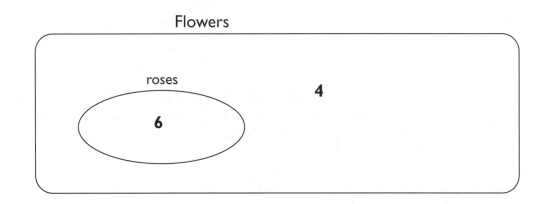

You can go outside to do a fun activity to teach Venn diagrams. Draw any sort of looping relationships with chalk (or use rope or hoses). You can tell students what the loops represent and let them find the appropriate region to stand in. Better yet, keep the loop relationships to yourself, then direct students to the appropriate regions and leave it to them to figure out what the regions represent.

Are Venn diagrams used in real life? Yes! They are frequently used in scientific classifications, in sociology, political science, and in information science. Computerized searches can be modeled with Venn diagrams. If there are listings for 1200 articles on depletion of the ozone layer and 800 articles on genetic mutation, by asking for the articles that have both characteristics you should be able to get a smaller listing that is a subset of both groups. By including more categories or by including more specific categories, the numbers should get even smaller.

This is an example from political science.

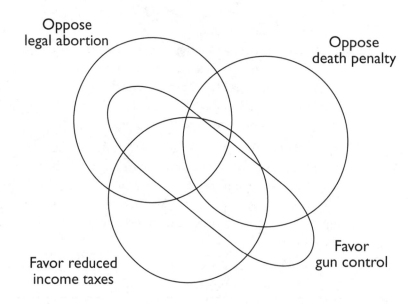

A person who fits into any one of these categories might be described as conservative or liberal. But there are 15 different regions in the diagram (16 if you count the region outside of any loop). Making the Venn diagram helps reveal the complexity of the relationships.

Text Problems

BASIC RELATIONSHIPS

Draw Venn diagrams that represent each of these statements. Your understanding of this process is critical to understanding the problems that are presented in the rest of the chapter.

1. Some birds are pets.
2. All accountants are college graduates.
3. No dogs are sheep.
4. All poodles are dogs.
5. Some dogs are poodles.

THREE CIRCLES

In how many ways can three circles be drawn? They can be inside each other, intersect in some way, or not intersect at all.

CATEGORIES

1. Household pets, dogs, animals, cats.
2. Living things, lizards, apes, chimpanzees, reptiles, dogs, mammals, terriers, dachshunds.
3. Place of birth, USA, Canada, Miami, Florida, Orlando, Montreal, Missouri.
4. Colleges, private school, state school, Yale, Kent State, Notre Dame.
5. Trumpet, piano, musical instruments, clarinet, violin, trombone, brass, woodwinds.
6. Water vessels, submarines, war boats, sailboats, battleships, ferries.
7. Cows, brown, black, white, dairy, old. (These cows can only be one color.)
8. Hamburgers, with cheese, double, homemade.

SCIENCE COURSES

In a group of students, 12 are taking chemistry, 10 are taking physics, 3 are taking both chemistry and physics, and 5 are taking neither chemistry nor physics. How many students are in the group?

MUSIC SURVEY

In a poll of 46 students, 23 liked rap music, 24 liked rock music, and 19 liked country music. Of all the students, 12 liked rap and country, 13 liked rap and rock, and 14 liked country and rock. Of those students, 9 liked all 3 types. How many students did not like any of these types?

HOMEROOM

There are 23 students in a homeroom. Eighteen are taking math and 15 are taking science. Six students are taking math but not science. How many are taking neither subject?

SPRING ROSTER

Frank Robinson, former manager of the Baltimore Orioles baseball team, looked over his roster at the beginning of spring training one season. He noticed the following facts. Every outfielder is a switch-hitter. Half of all infielders are switch-hitters. Half of all switch-hitters are outfielders. There are 14 infielders and 8 outfielders. No infielder is an outfielder. How many switch-hitters are neither outfielders nor infielders?

THE COMIC BOOK COLLECTORS

Bruce and Clark went to the comic book store to buy some classic comics. They found that they could buy a Batman and a Superman for $18. They also found they could buy a Batman and a Flash for $16,   and they could buy a Superman and a Flash for $22. How much did each of the comics cost separately?

Problem Set A, Version 2

1. JUNIOR PROM

There are 120 juniors in the current class. Of those, 66 are going to the junior prom. The same number (66) of juniors are going out to dinner that evening, including 48 of those going to the prom. How many juniors are neither going to the prom nor going out to dinner?

2. SODA SURVEY

In a recent consumer interview, 800 people took taste tests. Out of those, 723 said they like soda. Of the people who like soda, 316 like both root beer and cola, while another 87 said they like cola but do not like root beer. Furthermore, a total of 427 people in the survey like root beer. How many people in this survey like soda but do not like either root beer or cola?

3. COMPANY BARBEQUE

Before doing the ordering for a company barbeque, the president took a poll. She asked how many people would eat the ribs, hamburgers, and corn at the barbeque. She polled 64 people in the company that said they would probably attend. This poll revealed that 59 members would eat ribs, 56 would eat corn, 60 would eat hamburgers, 55 would eat ribs and corn, 54 would eat corn and hamburgers, 56 would eat ribs and hamburgers, and 53 would eat all three.

a. How many people did not want any of these foods?
b. How many people would eat ribs but not corn?
c. How many people would eat something so long as it was not a hamburger?
d. How many people would eat only corn?
e. How many people would eat exactly two foods?

4. SPIRIT OF WOODSTOCK

Of the six members in the "Spirit of Woodstock" rock band, four can play guitar. There are three who can play keyboards. All of the singers play guitar, and two of the guitarists also play keyboards. There are two members who do all three. Threr is one guitarist who doesn't sing. How many members sing but do not play keyboards?

5. COUNTRY CLUB

A survey was given among the members of the Silver Springs Country Club, asking which activities each club member participates in. The survey revealed that 67 play tennis, 64 play golf, and 52 like to swim. Of those, 29 like to play golf and tennis, 27 like tennis and swimming, 31 like to play golf and swim, and 14 participate in all three. There were 5 members who do not do any of the activities. How many members were surveyed?

6. EAST PARKING LOT

On the night our playoff was being held, there were a number of vehicles in the east parking lot of the gym. Half of the white vehicles were neither cars nor buses. There were 8 buses in all, and only 1 of those was yellow. There were 16 other yellow vehicles though, and 6 of those were cars. There were 9 cars that were not yellow or white out of a total of 20 cars. There were as many white buses as there were buses that were not white. Besides cars and buses, of course, there were vans and trucks. How many white vehicles were there?

7. SPLIT TICKET

In the fourth Dodgeville precinct the Green Party, the Democrats, and the Republicans all had candidates. The Green party congressional candidate, however, was the only actual Green party member running, and she was registered as Democrat and ran as Democrat. (So all Green party candidates were Democrats.) In the voting, one-seventh of the voters did not vote. Seven voted the straight Green party ticket (the Green Party candidate for congress and Democrats for senator and president). Forty-one people voted for at least one Republican candidate, though none of those were the ones who voted for the Green Party candidate. Thirty-seven voted for at least one Democrat, including the eighteen who split their ticket between Democrats and Republicans. How many people in all were registered in the fourth precinct?

8. BRAVE ALL-STARS

A number of people in the Atlanta Braves organization got together recently for a party. Of those, one-twelfth were all-stars. Two-thirds of the all-stars were hitters. Of the people at the party, half were players. Half of the players were neither hitters nor all-stars. One-fourth of the hitters were all-stars. There were 6 hitters who were not all stars. How many people were at the party?

9. EARTHQUAKE DAMAGES

After an earthquake, 32 homes in a remote area were checked by public safety officers before nightfall. They found that 22 of the houses had no gas, including 10 houses whose own gas lines were damaged. (A house loses its gas service if it has damage to its own line or if there is damage to the feeder line.) Of those houses that lost their gas, only four did not lose their electricity. Twenty-four houses in all had no electricity; the same number of them lost only their electricity as both lost electricity and had damage to their gas lines. How many of the houses checked did not lose either gas or electricity, and how many lost only their gas service?

Problem Set B, Version 2

1. THE TREASURE OF SIERRA MARBLES

Tom Sawyer, Huck Finn, and Becky Thatcher were feeling pretty pleased with themselves. They had just found a stash of great marbles buried in Tom's backyard in the Sierra Nevada mountains (they had moved from Missouri)—left, no doubt, by some previous tenant. They decided to sleep in the backyard that night to guard the marbles from theft. Unfortunately, they should have been guarding the marbles from each other. Soon after everyone had gone to sleep, Tom got up and decided to take his fair share of marbles. He separated the marbles into three piles. There was one marble left over, which he buried, and then he took one of the piles of marbles and went back to bed. A little while later, Huck got up and did the same thing. He separated the marbles into three piles. There was one left over, which he buried. He took one of the three piles and went back to bed. Becky got up last and found two marbles half buried in the ground. She put them into the remaining pile of marbles. Then she took one-third of the marbles that remained (the remainder was zero when she divvied them up) and went back to bed. In the morning the three friends got up and looked at the small pile of marbles that remained. An argument immediately broke out, as each friend accused the others of stealing some of the marbles. No one would admit guilt, so in the end they ended up splitting the remaining marbles evenly, which came to 16 more marbles per person. How many marbles did each person end up with?

2. TOOTHPICK SQUARES

What is the fewest number of toothpicks necessary to make 100 little squares? All squares are to be the same size. Toothpicks do not overlap. Discuss how you can know that your arrangement uses the fewest number of toothpicks. For example, to make five squares you need either 15 or 16 toothpicks as shown.

3. THE FRESHMAN CLASS

Ten students are taking neither band nor Spanish. Five students are taking neither algebra nor Spanish. Seven students are taking neither algebra nor band. All of the students are taking at least one of the three subjects. No student is taking all three subjects. Twenty-one students are not taking band. Seventeen students are taking algebra. Seventeen students are taking Spanish. How many students are taking band?

Several teachers invested together in a sandwich and soda shop. They call it the "Teacher's Sub Shop." They offer custom-made sandwiches. You can buy a sandwich with the following bases: pastrami, turkey, roast beef, or vegetarian. Along with that, they offer four kinds of cheese: Monterey Jack, Cheddar, Swiss, and American. You can also have mustard, mayonnaise, both, or neither. The patrons also get to choose white, wheat, or rye bread, but the rye is not offered with either pastrami or cheddar, as one of the owners objects under the rationale that the combinations of cheddar and rye or pastrami and rye are "gross." You also can't get mustard on turkey or mayonnaise on roast beef. A sandwich consists of one base, one cheese if desired, condiments if desired, and one bread. How many different types of sandwiches exist at this shop?

Five people from Sacramento recently ordered tickets to their favorite fine arts events: jazz concert, art exhibit, symphony concert, ballet, and musical comedy. None of the five people like to go to the same event. Their first names are Alan, Bev, Chris, Doreen, and Ernie, and their last names (in no special order) are Fillmore, Gunderson, Hatfield, Innis, and Jackson. The occupations of the five are publisher, engineer, reporter, doctor, and lawyer. Use this information and the clues below to determine each person's full name, occupation, and favorite fine arts event.

1. The kids of Jackson, Innis, and the man who is going to the jazz concert all play on the same soccer team.
2. Among the lawyer's clients are Alan and the art enthusiast.
3. Doreen and the reporter and the person who likes the symphony all have their tickets already.
4. Alan, Hatfield, and the jazz fan all attended the first Sacramento Surge football game together.
5. Neither Ernie nor the reporter has kids.
6. Of the five, only the doctor has never attended the symphony. The engineer, who is not Chris, has attended ballets and art exhibits, but really didn't like either.
7. The person who enjoys musical comedy (especially musicals written by Stephen Sondheim) and the doctor both have their tickets and are going to attend their events in the next few days.
8. The doctor (who is not Innis) and Ernie (who has never heard of Stephen Sondheim) went fishing the day of the first Sacramento Surge football game because both of them hate football.
9. Fillmore and the engineer just recently ordered their tickets and have not received them yet.

Problem Set B, Version 3

1. HUNGRY BROTHERS

Four hungry brothers went to bed, thinking about the batch of cookies that their mother had just baked. In the middle of the night, each of them got up and ate some of the cookies. Alan got up first. He separated the cookies into three piles and found there was one left over. He gave the leftover cookie to the dog, then ate one-third of the remaining cookies and went back to bed. Burt was the next to get up, and he ate one-fourth of the cookies. (The dog didn't get any from him because he thought the dog looked stuffed.) Chris then got up and gave two to the dog. Then he ate one-fifth of the remaining cookies. Daniel was the last to get up, and he ate just four cookies and then gave one to the dog, who was beginning to look really sick. When their mother went into the kitchen the next morning, she found a lot of crumbs, ants, a pale-looking dog, and only 15 cookies. How many cookies had she baked originally?

2. LET GO MY LEGO

Gary built a pyramid out of Legos. He used rectangular Legos that were four bumps by two bumps. He started with one Lego in the top level. Underneath that he put in as many Legos as needed to leave one row of bumps all the way around the outside. He continued to build the pyramid in such a way so that there was always one row of bumps all the way around the outside on each level. He was able to make ten layers on his pyramid before he ran out of Legos. The inside of the pyramid is completely filled in with Legos, many of which are not visible to someone looking at the top of the pyramid.

How many Legos are in the pyramid?

How many bumps total on all levels are visible on the outside of the pyramid?

3. COUNTRY MUSIC

Maile was driving through the Midwest recently and happened to tune in to a country music station. She likes country music, so she really enjoyed getting a chance to listen to some. After having listened to the station for an hour, Maile had heard 25 songs. All but one was about either truck drivers, being in love, prisoners in jail, or some combination of the three. She noted the following information.

All of the truck drivers were in love. Three-fourths of the truck drivers were not in jail. There were six prisoners in love. Of the prisoners who were not truck drivers, half of them were in love. Eighty percent of all the songs concerned people in love.How many songs concerned people who were in love but were not truck drivers or prisoners?

HOW MUCH STEREO CAN YOU AFFORD?

You are interested in buying a stereo system for your college dorm room. You want to buy a receiver, a compact disc player, and a pair of small book-shelf speakers. You consult a consumer magazine and determine that there are several kinds of each item that you are interested in. The list is shown below with prices.

CD Players	Receivers	Speakers (pair)
$400 Megavox	$300 Yohaha	$450 Allinfun
$330 BLT	$400 Technical	$350 Infinitesimal
$500 Bashiba	$250 Shark	$690 Mandarin
$550 Denmom	$490 Pilgrim	$200 ERP
	$350 Oinko	$300 Scoot
		$500 Mansion

After visiting your friendly neighborhood stereo store, you find they are out of the BLT CD player, and you don't like the Yohaha receiver or the Mansion speakers. You have $1100 to spend on your stereo system. In how many different ways can you buy a system that you will be happy with? (You do not have to spend all of the money.)

5. **POLITICAL PARTIES**

Five friends in a political party all have known each other for several years. Like most friends, they have a lot in common and a lot of differences. As they were talking at a rally, they noticed some things that they all did differently. Each goes to work in a different way: There is a car driver, a biker, a walker, a subway rider, and a bus rider. Their first names, not in any special order, are Walter, Teresa, Valerie, Jasper, and Maria. Their last names are Doyle, Peterson, Sinderson, Archer, and Lamson. And although they all are political activists, each one votes in a different area: Queens, the Bronx, Manhattan, Long Island, and Seaside. From the clues below, determine each person's full name, the way they get to work, and where they vote.

1. Teresa, the biker, and the person who votes in Manhattan have sent in their absentee votes. Archer and the person who takes the bus haven't voted yet.
2. The person who votes in the Bronx, Doyle, and Sinderson have all held office before.
3. The subway rider and the car driver meet Doyle and the person who votes in the Bronx for lunch every Tuesday. Walter cannot attend because he works on the other side of the city.
4. The person who votes in Queens and the subway rider voted absentee. They discussed their votes with the woman from Seaside (who hasn't voted yet).
5. Neither Valerie nor the person who bikes to work has ever held office.

6. Jasper (whose last name is not Sinderson) and Mr. Peterson and the person who votes in the Bronx first met at a victory party ten years ago.
7. Maria could take the subway but prefers her normal mode of transportation.
8. The person who rides a bus to work does not live in Long Island or Seaside.

Problem Set B, Version 4

1. FOUR FRIENDS

Four friends (one is named Sara) drove to the grocery store to buy their favorite food and drink. Two sat in the front seat, and two sat in the back seat. Each bought a different food (one bought chili), and each bought a different soda (one bought root beer). Use the clues below to determine what food each person bought, each person's soda flavor, and where each person was sitting.

1. The person who bought soup sat next to Mark.
2. Roberto sat diagonally from the person who had the lemon-lime soda.
3. The person who bought cola sat on the same side of the car as the person who preferred macaroni and cheese.
4. The person who had the orange soda sat on the same side of the car as the person who bought soup.
5. Roberto sat on the same side of the car as the person who bought spaghetti.
6. Areatha sat next to the person with the cola.
7. The driver did not buy a kind of pasta.
8. The person with the root beer sat in the back seat.

2. SOCCER TEAM

On a soccer team there are four positions: goalie, fullback, halfback, and forward. Each player on the team often plays more than one position during the course of the season. On one soccer team there are 16 members. All of the goalies also play forward, and one goalie plays fullback as well. No goalie plays halfback. There are as many fullbacks as halfbacks. The total number of halfbacks is two-thirds the total number of forwards. Half of the team plays halfback. No one plays only fullback. Three people play three positions. Three people play only one position. The number of halfbacks who play forward but not fullback is equal to the number of halfbacks who play fullback but not forward and is equal to the number of halfbacks who don't play anything else.

How many people play goalie? How many people play fullback and forward but nothing else?

3. ORANGE TREASURE

Three pirates were stranded on a desert island just outside of Pittsburgh. They found a treasure chest, which they opened and found to be full of oranges. Imagine their surprise. These pirates were overjoyed, however, as they loved oranges. Unfortunately, they couldn't decide how to split them up, so they left them in the chest. On the first afternoon, one pirate, Ahab, snuck away from the others and went to the treasure chest. He separated the oranges into three equal piles. There was one extra orange, which he gave to a passing monkey. Then he ate one of the three equal piles of oranges, put the rest back into the chest, and went back to camp. A short time later a second pirate, Bluebeard, snuck away from camp and went to the chest. He separated the oranges into four equal piles. (He wasn't quite as greedy as Ahab.) There were two extra oranges, which he gave to a passing monkey. He then ate one of the four piles and put the rest back into the chest. Still later the third pirate, Hook, went to the chest and separated the oranges into five equal piles. (He was even less greedy.) There were three leftover, which he gave to a passing monkey. Then he ate one of the piles and put the rest back into the chest. The next day the three pirates split the remaining oranges equally. Each pirate got twenty oranges. How many oranges were in the chest originally and how many did each of the pirates receive?

4. PENTAGON

If all the diagonals of a regular pentagon are drawn, how many triangles are formed? (**Regular** means all sides and all angles are the same.)

5. DIGIT 8

If all of the numbers from 1 to 999,999 were written down, how many times would the digit 8 appear in the list?

(Examples: 38 has one 8; 35,828 has two 8's; 88,348 has three 8's; 2,345,921 has zero 8's.)

algebra

A LGEBRA IS AN outrageously powerful problem-solving strategy—so powerful that it has monopolized the field for years, to the detriment of other problem-solving strategies and to algebra itself. Our intent with this chapter is not to teach algebra; we know a few books that already do that, and we recommend algebra as a prerequisite for students taking this course. Instead we use the chapter to demonstrate how other problem-solving strategies, especially guess and check, can be used in conjunction with algebra.

Many current algebra textbooks include a page on guess and check. The page may include "coin" problems, "age" problems, "work" problems, and a few other types. Entire lessons in the book might be devoted to these problem types, but guess and check is treated as a sidelight, without much explanation of how it can be applied to these problems.

In *Problem Solving Strategies*, algebra is used in conjunction with guess and check, making algebra more powerful and more accessible. Students understand guess and check better than they do algebra, so using guess and check to develop algebraic equations helps transfer this understanding to the algebra.

The biggest weakness of guess and check is in the handling of fractional answers. It is tough to do guess and check when the answer you're looking for is $^{211}/_{315}$ and the closest you can come is $^{322}/_{480}$. One way around this is to determine to what decimal place you want the answer. Answers to the nearest tenth are often reasonable. For better precision, you should probably convert the guess and check procedure to an algebraic equation.

Virtually any problem in an algebra text can also be solved with guess and check. A student who successfully solves a problem with guess and check should also be able to set up an equation. Use a variable for the guess. For each column in the chart, apply the operations you applied to your previous guesses to the variable. Write the result in that column as an algebraic expression. You should think, "what did we do to get this column?" in order to come up with an algebraic expression. The equation is usually right there in one or two of the columns. The only thing left to do is to figure out what column you've been doing the check on. That column often contains both sides of the equation. One side is the result of the algebraic guess. The other side is what the result of the guess is supposed to be equal to. If you've been trying to make two columns equal each other, those columns most likely contain the two sides of the equation.

Guess and check takes practice just as writing and solving equations do. Students might solve some problems in this chapter by guess and check alone, but you might require them to write algebraic guesses anyway so they get enough experience with this powerful strategy.

On a practical note, point out to students that someday in the future they may be called upon to do some algebra on the job. Even if they've forgotten their algebra, guess and check can be used in many instances and can help them remember how to set up equations for problems with non-integer answers.

Notes on Text Problems

SATURDAY AT THE "FIVE AND DIME" GARAGE SALE

This problem, like many others, can be set up algebraically in either one or two variables.

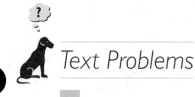

Text Problems

SATURDAY AT THE "FIVE AND DIME" GARAGE SALE

Sandy held a garage sale during which she charged a dime for everything, but accepted a nickel if the buyer bargained well. At the end of the day, she realized she had sold all 12 items and raked in a grand total of 95 cents. She had only dimes and nickels. How many of each did she have?

See if you can recreate the guess and check chart for this problem without looking back at the Guess and Check chapter.

FARMER JONES

Farmer Jones raises ducks and cows. She tries not to clutter her mind with too many details, but she does think it's important to remember how many animals she has, and how many feet those animals have. She thinks she remembers having 54 animals with 122 feet. How many of each type of animal does Farmer Jones have?

Again, recreate the guess and check chart. Then set up the equation(s) to solve the problem algebraically.

ALL AROUND THE PLAYING FIELD

The perimeter of a rectangular playing field is 504 yards. Its length is 6 yards shorter than twice its width. What is its area?

Set up the guess and check chart for this problem and then write the equation.

ORIGAMI

A group of exchange students from Japan went to a convalescent home to sing songs for the seniors and to demonstrate origami (Japanese paper folding). As it turned out, there was either one Japanese student at a table with three seniors, or two students at a table with four seniors. There were 23 students and 61 seniors in all. How many tables were being used to demonstrate origami?

ZEKE AND CLOE REVEAL THEIR AGES

Cloe is two years less than four times as old as Zeke. Cloe is also one year more than three times as old as Zeke. How old is each?

Solve this problem using guess and check to set up the algebra.

CHOCOLATE MILK

Augustus is trying to make chocolate milk. So far he has made a 10% chocolate milk solution (this means that the solution is 10% chocolate and 90% milk). He has also made a 25% chocolate milk solution. Unfortunately, the 10% solution is too weak, and the 25% solution is way too chocolatey. He has a whole lot of the 10% solution, but he only has 30 gallons of the 25% solution. How many gallons of 10% solution should he add to the 25% solution, to make a mixture that is 15% chocolate (which Augustus is sure will be absolutely perfect)?

SALT SOLUTION

A pet store sells salt water for fish tanks. Unfortunately, recently hired Flounder (a character from the movie Animal House) mixed a salt solution that was too weak. He made 150 pounds of 4% salt solution. The boss wants a 7% salt solution. Help Flounder out by giving him two options for reaching the 7% solution.
   a. Add some salt. How much?
   b. Evaporate some water. How much?

THE SEASON'S STATS

Franny, Carl, and Amichung compared their season statistics during the post-season banquet for their high school baseball team. Franny had three times as many singles as Carl. Carl had four times as many doubles as Amichung. Each of them had exactly the same number of hits. None of the three had any hits besides singles and doubles (they were slap hitters). The three of them as a group had exactly as many singles as doubles. Added together, the three of them had fewer than 200 hits in all. How many singles and how many doubles did each of them have?

THE SHADOW

A man 6 feet tall is walking away from a street light that is 15 feet tall. How long is the man's shadow when he is 10 feet away from the light?
   Note: Guess and check doesn't really help here, but a diagram helps a lot.

WORKING OUT

Brian is supposed to run around the basketball court inside the gym at the beginning of each day's volleyball practice. The court measures 70 feet by 120 feet. Brian is rather lazy, however, and cuts off each corner as he runs around. When he is 6 feet from the end of the court, he runs diagonally to a point 6 feet from the side of the court. He does this on each of the four corners. How many feet does Brian cut off one lap?

Problem Set A, Version 2

1. MORE AND MORE COINS

Rufus has $3.45 in quarters and dimes. He has four more quarters than dimes. How many of each coin does he have?

2. COMPLEMENTS

The larger of two complementary angles is 3 degrees more than twice the smaller of the 2 angles. What is the measure of each angle?

3. MARYLOU'S INVESTMENTS

MaryLou made some money on her investments. She made twice as much money on her investment at 8% than on her 5% investment. In all she made $600 in one year. How much did she have invested at each percentage rate?

4. A SMALL WOODWORKING COMPANY

A Small Woodworking Company must ship two different size packages: The small ones cost them $.45 each and weigh 6 ounces, and the large ones weigh 25 ounces and cost $1.20 each. The total shipment this morning weighed 20 pounds, 7 ounces and cost $18.45. How many packages of each size were shipped?

5. SPEEDING TIX

The fines for speeding tickets inside the Kreith Township are computed as follows: The speed you were going is added to how much over the speed limit that speed is. The sum is then squared. The answer is the fine. Chris's fine for going 23 miles per hour over the posted speed limit was $5041. How fast was he going and what was the speed limit?

6. DAD GETS LOTS OF HELP

Dad and Junior together can wash the car in 40 minutes. Junior can wash it by himself in 70 minutes. How long would it take Dad to do it by himself?

7. MOM GETS HELP?

Mom can rake all the leaves from the vast front yard in about 30 minutes. With help from her youngest child, Sonny, she can rake the yard in about 40 minutes. How much work does Sonny contribute to getting the job done? How long would it take Sonny working by himself?

8. TAXING BERNICE

Bernice paid $2970 in state income tax last year. The first part of her income was taxed at 7%, and the next (higher) part of her income was taxed at the rate of 9%. She had $42,000 in taxable income. How much was taxed at 7%, and how much was taxed at 9%?

9. TERRY'S BOOBOO

Terry goofed up mixing 10 gallons of grape juice. He made a punch mix that was 20% juice concentrate instead of the usual 30% punch concentrate. How much juice concentrate does he need to add to the 10 gallons already mixed in order to bring it up to 30% juice concentrate?

10. ALGEBRA AREA

A rectangle with perimeter 104 centimeters has a width 18 centimeters less than its length. What is its area?

11. MICHEALA'S SEASON

Michaela had 24 hits last baseball season. She had no home runs but still managed to have 35 total bases out of those 24 hits. (A single counts for 1 base, a double counts for 2, and a triple counts for 3.) She had 7 doubles and triples total. How many each of singles, doubles, and triples did she have?

12. GOLD COUNTRY TIRE

Darcy runs a tire store. One week she counted up 35 bills of sale. She knew that all of the customers had either bought 4 new tires or 2 new tires. There were 82 old tires to be disposed of in the yard. How many customers bought 2 tires and how many bought 4 tires?

13. CLARENCE AND STEPHANIE ARE THINKING

Clarence and Stephanie are each thinking of a number. If you multiply Stephanie's number by 3 and subtract 2, you get Clarence's number. If you take half of Clarence's number and then subtract 2, you get Stephanie's number. What number is each thinking of?

14. SUGAR PUNCH

Mindy is mixing up some sugary punch for tomorrow's fund-raiser. She took over for someone who goofed up. She knows that she already has 20 liters of an 18% punch mix and 50 liters of a 30% punch mix. How can she make both batches into a 25% mixture by mixing the existing punches and adding only water?

15. SLED RUN

Vanessa and Kelsey set up a sled run for themselves and their friends. On the first part, they figured it dropped vertically about 16 feet over an 80-foot horizontal distance. The second part was flat for about 60 feet, then the third part was about 150 feet horizontally with a 22-foot drop. About how far will the sled travel on this course?

16. CAFE STANDARDS

Federal standards require Gigantic Motors to sell cars that average 27.5 miles per gallon. If the fleet average was 25 miles per gallon for the first 150,000 cars they sold, how many cars averaging 35 miles per gallon must they sell in order to bring the fleet average up to 27.5 miles per gallon?

Problem Set B, Version 2

1. THE DRAMA PRODUCTION

Daffany and her friends are in a drama production. At the beginning of the show, she and the others all line up behind Angie, march on stage, and then peel off from a marching circle until there is one person left. Actually, every other person starting with the lead person peels off. The others keep marching around in the circle until it is their turn to peel off. As they peel off from the marching circle, they form a line from left to right across the stage. The final order is supposed to be: Augie, Beatrice, Corrinne, Daffany, Estefan, Fiona, Gwendolyn, Heather, Ilana, Jackie, Kent, and Lorena. In what order do they need to line up originally?

2. SELLING STEAK

Karl ran a dairy delivery truck. He used to make a lot of regular stops at some regular places. Karl was a pretty clever guy and liked to make up puzzles for his customers. His customers generally liked his puzzles, which usually gave them a little bit more to think about while doing their jobs. Everybody knew Karl and liked Karl, and they usually enjoyed the puzzles he made up. One day Karl bought some steaks cheap at one of his stops, figuring he could sell them at a mild profit at a later stop. Later he found that Freda was interested in them, so he told her "You need to figure out two things: the price per box (in dollars) and how many boxes there are." Karl continued, "If you multiply what I'm going to charge you per box times the number of boxes, that's the total price. Of course, these boxes are on sale. The regular price per box is the same as the number of boxes. Well, the total price is 15 times as much as the amount you're saving on each box. If you add the regular price of each box to how much I'm charging you for each box, the result is 4 times the amount you're saving on each box. I'm going to start unloading your order. Let me know by the time I'm ready to go if you want the steaks." How many boxes are there and what is the sale price of each box?

3. DICEY PRIMES

Of three dice, two are labeled normally: 1, 2, 3, 4, 5, 6. The third die has sides labeled 2, 4, 6, 8, 10, 12. Two dice are rolled and their values added. Find the ratio of the frequency of primes rolled using the first two (ordinary) dice to the frequency of primes rolled using the unusual die and one ordinary die.

4. ICE CREAM COUPONS

A local ice creamery gave the principal of the high school 295 ice cream certificates, good for a huge order of ice cream, to be awarded to any student with a "B" average or better. As it happened, there were 297 students who had at least a "B" average. Since there were two more students than ice cream certificates, the principal started a long, agonizing process of giving them out and determining who didn't get one. Each day the principal chose three students at random. If all three were freshmen, they were each awarded a certificate. If two of the three were sophomores, the principal awarded the certificates to two of the sophomores and put the third's name back in the hat. If all three were from a different class, he awarded all three. If any other combination of students was selected, no certificates were awarded that day and the names went back in the hat. At the end off many days, there were only two "B" average students left who had not received a certificate. They had started with 101 freshmen, 99 sophomores, and 97 juniors. From which class were the two remaining students?

5. HALFWAY LINES

In the grid below, exchange the places of one pair of numbers so that you can draw a vertical line that divides the grid into two parts with equal sums and a horizontal line that also divides the grid into two parts with equal sums.

1	3	2	4
5	7	6	8
9	11	10	12

Problem Set B, Version 3

1. LATE TO THE GATE

Tiffany hated being late for her plane, but her first flight into Atlanta's Hartsfield Airport was late. She went to the ticket counter to find out what gate her connecting flight left from. The ticket agent told her to go to gate 47, which was pretty far away. She walked and after a while reached a moving sidewalk. She got on the moving sidewalk and continued walking. She looked at her watch and noticed it took her 16 minutes to get from the ticket counter to gate 47. Unfortunately, that wasn't fast enough, as by the time she reached the gate her plane had already left and was taxiing on the runway. She walked all the way back (without using the moving sidewalk) to the ticket counter to register a complaint and book a new flight. It took her 25 minutes to walk from the gate back to the ticket counter. About 2 hours later, she left the snack stand by the ticket counter and walked and rode the moving sidewalk back to gate 47. This time she didn't walk while she was on the moving sidewalk, and the trip took her 20 minutes. She knows she walks about 3 miles per hour. What is the speed of the moving sidewalk?

2. CARD ARRANGEMENT

You have ten cards, numbered 1, 2, 3, 4, 5, 6, 7, 8, 9, 10. Your task is to arrange them in a particular order and put them in a stack, hold the stack in your hand, and then do the following. Put the top card face up on the table, put the next card on the bottom of the stack in your hand, put the next card on the table, put the next card on the bottom of the stack, and so on, continuing to alternate cards that go on the table and under the stack, until all ten cards are on the table. That, of course, would be really easy to do, so the trick is, when the cards are put on the table they are to be in numerical order. In other words, the first card you put on the table will be number 1, the next card you put on the table will be number 2, the next card you put on the table will be number 3, and so on, until the last card placed on the table is number 10. In what order should the cards be arranged in the original stack so that this will happen?

3. RECTANGLE RATIOS

A certain rectangle has its area, its perimeter, and the difference of its dimensions in a ratio of 15 to 12 to 4. Find the length and width.

4. **TRIOMINOES**

How many different figures can be made using six equilateral triangles placed so that at least one edge of each triangle adjoins the edge of another triangle?

See the examples below. Reflections and rotations don't count as different.

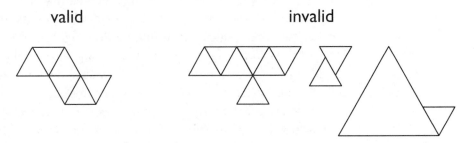

5. **NEMATOAD**

No one seems to know how this game got its name, but it doesn't really matter. It is played like this: Two players place 25 beans between them. They then take turns picking up 1 to 4 beans until there are none left. Whoever picks up the last bean is the winner. You are going to go second. What should your strategy be?

Problem Set B, Version 4

1. AMAZING NUMBERS

From each square in this maze, you can travel in a straight line in one direction (vertically, horizontally, or diagonally) exactly the number of spaces indicated by the number in the square. For example, from the 6 in the lower left-hand corner, you could move vertically 6 spaces up to the 4, or 6 spaces diagonally to the 3, or 6 spaces horizontally to the right to the 2. Any of those would be considered 1 move.

Your task is to start at the 3 in the upper left-hand corner and reach the E in the lower right hand corner in exactly 6 moves.

3	5	6	4	2	6	7	5
4	7	3	5	2	6	3	7
5	2	2	3	2	1	7	4
7	1	4	5	4	2	5	5
4	1	4	3	5	4	4	6
3	2	6	5	3	6	3	5
7	1	2	4	6	2	3	2
6	4	5	3	7	1	2	E

2. LID ASTRAY

In my kitchen cabinet I have lots of different sizes of plastic containers. The lids for all of these (as well as for some containers that I don't even have anymore) are in a drawer. The other day, I needed several containers for freezing spaghetti sauce. I pulled out three different sized containers. I then went to the lid drawer and was confronted with a large mass of lids. I pulled out five lids, all different sizes. I knew that the lids for the three containers that I had were among the five lids. Devise a strategy for getting the right lids on the right containers as efficiently as possible. (Note: These old containers have no labels and are all the same color.)

3. RADIATOR

The capacity of my car radiator is 24 quarts. The mixture of antifreeze and water in the radiator was 25% antifreeze. Since winter is approaching, I wanted a larger percentage of antifreeze. My mechanic suggested a 38% mixture. I therefore needed to drain off some of the current mixture and replace it with pure antifreeze. How much of the current mixture do I need to drain off? (Answer exactly.)

4. LSAT TEST

Problems similar to this appear on the LSAT test each year. The LSAT is the test you must pass in order to get into law school.

A flagpole has spaces for seven colored flags arranged in a vertical line. Two of the flags are yellow, two are green, one is red, one is orange, and one is brown. Flags are to be placed on the pole under the following conditions. The orange flag is to be placed immediately below the brown flag. The red flag is not allowed to be immediately above or below either green flag. The two green flags must be together. The two yellow flags must not be together. The red flag is not allowed to be at the top or the bottom of the pole. How many acceptable flag arrangements are there?

5. LARGE POWER OF TWO

Perhaps you have seen the notation 4! (read four factorial) which means $4 \times 3 \times 2 \times 1$. Similarly, $10! = 10 \times 9 \times 8 \times 7 \times 6 \times 5 \times 4 \times 3 \times 2 \times 1$.

A factorial always starts with an integer and multiplies it by all preceding positive integers all the way down to one.

$n! = n(n - 1)(n - 2)(n - 3) \dots (3)(2)(1)$

As you can imagine, 800! is a very large number. Find the largest power of 2 that divides 800! without a remainder.

finite differences

FINITE DIFFERENCES are a means for determining the equation of a polynomial function by examining the changes in the dependent variable. This method does not work for trigonometric or exponential functions. A polynomial function can be analyzed by considering the differences between successive values of the function. In linear functions, the successive values have a constant difference. In quadratic functions, the first layer of differences creates a linear function and the difference reveals a constant.

Note that we use the letters g, f, and e when doing second-degree equations. This is to avoid confusion with linear equations in which m and b are used and with the quadratic formula where a, b, and c are used.

When you do a problem using finite differences, you will want to set up a master chart of differences using only variables. Compare the master to the specific differences for the function you are examining. The comparison of the two gives you a choice of a number of equations to work with.

Finite differences should also be a help in teaching students about the concept of variables and about functions. You will also notice a correspondence between finite differences and solving systems of equations.

You can apply finite differences to a number of functions in which the input and output are known but the function's equation is not. For example, finite differences can be applied to the price of chicken nuggets. If there's a constant difference in price corresponding with successive different-sized orders, you might be able to calculate a price per nugget (the slope of the linear function). The number added to this (the y-intercept) might be the markup. Realize, of course, that this is a gross over-simplification. But polynomial functions are at least a starting point for many pricing strategies.

Text Problems

x	y	x	y	x	y
0	3	0	-2	0	-4
1	7	1	5	1	1
2	11	2	12	2	12
3	15	3	19	3	29
4	19	4	26	4	52
5	?	5	?	5	?
137	?	137	?	137	?

Find the pattern in each function and then fill in the *y* values for the *x* values 5 and 137.

MORE FUNCTIONS

Find the equations for the two functions below. Then use your equation to find the *y* value for the other *x* value listed in each table.

x	y	x	y
0	-5	2	14
1	-2	3	11
2	5	4	8
3	16	5	5
4	31	6	2
5	50	7	-1
48	?	82	?

HANDSHAKES

At the first meeting of the House of Representatives, all 435 members shook hands with each of the other members. How many handshakes took place?

HOW MANY SQUARES?

Find a formula for the number of squares on any size *n* by *n* checkerboard.

Problem Set A, Version 2

1. A COVEY OF FUNCTIONS

Find the equation for each function.

a.

x	y
0	3
1	7
2	11
3	15
4	19
5	23

b.

x	y
0	4
1	-1
2	-6
3	-11
4	-16
5	-21

c.

x	y
0	3
1	5
2	15
3	33
4	59
5	93

d.

x	y
0	7
1	7.5
2	8
3	8.5
4	9
5	9.5

e.

x	y
0	2
1	0
2	-2
3	-4
4	-6
5	-8

f.

x	y
0	7
1	12
2	21
3	34
4	51
5	72

g.

x	y
0	-1
1	11
2	41
3	101
4	203
5	359

h.

x	y
0	-2
1	-3.5
2	-5
3	-6.5
4	-8
5	-9.5

2. BLOCK PYRAMID

The drawings below show a 1-layer pyramid, a 2-layer pyramid, and a 3-layer pyramid made out of building blocks. Notice that there is one visible block on the first one, five visible blocks on the second one, and thirteen visible blocks on the third one. There is one hidden block in the middle of the bottom layer of the third pyramid. "Visible" blocks are those that you would be able to see if you were to walk around the pyramid. How many blocks would be visible on a 35-layer pyramid?

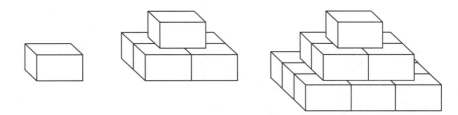

A BEVY OF FUNCTIONS

Find equations for these functions:

i.

x	y
0	1
1	3
2	5
3	7
4	9
5	11

j.

x	y
0	0
1	3
2	4
3	3
4	0
5	-5

k.

x	y
0	-7
1	-3
2	1
3	5
4	9
5	13

l.

x	y
0	-3
1	2
2	9
3	18
4	29
5	42

m.

x	y
0	1
1	-2
2	-5
3	-8
4	-11
5	-14

n.

x	y
0	-2
1	-7.5
2	-12
3	-15.5
4	-18
5	-19.5

4. **HEXAGONAL NUMBERS**

The figures below represent the first four hexagonal numbers. Find a formula for the hexagonal numbers.

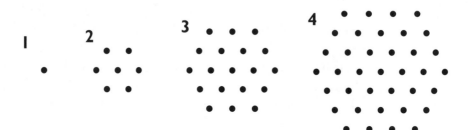

p.	
x	y
0	23
1	30
2	31
3	14
4	-33
5	-122

q.	
x	y
0	8
1	11
2	16
3	17
4	8
5	-17

r.	
x	y
0	-5
1	-3
2	13
3	49
4	111
5	205

s.	
x	y
0	5
1	-2.5
2	-19
3	-41.5
4	-67
5	-92.5

Problem Set B, Version 2

1. WORMS

Wally "wuvs" worms. Every week, when exposed to sunlight for one hour, each worm splits into four parts. Each part becomes a full-fledged worm. Wally decides to run a worm farm. He figures he can sell his worms to bait and tackle shops in the area. Wally starts with 14 worms, and every week he exposes them to sunlight for 1 hour and watches them split. After 6 weeks, he takes all of his worms and packs them up. Each worm weighs 3 ounces. He packs them in 2-pound cartons and packs the cartons into cases: 40 cartons to a case. How many cases of worms does he have at the end of 6 weeks?

2. PRODUCE

At the grocery store you can buy

1. an orange and an apple for the price of a grapefruit.
2. an orange for the price of an apple and a peach.
3. two grapefruits for the price of three peaches.

One orange would cost the same as a certain number of a certain fruit. How many of which fruit?

3. ANTIFREEZE

I like to keep my car's radiator full of an antifreeze-water mixture that is 25% antifreeze and 75% water. Recently, I left the cap off while I was driving, and a bunch of the mixture leaked out. I filled it up with nine quarts of water (I was out of antifreeze) and then found that the mixture was only 12% antifreeze. What is the capacity of the radiator?

4. STRANGE NUMBER

There is a 5-digit number that has the following strange property. Put a 2 in front of this 5-digit number. Multiply the resulting 6-digit number by 3. The product is a 6-digit number consisting of the original 5-digit number followed by 2. What is the 5-digit number?

5. TWO SEQUENCES

Consider the two sequences 21, 32, 45, 60, 77, 96, ... and 1505, 1540, 1575, 1610, 1645, 1680, ...

How many terms will it take for the first sequence to overtake the second sequence?

Problem Set B, Version 3

1. OLD CHEVY

My old Chevy Malibu loves super premium gas. Unfortunately, my sister drove it one day and filled it up with 5 gallons of regular gas. The tank holds 16 gallons. My car gets 17 miles per gallon. How many miles will I have to drive the car so that when I fill up the gas tank with super premium gas, the mixture in the gas tank will be at least 95% super premium gas?

2. COUNTY FAIR

John and Marcia took her two kids to the county fair. They first had to pay admission to the fair. John and Marcia spent ⅙ of their money on adult tickets, and $6.50 on kids' tickets. They spent ⅜ of their remaining money on ride tickets. Then they spent $4.00 each on lunch. Then they spent ⅕ of their remaining money on a T-shirt for John. Then Marcia wanted a T-shirt too, so they bought another one for the same price. Then one child found a quarter and the other child found a dime. They each gave the money to their mom, whereupon John and Marcia each gave each child a dollar. John and Marcia then spent ⅖ of their money on ice cream sundaes. When they left the park, they had to pay their parking tab, which amounted to $1.50 an hour. They had been there for 7 hours. When they got to the home of Marcia, John and Marcia had $3.15 left between them. How much money did they spend at the fair?

3. HOW MANY SEGMENTS?

There are n points on a piece of paper, no three of which are in a straight line. How many line segments can be drawn joining every possible point on the paper.

4. MYSTERY SUM

The sum below features consecutive numbers in each column. The numbers can be consecutive reading down or reading up, but the entire column (including the digit in the answer) is consecutive in one or the other order. Note: 0 and 9 are not considered to be consecutive. Fill in the spaces. Two fives have been filled in to help you.

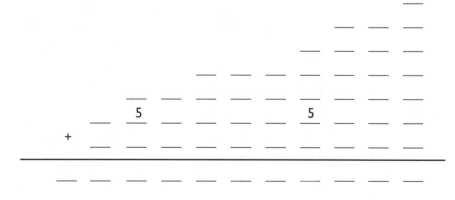

Nine ordinary people get to be the celebrities on the game show Hollywood Squares. They sit in a tic-tac-toe board in three rows, with three people on the top row, three people in the middle row, and three people on the bottom row. The following clues refer to the positions of the nine people. Names beginning with the letters A through I are first names, and names beginning with J through W (not all letters are used) are last names. (Note: if a clue states that a person is between two other people, you don't know who is on the left and who is on the right, but you would of course know who is in the middle.)

1. Betty is between Madison and Kennedy.
2. Lincoln is between Anh and Ellen.
3. Jefferson is between Gregorio and Taft.
4. Frank is on the bottom row next to Roosevelt.
5. Isabel is under Gregorio and over Pierce.
6. Della is on the top row next to Howard.
7. Clara is in the middle row next to Nixon.
8. Isabel, whose name is not Madison, is on the far left side.
9. Anh is not Pierce nor Wilson.
10. Della is not in the same column as Roosevelt.

Determine each person's full name and his or her seating position.

Problem Set B, Version 4

1. ANTS

A long stick is leaning against a wall. A group of ants spies the stick, and they figure they could climb up the stick to reach a hole in the wall. Unfortunately, the stick does not quite reach the hole. The ants measure the distance from the bottom of the stick to the bottom of the wall and find it to be 15 inches. They estimate that the top of the stick is 4 inches below the hole. So they decide to push the bottom of the stick toward the wall. They push the bottom of the stick toward the wall at a rate of ½ inch per minute. This causes the top of the stick to slide up the wall. It reaches the hole in 16 minutes. How long is the stick?

2. SEQUENCE RACING

Consider the two sequences 4, 8, 14, 22, 32, … and 5000, 5200, 5400, 5600, 5800, 6000, ….

How many terms will it take for the first sequence to overtake the second sequence?

3. CORNER CAFE

The new waiter at the Corner Cafe had a problem getting orders straight. When he brought out the order to table 14 (a square table with one person on each side) every order was messed up. He brought French toast and strawberries to Karen, eggs and hashbrowns to Gil, an omelette and a muffin to Donna, and pancakes and sausage to Stan. No person received either item that they ordered, but no one received both of the items that were ordered by someone else. The four diners managed to sort out the confusion and rearrange the food. When order was restored, Karen was sitting between hashbrowns and pancakes, Donna was sitting between eggs and French toast, the person sitting on Stan's right had sausage, and the person across from Gil had a muffin. No one had ordered two main items (which are French toast, eggs, omelette, and pancakes). Who ordered what?

4. THE GREAT NUMBERINI'S NUMBER

"I am the great 'Numberini.' I am thinking of a 5-digit number with 5 different digits. Place a 2 in front of my number to make a 6-digit number. Multiply the 6-digit number by 16. The answer is a 7-digit number that begins with my 5-digit number, followed by a 2 and then a 0. What is my five digit number?"

Last winter we went skiing in Flagstaff, Arizona. In the parking lot I noticed there were license plates from Arizona as well as from various other states. There were also some license plates from other countries. Some of the vehicles were trucks, and the rest were not trucks. Some of the vehicles were four-wheel drive (FWD), and the rest were not. Here are some other observations:

1. There were 56 total vehicles.
2. Every truck had FWD.
3. Thirty-five of the vehicles were FWD and 21 were not.
4. There were 20 trucks.
5. There were 42 vehicles from the U.S., 28 of which were from Arizona.
6. There were four times as many Arizona trucks as trucks from other states in the U.S.
7. There were two more non-FWD vehicles from Arizona than there were FWD vehicles that were not trucks and not from the U.S.
8. The number of trucks was 8 less than the number of vehicles from Arizona.
9. There were 7 more Arizona trucks than there were trucks from other countries.
10. The Arizona vehicles that were not trucks were split evenly between FWD and non-FWD.

How many of the U.S. vehicles that weren't from Arizona were not trucks? How many foreign FWD vehicles were there?

other ways to organize information

M UCH OF PROBLEM SOLVING involves organizing a problem's information in some different manner than it is presented in. For example, if you draw a diagram to solve a problem, part of what you do is to organize the information in a different way. Just as a picture is worth a thousand words, organized information presents a better picture. We are accustomed to much information being presented in linear form: Sentences, paragraphs, chapters, and books are all linear. Music is linear. On the other hand, some of the problems in this chapter are done by organizing the information in two dimensions. The Mathlete example on page 423 of the student text and the Three Squares problem on page 419 are examples of two-dimensional organization schemes. Such schemes are easily represented on a piece of paper (as paper—at least the part useful to us—is two dimensional).

At the end of the chapter we present tree diagrams (also presented in chapter 2). Tree diagrams are another good way to use two dimensions to organize a problem. Time is often one of the dimensions represented in a tree diagram. In the tournament example, the horizontal dimension represents time (successive rounds of the tournament) while the vertical placement signifies the person's placement within the playoff schedule. Music is also written using two dimensions in which the horizontal dimension represents order in time and the vertical represents pitch.

Organizing information is one of the broad "umbrella" categories of problem-solving strategies. Some of the strategies based on organizing information include systematic lists, eliminate possibilities, matrix logic, look for a pattern, guess and check, unit analysis, algebra, and finite differences. There are also elements of organizing information present in working backwards. Organizing information makes a problem more manageable.

Reorganizing information might be a better name for this strategy. Information in a problem may already be organized in some way, but what you need to do is to approach the problem aggressively with the assumption that it can be organized better.

TV schedules are an example of how information was organized in a certain way before it occurred to someone to organize it differently. For years, schedules were invariably written out as a linearly organized listing based on times:

8:00

③ Lifestyles of the Guess and Checkers: TV's cleverest characters are highlighted in this display of designer jeans on Rodeo Drive. We also pay a visit to an ex-presidential dog.

⑩ Wheel of Diagrams: So popular has buying a vowel become that a shortage arises. Imported o's with umlauts (ö) make their debut.

⑬ All My Physical Representations: Storm has been caught with his physical representations . . . well, let's just say this show should be previewed by sensible parents.

9:00

⑩ Crossing the River with Dogs (adventure): The President stops off in Rocklin in order to seek wisdom from our heroes, Ted and Ken.

⑬ I Dream of Systematic Lists: Art, Brad, Cindy, and Donna find several ways to line up at a drinking fountain, and Penny Stimes pays a return visit.

9:30

⑩ As the Diagram Draws: Leslie finds out what Rob and Kelsey have known all along and what Mom, Gus, and Rover suspected. Never mind, just watch the show.

10:00

⑬ Wide World of Subproblems: New show features loading a truck in Chicago, planning a Rocky Mountain camping trip, diagnosing a malfunctioning car in Phoenix.

10:30

③ Wyatt ERP: Famous lawman seeks to solve problems the easy way.

⑩ The Simplesons: At a new time—Bart and his family go head-to-head solving simpler problems.

More recently, most TV schedules have been revamped to list times along the top and stations on the left. This two-dimensional model is more efficient for presenting the essential information.

	8:00	8:30	9:00	9:30	10:00	10:30	11:00
③	Lifestyles of the Guess and Checkers			As the Diagram Draws		Wyatt ERP	
⑩	Wheel of Diagrams		Crossing the River with Dogs (adventure)			The Simplesons	
⑬	All My Physical Representations		I Dream of Systematic Lists		Wide World of Subproblems		

The length of the show is represented by the length of the bar that bears its name. In the linear scheme the length of a show was not presented. The only way to determine a show's length was to look through the list until the next time a show appeared on that channel.

Notes on Text Problems and Problem Set A

THE THREE SQUARES

This was originally solved by systematic lists and eliminating possibilities in Chapter 3. Now a solution is presented using organizing information. It is important that students know and see problems solved in a variety of ways. This is a good example of organizing the information differently so that the organization highlights different elements of the problem. Notice also that seeking contradictions (indirect proof) shows up in this problem.

TWO BILLS

Many students will miss the point of this problem as written. It may be helpful to suggest looking for the maximum age Bill could be and the minimum age Bill could be. The same is true for Dolores' Age in Problem Set A, Version 2.

Text Problems

Franny, Carl and Amichung compared their season's statistics during the post-season banquet for their high school baseball team. Franny had three times as many singles as Carl. Carl had four times as many doubles as Amichung. Each of them had exactly the same number of hits. None of the three of them had any hits besides singles and doubles (they were slap hitters). The three of them as a group had exactly as many singles as doubles. The three of them had fewer than 200 hits in all. How many singles and how many doubles did each of them have?

THE THREE SQUARES

Three cousins, Bob, Chris, and Phyllis, were sitting around watching football on TV. The game was really boring, and so they started talking about how old they were. Bob (the oldest) noticed that they were all between the ages of 11 and 30. Phyllis noticed that the sum of their ages was 70. Suddenly, Chris(the youngest) burst out, "Gee, if you write the square of each of our ages, all of the digits from 1 to 9 will appear exactly once in the digits of the three squares." How old was each person? See if you can organize the information in a new way.

I. THE CLASSIC HOMEWORK EXCUSE

Alan claims that his puppy chewed up his homework and then stepped all over it with muddy paws (he has his parents' couch to prove it!). The homework assignment had been to prepare a totals chart for doughnuts and coffee. As much of the chart as could be read is reproduced below. As a result of being "dogged," some of these numbers may have been misread by the typesetter. Determine the price of one doughnut and the price of one coffee, and fix any numbers that are inaccurate. (Note: When you re-create this matrix, do it assuming that as few of the numbers are mistyped as possible. Without this assumption, someone could make this problem very easy – assume that all numbers are mistyped, and set new prices for coffee and doughnuts.)

DOUGHNUTS

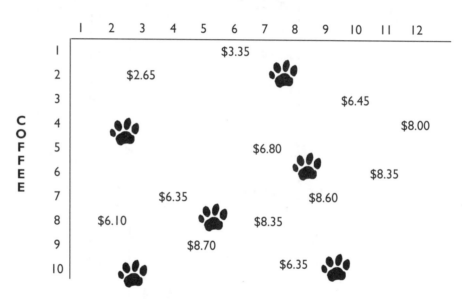

2. SON OF TWO-INPUT FUNCTIONS

The following are functions with two inputs. The first input is *x,* and the second input is *y*. What is the rule for calculating the output?

a.

Input	Output
5, 6	16
-5, 1	-9
8, 2	18
10, 1	21
4, 7	15
-5, -4	-14
-1, 6	4
-1, 0	-2
-1, 3	1
4, 8	16
8, 9	25
9, 8	26
2, 6	10
-3, 1	-5
-5, -2	-12

b.

Input	Output
-1, 3	10
4, 8	20
3, 6	15
8, 9	19
-3, 4	15
9, 8	15
2, 6	16
-3, 1	6
-5, -2	-1
10, 7	11
2, 3	7
5, 6	13
-4, 0	4
10, 7	11
1, 5	14

c.

Input	Output
-1, 3	4
4, 8	4
3, 6	3
8, 9	1
-3, 4	7
9, 8	-1
2, 6	4
-3, 1	4
-5, -2	3
10, 7	-3
2, 3	1
5, 6	1
10, 7	-3
1, 5	4
6, 5	-1

d.

Input	Output
10, 7	13
1, 5	-3
6, 5	7
2, 5	-1
6, 4	8
-3, 3	-9
3, 4	2
-4, -1	-7
7, 7	7
10, 0	20
9, 9	13
-5, -5	-12
-4, -4	-5
-1, -1	-7
9, 9	17

2. SON OF TWO-INPUT FUNCTIONS (CONTINUED)

The following are functions with two inputs. The first input is x, and the second input is y. What is the rule for calculating the output?

e.	
Input	**Output**
-2, 4	8
10, -1	17
8, 6	34
9, 8	42
3, 7	27
-5, -1	-13
-3, 4	6
-3, 0	-6
-4, 3	1
9, 2	24
-1, 6	16
2, 7	25
3, 6	24
3, 8	30

f.	
Input	**Output**
1, 5	6
1, 8	9
0, 4	4
4, 5	21
5, -7	18
6, 9	45
7, 2	51
8, 9	73
3, 7	16
-1, 2	3
-4, 3	19
5, 5	30
-2, 3	7
7, 8	57

3. DOLORES' AGE

Dolores told me several things about herself without telling me her age:

She said, "I played soccer in the 7 to 8 year-olds league." I knew that she had to be 7 or 8 when the league started August 1 and that it continued through November.

She also said, "I was the best basketball player in the 8 to 9 year-olds league." Basketball went from January through March, and you had to be 8 or 9 upon entering on January 1.

Later on she said, "I turned 8 in second grade." I knew she started second grade in September 1988, and she told me this in 1993. How old could Dolores have been when this conversation took place?

4. LOG RIDE

Six people were on the log ride. There were three rows of seats and two people in each seat. The ages of the people on the left side differed in six-year increments with the youngest in front. The person in the front right was twice as old as his seatmate. The person in the middle right was one and a half times as old as her seatmate. The person on the right back seat was half as old as her seatmate. The sum of the six peoples's ages is 145. How old are the youngest and oldest people?

COMPUTER PRINT-OUT

The computer printout for the adults and children's prices at the county fair is totally messed up, but still accurate if you can decode the information. The columns and rows are the prices for a certain number of adults and for a certain number of kids. What is the admission price for a child and what is the admission price for an adult?

```
ADULTS
012345678910
C006121824303642485460
H14101622283440465258647076
I2814202632384450566268
L31218243036424854606672
D416222834404652586470
R520263238445056626874 80
E62430364248546066727884
N7283440465258647076 8288
8323844505662687480 8692
93642485460667278849096
10404652586470768288 94100
```

STAMP COMBINATION

Suppose you have only an 8-cent stamp, a 10-cent stamp, a 7-cent stamp, and 3-cent stamp. What are the different amounts of postage you can make using these four stamps?

GOOD AND YUMMY RESTAURANT

The Good and Yummy Restaurant claims to make the best burritos in the world. Fortunately, most people know better. They start with a tortilla, put in beans, then give the customers some choices: Monterey Jack cheese, cheddar cheese, or both kinds of cheese and then hot sauce, barbeque sauce, or neither.

a. Set up a tree diagram showing all of the different types of burritos the Good and Yummy Restaurant offers.

b. Organize a chart to show the different types of burritos available.

Problem Set B, Version 2

1. ALONA'S FENCE

Alona told her son Frank to paint the fence. Frank whined and complained. So she said, "OK, you don't have to do it today. Instead, paint $^1/_2$ of one board today. Tomorrow paint $^1/_3$ of a board and $^2/_3$ of a board. I don't care which boards you paint. The next day paint $^1/_4$ of a board, $^2/_4$ of a board, and $^3/_4$ of a board. That will cover 3 days; continue like that for another 22 days. I'll do the rest." If you add up all of the boards Frank completed and the parts he painted, Frank painted the equivalent of how many boards?

2. STOCKS

Four stockbrokers were having a conversation about how their pet stocks were doing.

Alex: My stock is worth 3 or 4 times as much as Billie Jo's stock.
Billie Jo: Yeah, but my stock is worth 3 or 4 dollars more than Cayla's stock.
Cayla: But Alex's stock is worth 3 or 4 dollars less than Derwood's stock.
Derwood: And my stock is worth 3 or 4 times as much as your stock, Cayla.

All the stock prices are whole dollar amounts. None of the prices contain a digit of 3 or 4. What are the prices for each stock?

3. ZNORS

All Znors are Zmuds. Half of the Zorfs are Zmuds. There are 24 Zorfs. No Zlogs are Znors. There are 16 Zorfs that are not Zlogs. All Zlogs are Zmuds. Half of the Zlogs are Zorfs. No Znors are Zorfs. There are 9 Zmuds that are not Znors or Zorfs or Zlogs. There are 15 Znors.

How many Zmuds are there? How many Zmuds are also Zlogs and Zorfs?

4. CONFERENCE

At a company meeting of photocopy repair persons, there were 17 people from 4 different cities (New York, Peoria, Topeka, San Diego). The facts below refer to these 17 people.

1. More than half of the participants were from the Midwest.
2. The farther east the city, the more participants.
3. There was at least one person from each location.

One person was due to be transferred from one city to a city farther east, but all of the above would still be true. The person being transferred was given a going-away potluck by the other repair technicians in his office. Unfortunately, they all brought chips. From which city to which other city was the transfer?

In a 4 by 4 grid, place the numbers from 1 to 16 with the following constraints.

a. No row or column contains 2 consecutive numbers.

b. No row or column contains 2 multiples of 4.

c. There are no multiples of 3 in either row 1 or row 3.

d. The numbers 2 and 13 are in the third column.

e. The corners all contain prime numbers.

f. The numbers 6 and 11 are in the bottom row.

g. The numbers 4 and 15 are in the first column.

h. The numbers 14 and 10 are in the same row.

i. No 2 adjacent columns have the same number of odd numbers.

Problem Set B, Version 3—Dad's Birthday

1. DEAR OLD DAD

My father liked to puzzle people. He indeed was very puzzling. For example, he had a new puzzle cooked up for the birthday party we threw him. Attending the birthday party were my aunt Jasmine, my uncle Pedro, my grandma, and all of us kids. (Grandma is the mother of my dad, my aunt Jasmine, and my uncle Pedro.) My dad said, "Suppose you multiply together the digits in my age. Subtract that from my age and the answer is 18." Basically, our response was "Big deal!" However, he continued, "I did the same thing when I was my brother's age, only the answer was 16." Again, our basic response was "Big deal!" Undaunted, my father continued speaking. "If I do it again when my brother is my age, the answer again will be 16." It started sounding intriguing now, because nobody had heard anything from his brother, and I sure didn't know what age Uncle Pedro was. Then my grandma spoke up. "It's weird, but I just did the same thing with my age and the answer is also 18. If I'd done it when I was my daughter Jasmine's age, the answer would have been 16. And if I do it again when Jasmine is my age, the answer will be 16 again."

How old are my Uncle Pedro and my Aunt Jasmine?

2. SIXTEEN CANDLES

We put 16 candles on Dad's birthday cake: 4 each of blue, green, yellow and purple. Just for fun, we decided to arrange them in a line so that primary colors were only next to related secondary colors.

What order were they in?

3. REAL DOLLS

My cousin Pat was also at the party. Pat brought a large collection of 36 dolls. Pat gave us some clues about the dolls. "Some of them are Barbies; in fact, half of the female dolls are Barbies. Half of the Cabbage Patch dolls are female. There are as many females that are not Barbies or Cabbage Patch dolls as there are Cabbage Patch dolls. Half of the dolls are not female. All of the dolls except two (which I found at a garage sale and whose gender I found it impossible to determine) are either male or female. One of those two genderless dolls is a Cabbage Patch doll. How many male, non-Cabbage Patch dolls are there?

4. **WHH**

Another cousin, Dave, was also at Dad's party. He said he found this problem on the bulletin board at work.

Find pairs of integer values that work for this equation.

$$wh + h + h = w^2 \qquad \text{(Note: } wh \text{ means } w \text{ times } h\text{)}$$

5. **ONE HUNDRED FACTORS**

Dad was impressed at our problem-solving ability so far. He was reading a magazine after dinner and found the next problem in the magazine:

"What is the smallest number that has 100 different positive, integral factors, including 1 and itself?"

Problem Set B, Version 4

1. MARBLES

I overheard this story on the playground one day. Three kids were talking. I heard the voices but didn't see who was talking. The voices were discussing a marble match that had just occurred.

One voice said, "Wow, what a weird game. First Zeus won half of Venus's marbles."

Another voice said, "Then Venus won ⅓ of David's marbles.

A third voice said, "Then David won ¼ of Zeus's marbles."

Then one of the three voices said, "We all ended up with the same number of marbles. I started with 34 marbles."

How many marbles did each one end up with?

2. COUSINS

Five kids from the Gleane family (Tom, Bonnie, Janet, Stefan, and Michael) went to a family reunion with their cousins, the Jenicks (Ryan, Torrey, Will, Daniel, and Gary). They stayed in a townhouse near a lake for five days. There were five great hikes to take: around the lake, to the top of the waterfall, to the top of Lover's Leap, along the river, and to the store. Each day the cousins paired off, with one Gleane cousin matched up with one Jenick cousin, and went for a hike. Arrange a daily hiking schedule for the five days so that each Jenick is matched once with each Gleane, and all ten kids get to go on each hike once.

3. ANT GRAPEVINE

Em, Mame, and Bea are all ants and live in an anthill. They learned a new verse to the song, The Ants Go Marching, and wanted to teach it to all of the other ants in the neighborhood. Each of the three ants decided to teach the song to two other ants on the first day. Each ant that learned the song then had to teach two other ants the next day. This continued for days and days, with each learner becoming a teacher the next day. After how many days would all four billion ants in the neighborhood know the song?

4. LONG LIST OF NUMBERS

The numbers from one to one billion were written out in alphabetical order. (The word "and" was not used, and no dashes were used, so the number 431 was written as four hundred thirty one, and 54187 was written as fifty four thousand one hundred eighty seven.) What was the last number written in the list?

The figure below shows the alphabet split into regions. The regions are formed by two circles, two rectangles, two squares, and two equilateral triangles. Vertices of the rectangles, squares, and triangles are noted by dots. Don't count any smaller triangles or quadrilaterals that are formed by the crossing of the lines. For the purposes of this problem, all references to rectangles refer to rectangles that are not squares.

The five clues below each describe a different letter. Take these five letters and rearrange them to form a word. (By the way, the word is not plural.) No two clues refer to the same letter.

1. A letter that is inside one less triangle than square and inside one more circle than triangle.
2. A letter that is inside the same number of triangles and rectangles and inside the same number of squares and circles and is inside fewer squares than triangles.
3. A letter that is inside more circles than triangles and inside more triangles than both squares and rectangles.
4. A letter that is inside a total of four figures but only two different kinds.
5. No letter is inside more figures than this one. This letter is not in a rectangle.

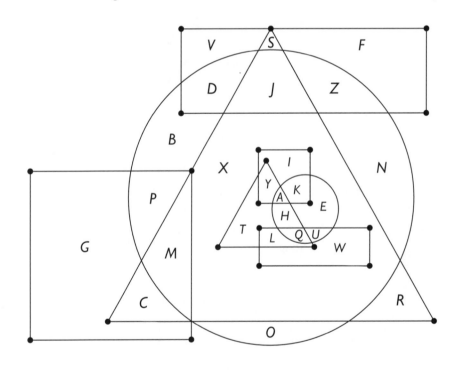

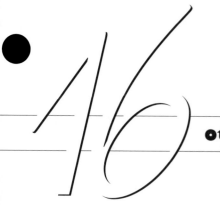

other ways to change focus

IN HIS INAUGURAL SPEECH in 1961, President John Kennedy said, "Ask not what your country can do for you; ask what you can do for your country." His statement illustrates well the concept of changing focus. He wanted people to stop focusing on the government as the solver of problems and focus instead on their own roles as individuals in dealing with the country's problems.

This chapter (and strategy) is divided into three parts: Change Your Point of View, Solve the Complementary Problem, and Change the Representation.

Changing your point of view means looking at a problem from another perspective. Instead of focusing on the time spent driving, look at the distance driven. Instead of asking what your country can do for you, ask what you can do for your country.

Solving the complementary problem means looking at the rest of the picture. Instead of focusing on what's there, focus on what's not there. Instead of asking what your country can do for you, ask what your country cannot do for you. To evaluate the effectiveness of a medicine, look for instances when it is not effective.

Changing the representation involves finding another way to represent the information in a problem so that you can solve the problem more efficiently or understand it better. Drawing a diagram is a way to change the representation and thus change focus. The diagram brings out the spatial relationships between key elements of the problem. Using manipulatives is another way to change the representation.

By changing focus, you give a problem a whole different look. The problem may be easier to solve if you can find a different way to look at it.

Changing focus is one of three umbrella categories of problem-solving strategies presented in this book, the other two being organizing information and spatial organization. Other strategies that employ changing focus are subproblems (looking at the inside of the problem), easier related problems (looking at other problems first), and working backwards (looking at the problem in reverse).

Changing focus is a strategy we use often in our lives, not necessarily in concrete problem-solving situations, but in more subjective realms. A parent might have to change focus to deal with a child's misbehavior. Instead of focusing on the behavior (teasing or hitting, say), the parent may deal with the problem more effectively by focusing on the cause. Perhaps the child is jealous of the person he or she is teasing. Focusing on the child's feelings may help the child learn more civilized ways of dealing with jealousy.

You can even take this strategy out to the backyard. If a dog is digging up new plants, look to see if there is some other cause besides a dog just plain acting like a dog. Perhaps the creature needs some place to dig. Maybe it needs a place to lie down when it's hot outside.

Robert Kennedy said, "Some people look at this country the way it is and say 'why?' I look at this country the way it can be and say 'why not?'" Besides being good rhetoric, being able to look beyond perceived constraints in a problem is often looked upon as a sign of genius and good leadership.

Notes on Text Problems

NINE DOTS

In this problem, people often feel constrained to stay within the bounds created by the dots. Truly creative problem solvers are able to look beyond perceived constraints. This problem is a simple, effective demonstration of this principle. It can serve as a lead-in to dealing with the concept of constraints, real or imagined.

Text Problems

NINE DOTS

Without lifting your pencil from start to finish, draw four line segments through all nine dots.

.   .   .

.   .   .

.   .   .

The solution, by the way, has nothing to do with how wide the dots are or that possibly the lines determined by them are not parallel. The dots are mathematically defined—they have no width, and they determine sets of parallel lines.

THE HUMAN FACTOR

Mayra is a human computer. She has appeared on talk shows with her amazing ability with numbers. One of the problems that Mayra is very adept at is the following: A person from the audience will give Mayra a number and Mayra will immediately be able to tell how many one-digit factors that number has. For example, if you were in the audience and you said 50, Mayra would say three, because 50 has three one-digit factors (namely 1, 2, and 5). One day, Mayra was on a well-known talk show, and some wise guy in the audience asked Mayra to tell him how many one-digit factors the numbers from 1 to 100 had. The answer was not nine, since Mayra had to count every factor as it appeared for a particular number, and sum that with the number of factors for each of the other numbers from 1 to 100. So for instance, even though the factor 5 appears in 50, it also appears in 45, and so must be counted each time. Mayra quickly "programmed" her brain to give her the answer, and she had it in a few moments. What was her answer?

AVERAGE SPEED

Jacques left his home in Austin and drove to San Antonio. On the way there he drove 40 miles per hour (there was a lot of traffic). On the way back he drove 60 miles per hour. What was his average speed?

BOOK REPORT

Seiko had to do a book report. She was supposed to read five books (in any order), then write an essay comparing and contrasting the books. She could choose from the list below. In how many ways could she choose five books?

Pride and Prejudice
The Scarlet Letter
Huck Finn
No Exit
Call of the Wild
Catch-22.

AREA

Find the area of the shaded region.

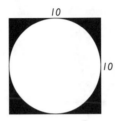

OFFICE COMPUTER

I hate our office computer system. It seems to be "down" more than it is "up." Take the last eight days since I came back from vacation, for example. I work an 8-hour shift, but the computer works less. The first three days back were fine. It was working the whole time I was. But the fourth day, it was down for the first half-hour of my shift, and then went down again 15 minutes before I left. The next day I had to wait a half-hour longer than I had to wait the previous day for it to come up, and it went down 15 minutes earlier than the day before. The computer almost seems to have a brain. The sixth day it did the same thing: It came up half an hour later than on the fifth day, and went down 15 minutes earlier. That same pattern carried on to the seventh day. How many hours total was the computer operational during my last seven shifts?

THE TENNIS TOURNAMENT

A big regional tennis tournament in New Orleans drew 378 entries. It was a single elimination tournament, where a player is eliminated from the tournament when she loses a match. How many matches must be played to determine the champion?

You have ten cards, numbered 1, 2, 3, 4, 5, 6, 7, 8, 9, 10. Your task is to arrange them in a particular order and put them in a stack, hold the stack in your hand, and then do the following. Put the top card on the table face up, put the next card on the bottom of the stack in your hand, put the next card on the table, put the next card on the bottom of the stack, and so on, continuing to alternate cards that go on the table and under the stack, until all 10 cards are on the table.

That, of course, is really easy to do. The trick is to lay the cards on the table in numerical order. In other words, the first card you put on the table will be the 1, the next card you put on the table will be number 2, the next card you put on the table will be number 3, and so on, until the last card placed on the table will be number 10.

In what order should the cards be arranged in the original stack so that this will happen?

See if you can represent this problem in a completely different way (we used a diagram) and solve it more easily.

Problem Set A, Version 2

1. BASIC HEX

Without lifting your pencil from start to finish, draw four line segments through all seven dots. The solution has nothing to do with how wide the dots are or that possibly the lines determined by them are not parallel. The dots are mathematically defined—they have no width, and they determine sets of parallel lines.

2. TEN-DOT PUZZLE

Without lifting your pencil from start to finish, draw five line segments through all ten dots. The solution has nothing to do with how wide the dots are or that possibly the lines determined by them are not parallel. The dots are mathematically defined—they have no width, and they determine sets of parallel lines.

3. FOURTEEN-DOT PUZZLE

Without lifting your pencil from start to finish, draw 6 line segments through all 14 dots. The solution has nothing to do with how wide the dots are or that possibly the lines determined by them are not parallel. The dots are mathematically defined—they have no width, and they determine sets of parallel lines.

4. HOURGLASS

Without lifting your pencil from start to finish, draw four line segments through all eight dots. The solution has nothing to do with how wide the dots are or that possibly the lines determined by them are not parallel. The dots are mathematically defined—they have no width, and they determine sets of parallel lines.

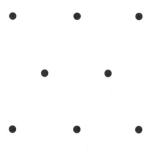

5. FRUIT STAND

The first customer bought $3.00 worth of oranges. She bought them in a bag, so she didn't know that the price came out to $.40 per pound. The next customer also bought a $3.00 bag of oranges, but he paid $.50 per pound for his oranges. Of the oranges sold so far, what has been the average price per pound?

6. BADMINTON TOURNAMENT

Bobbi needed to select six badminton players to represent the school at a badminton tournament. She felt she could choose from Steve, Debi, Amy, Mindy, Andy, Ravi, Brent, and Kendra. In how many ways can she choose her six players?

7. DANCING HEARTS

Pauline had seven dancers to choose from to fill the positions as cards in a production based on *Alice in Wonderland*. The cards were all hearts from the two through the eight. Their names in order from shortest to tallest were Brittney, Alyse, Katie, Aubrey, Wynnter, Jennifer, and Summer. How many different groups of dancers could she set up as the cards?

8. AREAS OF SHADED REGIONS

Find the area of the shaded region. The cutouts on the ends are semicircles.

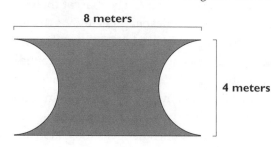

9. MORE AREA

Find the area of the shaded region.

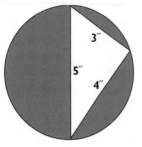

This problem requires some geometry knowledge. Can you determine if 5 inches is the diameter?

10. ATTENDANCE FIGURES

The attendance figures for Durango High were off the last two weeks. Usually there is a 97% attendance rate. However, on Monday it was 91%, on Tuesday it was 94%, on Wednesday it was 93%, on Thursday the attendance was 95%, and on Friday it was 92%. How many student-days were missed last week? (The enrollment is 1800 students.)

11. LIGHT BEARINGS

Sitting in a box are 141 ball bearings. A quality control worker claims that he accidentally dropped a defective ball (too light) into the box. Using a balance scale, what is the minimum number of weighings it will take to find the defective ball?

12. HEAVY BEARING

You have 12 ball bearings, 1 of which is heavier than the others. What is the minimum number of weighings you must do on a balance scale before you can be certain of finding the heavier one?

13. PADUCAH HALF-TIME

The twelve cheerleaders of Paducah High School do a maneuver at half-time. They run onto the field and run in a circle around the mascot. As the first person runs by, the mascot raises one paw. When the second person runs by, the mascot raises the second paw. The mascot then lowers both paws at once, pointing at the third cheerleader going by. As the mascot points, that cheerleader peels off and goes over to the 50-yard line where they will start another routine. The cheerleaders continue to run around the mascot in a circle, and the mascot repeats its actions until all 12 cheerleaders have peeled off. The 12 are Alex, Bobbi, Chris, Darryl, Evan, Fran, Gabby, Henny, Izzy, Jackie, Kris, and Les. In what order should they line up off-field in order to peel off in the correct order (which happens to be alphabetical order)?

14. WALKING HOME FROM SCHOOL

Every day mom used to sit on the front porch and wait for us to walk the 3 miles home from school. It took us about 45 minutes to do it. Our dog, Denny, waited for us at school every day. As soon as we came out he would greet us and then run home. It only took him about 10 minutes to get home. As soon as he told mom we were out of school, he would come back and meet us on our way home and then turn around and run home to report to mom on our progress. He continued doing this the whole time we walked home, even as we turned the corner at Mr. Jansen's house and came up the front walk. How far did Denny run each day?

15. MORE TOOTHPICKS

Using six toothpicks, make six triangles of the same size.

16. PERFECT CUBES

How many perfect cubes are there between 100 and 10,000,000?

17. SOME COMPLEMENTARY EVENTS

Find the complementary event for each of these situations:
a. A family has three kids, all girls.
b. The Family family watches three movies, all with "Friday the Thirteenth" in the title.
c. You find six coins, and none of them are dimes.
d. You meet four new people this last week and all are from Pennsylvania.

18. RUNNING GEORGE

George tries to run every day. He realizes that his body needs a break from running about twice a week, and usually his day-to-day schedule takes care of those breaks. He normally runs 6 miles each day. However, last week he couldn't run on Monday because he had to take Sue to the airport. On Wednesday, he cut his run short about 1½ miles because he twisted his ankle on an icy sidewalk. He then missed Thursday, but ran every day the rest of the week. He also cut his Saturday run short by 2 miles to make sure he could get Emily to her soccer game on time. How far did George actually run this week?

19. IS SHE, OR ISN'T SHE?

Brand A early pregnancy test is accurate 92% of the time when it shows positive. Brand B is accurate 95% of the time when it shows positive and accurate 87% of the time when it shows negative. If a woman tests positive with brand A and negative with brand B, what are the chances she really is pregnant?

20. ALPHABET FLASH CARDS

A deck of alphabet flash cards has 26 cards in it. Try this challenge: Count off the cards. As you count the first 2, place them on the bottom of the deck. The third one is placed face up on the table. Continue doing this until all 26 cards have been laid down. In what order would the cards have to be arranged to be laid on the table in alphabetical order?

21. ORGAN TRANSPLANTS

The one-year survival rate for heart transplant recipients is 82%. The one-year survival rate for lung transplant patients is 67%. The heart patient survival rate for the second year is 91%. If someone were to have a heart transplant with a lung transplant scheduled for a year later, what are the chances that person would still be alive two years after the heart transplant?

Problem Set B, Version 2

The Treasure of Mount Nessum-Sar

1. RECTANGULAR TILES

The tomb of Queen Neiledam is reputed to hold the missing clues leading to the buried treasure of Mount Nessum-Sar. By using the tiles described below, form a rectangle—no overlaps, no gaps. This rectangle is placed on the floor of the crypt. The scroll buried with the queen will reveal where to hold a torch, the light of which will reflect off the surface of the tiles onto the rough texture of the western wall of the crypt. The resulting design will be a map leading to the location of the buried treasure.

The dimensions of the tiles are as follows:

$9 \times 11, 11 \times 13, 7 \times 13, 5 \times 9, 4 \times 5, 2 \times 5,$
$2 \times 8, 4 \times 8, 3 \times 9, 5 \times 6, 5 \times 12, 1 \times 20,$
$2 \times 9, 2 \times 9, 4 \times 7, 4 \times 7, 4 \times 7$

Form these small rectangles into a large rectangle, then go search for the treasure.

Unfortunately, after you solved this problem, you did not have the map revealed to you. Instead, a great genie appeared. He said, "I am the great Tenneb. If you can solve the next puzzle, I will show you the map that leads to the buried treasure."

2. CONSECUTIVE INTEGERS

"Tell me," said the genie, "all of the integers between 1 and 600 that can not be represented as the sum of 2 or more consecutive positive integers."

"I don't understand," you protested.

"All right," Tenneb replied, "I will give you an example: 3 can be represented as 2 + 1 and 12 can be represented as 3 + 4 + 5. But I want all the numbers that cannot be represented in this way."

Find all such numbers.

After you solved the last puzzle, Tenneb turned to you and said, "Well, little one, you did very well. But I have another puzzle for you. If you solve this one, I will lead you to the treasure personally."

3. ALPHABETICAL NUMBERS

"Write out the numbers from 100 through 999 in alphabetical order. (By the way, don't use the word 'and.' So, for example, write the number 431 as four hundred thirty-one.) Next to that list, write the numbers from 1 through 900 in numerical order. Which number(s), if any, occupy the same position in both lists?"

"But writing out all those numbers could take all night," you protested.

"Well then, little one, see if you can find the answer without writing out the whole list."

"Very good," the genie said when you finished. "Now I have just one more puzzle for you. If you solve this one, there will be a big surprise in store."

4.   SAY THE MAGIC WORD

"I am thinking of five words," the genie said. "The five words are

PINT   RATE   TURN   NEST   WIND

"One of these words is the magic word. Your task is to figure it out."

"I need a hint," you said.

"All right," Tenneb said. "If I tell you any one letter in the magic word, then you can tell me the number of consonants in the magic word."

What was the magic word?

You solved this puzzle too and said, "Okay, I am ready for my big surprise. What is it?"

"Little one, you are in for a big surprise."

5.   WHERE SHOULD YOU STAND?

You were shown into a great cavern. "Counting yourself, there are 350 people in this cavern," the genie said.

You looked around and said, "These don't look like people, they look like mummies."

"Yes, they are mummies, little one. If you can't solve my next puzzle, you may become one of them. You will all line up in a single line. I will go down the line and count 1, 2, 3, 4, 5, 6, and so on. Every even-numbered person (or mummy) will step out of line. Whenever I reach the end of the line, I will go back to the beginning of the line and continue counting from wherever I left off. The even numbers will still step out of line. The last person left in line will get the buried treasure. You can stand anywhere you want, little one, but choose wisely."

The genie then shouted, "Line up," as you worked furiously trying to figure out what position to be in. The mummies all began to shuffle into position. The genie turned to you and said, "Well, little one, where do you wish to stand?"

What position in line is the lucky winner?

Problem Set B, Version 3

1. LARGE CORPORATION

In a certain corporation, ⅔ of the employees are men; the rest are women. Of the men, ⅝ are college educated; the rest are not. Of the women, ⅖ are college educated; the rest are not. Of the college-educated employees, ⅚ are in management. Of all non-college-educated employees, ⅑ are in management. Of all managers, ⅓ are women. If all of the college-educated women are in management, what percentage of the non-college-educated managers are women?

2. MOVIE STARS

Four people starred in a movie. Their first names are Bill, Ted, Grim, and Don. Their last names are Preston, Logan, Reaper, and Thanes. Their shirts are either red, green, yellow, or blue. The pattern on the shirt is either plain, striped, checkered, or print. Four kids watching the movie made comments about the people in the movie. Each comment referred to all four actors.

Kid 1: I saw Bill, a person in a plain shirt, Logan, and a person in a green shirt.

Kid 2: I saw Preston, a person wearing a blue shirt, another wearing a yellow shirt, and Ted.

Kid 3: I saw Grim, a person wearing a checkered shirt, a person wearing a red shirt, and Don.

Kid 4: I saw a person wearing a print shirt, a person wearing a red shirt, Grim, and Reaper.

Ted is not wearing the red shirt. Don is not wearing the plain shirt. Logan is not wearing the yellow shirt. Determine each person's full name and color and style of shirt.

3. SUMSUMS

The sumsum of a number is the sum of digits of the number added to the number itself. So the sumsum of 15 is 6 + 15 = 21. How many of the numbers from 1 to 500 are sumsums of some other number?

4. WRESTLING NEWSLETTER

Beth loves to watch wrestling on TV. She has a bunch of friends who like wrestling too. Beth gets to watch it more than they do though, so she often writes a short newsletter detailing the results of the day. The other day she caught the tail end of a wrestling match in which a wrestler named Mango Mulch beat another wrestler named Gyurk. Gyurk was so sad that he cried. Beth wrote the article for the newsletter and used this headline.

MANGO MULCH BELTS GYURK: WHINE

After she wrote the headline, Beth noticed that her headline contained five 5-letter words. The weird thing was, there is another 5-letter word that shares exactly two letters with each word in the headline. What is that word?

In the figure below are circles connected with lines that form a whole bunch of triangles. You are to fill in the circles with the digits 1 through 9. When you are done, each triangle will form a 3-digit number such that the difference between the smallest digit and the second smallest digit is greater than 2, and the difference between the second smallest digit and the largest digit is greater than 2. For example: one of your numbers could be 418, because the difference between 1 and 4 is 3 (more than 2) and the difference between 4 and 8 is 4 (also more than 2). On the other hand, 863 could not be one of the numbers. The difference between 3 and 6 is 3, which is fine, but the difference between 6 and 8 is only 2. The digit 3 has been placed to get you started.

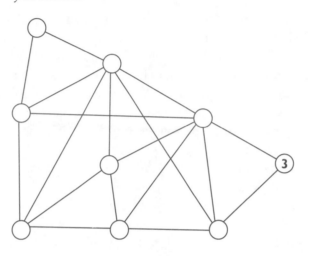

Problem Set B, Version 4

1. REUNION

Five people attended a high school class reunion. To get there, one person traveled for one hour, another person traveled for one and a half hours, another for two hours, another for two and a half hours, and the last for three hours. Three of the people came in the same car (with one person driving the car and picking up the other two people at different places along the way). The other two people came in a plane (with one person flying the plane and picking up the other person along the way). The car and the plane each traveled at a constant speed, and the plane's speed was five times the car speed. Each person traveled a whole number of miles, and the 5 people traveled a total of 1342 miles. What was the speed of the car? (Note: Travel times do not include stops and starts or takeoffs and landings or acceleration and deceleration.)

2. BAND

A marching band director is deciding what sort of rectangular arrays her band can form. She is interested in rectangles that have the same number of band members standing on the outside edge as the number of band members standing in the interior. What are the possible dimensions of rectangular arrays that allow this?

3. POKER

Five poker hands were dealt, each containing five cards.

The first hand had a full house, which included two kings. This hand had the six of clubs, which was the only black card in the five hands.

The second hand had a diamond straight flush.

The third hand had a straight. This hand could have been a straight flush that would have beat hand two, but the highest card was the wrong suit.

The fourth hand had two pair. All five cards were of equal or lower denomination than any card in any other hand, and lower than the two unused red cards.

The fifth hand had a heart flush.

Determine the cards in each of the five hands.

Note: a full house features two of a kind and three of a kind. A straight is five cards in consecutive order, but not all five cards are in the same suit. A flush is five cards of the same suit. A straight flush is five cards of the same suit in consecutive order. Two pair is two different sets of two of a kind and a fifth card that does not match either pair. The highest ranking card is the Ace, followed by the King, Queen, Jack, ten, nine, etc., down to two. An Ace can be used as a low card or a high card in a straight (such as A, 2, 3, 4, 5, or 10, J, K, Q, A).

4. DICE PRODUCTS

Kathlan is a third grader in Ms. Latimer's class. Yesterday Ms. Latimer gave the class an assignment to practice their addition and multiplication. Each student was given a pair of dice. The students were to roll the dice and multiply the two numbers together. They were to do this seven times and then add up the seven products. Kathlan did this and got a total of 39. She noticed that none of her products were repeated. What is the probability that her list of products included an 8, a 15, or both?

5. BOOK CHOICE

Max works in the library. Every day before he goes home he wants to pick a book to read at home. (He reads a book every day.) This week he is interested in science fiction. The science fiction books are arranged in alphabetical order by author's last name. It turns out that there are 13 books with author's names for each letter of the alphabet: There are 13 books with author names starting with A, 13 with B, etc. Max has a strange way of picking out the book he will read. Every day he does it differently. Today he uses this system. He walks down the row of books and takes out every second book and throws it on the floor. When he gets to the end of the row, he goes back to the beginning. If he throws out the last book in the row, then he skips the first book when he starts again at the beginning. If he skips the last book, then he throws out the first book and continues, throwing every second book on the floor. He continues in this way until there is only one book left on the shelf. That is the book that he takes home to read (after picking all the books off the floor and arranging them back on the shelf again). What is the first letter of the last name of the author of the book he chose?

17 other forms of spatial organization

M ANY PROBLEM-SOLVING strategies revolve around organizing information spatially. Spatial organization accentuates different aspects of a problem so that our strong visual sense and visual experience become more involved in solving the problem. Graphs are one form of spatial organization. Instead of (or in addition to) organizing data in a chart, you can use a graph to organize data in a picture. Organized this way, the data is worth a thousand words. Higher-level thinking skills like graphing data and interpreting graphs are becoming more important as technology takes more of the burden of computation.

Besides making a graph, other strategies that rely heavily on some form of spatial organization include drawing a diagram, physical representations, and Venn diagrams. Scale drawings also appear in this chapter.

This chapter and strategy abound with practical implications. Each of the problems in the first half of this chapter could be a realistically solved by graphing, with the possible exception of the telephone bill problem (why not just call the phone company or look in the phone book to find out their rates?).

Problem Set A includes a number of problems that you might view as trigonometry problems. Encourage your students to make scale drawings instead of using trigonometry. (Besides, they may not have had trigonometry.) The experience of using drawings will carry over into trigonometry problems. By making scale drawings, students will not only form mental images of the problem but will also develop organizational schemes for such problems. The skills and experience of drawing appropriate diagrams will give the students insights to complement a trigonometric approach.

Notes on Text Problems

CHICKEN NUGGETS

The most convincing solutions to this problem tend to be those where graphs and algebra are combined. We believe something more readily if we can see it, and the graph makes that possible.

PHONE CALLS

You may wish to discuss step functions with the students. The phone call charges function is an excellent, easy-to-understand example of a step function that comes from real life.

VACATION

The main feature of this problem is that graphs can be used to extend data, both between known data points and beyond the boundary of known data points.

ROSEVILLE HIGH SCHOOL

Graphs are proof that "seeing is believing." In this case, the graph makes "seeing is doubting" a reality, also.

Text Problems

A local fast-food vendor sells chicken nuggets for the following prices.

SERVING SIZE	PRICE
6 nuggets	$2.40
10 nuggets	$3.60
15 nuggets	$5.10
24 nuggets	$7.80

Draw a graph of this information. Then answer the questions below.

a. What is the equation for this graph?

b. What is the slope for the graph?

c. What is the real-world significance for the slope?

d. What is the y-intercept for this graph?

e. What is the real-world significance for the y-intercept?

f. How much would it cost to buy a serving size of 50 chicken nuggets?

g. Another restaurant sells 13 nuggets for $4.25 and 20 nuggets for $6.75.

Use the graph to find out whether these are good deals compared to the restaurant above. Then use the equation to check yourself.

Lisa Family just got a new phone installed in her room. Her boyfriend, Ernie, loved to call her, and she needed her own phone because Ed was always monopolizing the Family family phone talking to his girlfriend, Candy. During spring break, Ernie went on vacation. Lisa was very sad, because she wasn't going to see him for five days. Fortunately, she could call him, although it was a long-distance call. During the five days that he was gone, she called him each day. The shortest call was 6 minutes, which cost $1.26. A 7-minute call cost Lisa $2.07. Here's a chart of the other three calls she made to Ernie:

Time (minutes)	Charge
11	$2.26
17	$4.57
22	$4.46

Determine the connect fee and the cost-per-minute for the two rate schedules she called under: day rate and evening rate. (A connect fee is the charge levied the instant a phone conversation begins.)

The Family family wants to take another vacation. They have decided to take their van and drive to a destination that is 600 miles away. Plot a graph that shows various speeds on the x-axis and time spent driving on the y-axis.

FAT CONTENT

You may have seen ads for food indicating % fat or % fat free. For example: "Our burgers are 90% fat free," or perhaps, "Our lean hamburger is only 15% fat." A person reading these ads would probably assume that the percent of calories coming from fat is also only 10% in the first case and 15% in the second case. Unfortunately, this is not the case. The percentage of fat indicated in the ads is percent fat by weight, not by calories. Fat has 9 calories per gram. On the other hand, carbohydrates and protein each have only 4 calories per gram. So, for example, 10 grams of an apple, which is carbohydrates, is only 40 calories. Ten grams of butter (which is fat) is 90 calories. So a person will gain weight a lot faster by eating food high in fat.

Draw a graph that shows the percent fat by weight on the x-axis and the percent fat by calories on the y-axis. Then use your graph to find what percent of fat by weight gives 50% of the calories from fat.

ROSEVILLE HIGH SCHOOL

The population served by the Roseville High School District has grown drastically. Roseville High School itself has grown quickly. The neighboring school, Del Oro High School, has also been growing. Here's the enrollment data for the two schools for the last several years.

YEAR	ROSEVILLE	DEL ORO
1986	1402	1718
1987	1462	1741
1988	1467	1745
1989	1548	1782
1990	1661	1765
1991	1801	1778

Use this to project the number of students for the next five years.

DUCKS AND COWS

Farmer Brown has ducks and cows. The animals have a total of 12 heads and 32 feet. How many ducks and how many cows does Farmer Brown have? Solve this problem with a graph.

INTERSECTION

Find the solution(s) for x.
$$1 + 2^x = x + 5$$
If possible, use a graphing calculator or a computer.

MAXIMUM AREA

A farmer with 100 feet of fence to use wants to build a rectangular garden. What should the dimensions of the garden be in order to enclose maximum area?

DUCKS AND COWS

Farmer Brown has ducks and cows. The animals have a total of 12 heads and 32 feet. How many ducks and how many cows does Farmer Brown have?

Read the following explanation of how to solve the problem with a special kind of scale drawing.

MY PATIO

Make a scale drawing of my backyard patio. I have a rectangular patio that is 18 feet by 12 feet. On the patio is a rectangular lounge chair that measures 2 feet by 4 feet 3 inches and a circular picnic table measuring 5 feet 8 inches in diameter.

Make a scale drawing.

MAYDAY

"Mayday, Mayday!" the call came in. It startled Ned in the Coast Guard office. He immediately got on the radio. "Coast Guard here. What is your position? Over."

"I'm not sure. We left the port at Miami at 7:30. We sailed due southeast for 2 hours at 35 knots. Then we turned about 30 degrees to starboard (right) and sailed for 4 hours at 25 knots. Then we lost our engines and we have been adrift for about an hour and a half. We would have called earlier, but our radio was out. Can you send us some help?"

Ned replied, "I'll work out your position and send out a chopper right away. Over."

"Thanks a lot."

Ned knew that the current in the ocean at that time of day was approximately 5 knots due south. A knot, or 1 nautical mile, equals 1.151 land miles. The helicopter speedometer measures land miles per hour. The likely speed of the helicopter was 80 miles per hour (that is, land miles). In what direction should Ned send the helicopter and how many minutes will it take it to get to the stranded boat?

Make a scale drawing and solve this problem.

Problem Set A, Version 2

1. **DENISE'S AUTO REPAIR**

Sometimes auto repairs take a while because the mechanic has to test a car, let it cool, then investigate the problem. Other times repairs are delayed while the mechanic waits for parts to be delivered. When Denise opened her auto shop, she tried to keep a few cars in the shop so she always had at least one to be working on. Some customers, she found, were very demanding about getting their cars back right away, while others, though they needed their cars, were very patient about waiting. Denise decided to do things a little bit differently. She decided to charge those customers who wanted their cars right away more money and to charge those who were more patient less money. At the time she wanted to make an average of about $20 per hour. The customers who could wait 4 days before getting their car back would be charged only $15 per hour. Those who wanted their cars back within 2 days (48 hours) would be charged $60 per hour. At these rates, Denise figured that she could hire people to do things around her house. For example, if someone was really willing to pay $144 an hour in return for the guarantee of repair within 10 hours, Denise would in turn hire a couple of neighbors to watch her kids after school, cook dinner, clean house, etc., and she could pay them generous rates and still be making some pretty good money for herself. So Denise made up a table:

Denise's Auto Repair
Hourly Rates

Choose the schedule. I will guarantee your
car back within that amount of time

Repair within	Hourly charge
6 hours	$240
10 hours	$144
18 hours	$80
24 hours	$60
30 hours	$48
36 hours	$40
96 hours	$15

a. Graph the information and estimate what she charged per hour for someone who wanted his or her car back within 12 hours.

b. Estimate how much she would charge for someone who wanted his or her car back within 60 hours.

c. Estimate how much she would charge someone who wanted his or her car back within 72 hours.

RUNNING ON M.T.

Marie Taylor (M.T.) runs for health and also trains for middle distance races. Graph these times for M.T.'s various exercise distances.

Time(Minutes)	Distance(Miles)
5.5	1
11.5	2
18	3
27	4
35	5
64	8
108	12
150	15

a. What would be a reasonable time for M.T. to run 18 miles in?

b. If M.T. had timed herself running for 70 minutes, how far do you think she would have run?

3. **KATHY'S CATERING SERVICE**

Kathy is considering opening a catering service. In the beginning, she will only be catering to small groups. In order to get an idea what to charge, she called other caterers to get their rates for various size groups with a comparable menu.

Jake's Catering		Sybil's Slicery	
# of people	Price/Person	# of people	Price/Person
40–49	$11.95	40–59	$11.50
50–69	$10.95	60–79	$10.50
70 and up	$10.59	80–99	$9.99
		100 and up	$9.50

What should Kathy charge for groups of 10 to 19, for groups of 20 to 29, and for groups of 30 to 39?

4. **GROUND TURKEY**

If ground turkey meat is kept at 35 degrees, it is estimated that it will stay good for about 20 days. On the other hand, if it is kept at 90 degrees constant temperature, it is estimated to have a 6-hour usefulness (after that the bacteria count will be dangerously high). Graph the following information:

Temperature	Days
40	8
50	4
70	1

a. How long would you expect the meat to last if it were stored at 80°?

b. How long would you expect the meat to last if it were stored at 30°?

c. At what temperature would you expect it to last 5 days?

5. SELLING SODAS AT THE PARADE

Darlene decided to sell sodas at the parade. She paid $1.20 for each six-pack and $1.50 for ice. She is charging $.35 per soda. What is her break-even point?

6. ANOTHER CUBIC

Solve using a graph: $(¼)x^3 + 3x + 4 = 0$

7. PIZZA

The prices for the local pizza parlor are listed below. Sizes are given as the diameter in inches.

	small (10")	medium (13")	large (15")
Cheese pizza	$6.75	$9.75	$12.25
Special	$10.00	$13.50	$16.50
Galleon	$9.25	$13.25	$16.25
Lighthouse	$8.25	$12.25	$14.50

Graph this information on two graphs. On one graph, plot diameter versus price. On the other graph, plot area versus price.
  a. Which graph do you think is a truer picture of the information?
  b. For each kind of pizza, decide which size you feel is the best buy.
  c. Suppose you were the manager and you decided to offer a mini cheese pizza that would be 6 inches in diameter. What would you charge for it and why?

8. THE CHICKEN COOP

The Family family just acquired 240 feet of chicken wire with which to make an outside pen for their chickens. It will be rectangular in shape, and the wire must only cover three sides, as the existing coop will be the fourth side. Building in a rectangular shape, they want to make it the largest size possible (in area). One possibility for the size of the pen is to make it measure 20' by 200'. What should the dimensions be in order to make the area as large as possible?

9. LAUNCHING ROCKETS

Melissa and her friends Janet, Delbert, and Sharla are launching rockets. Janet's parachute got stuck in a tree. She is going to use a pole (made out of plastic irrigation pipes) to retrieve it. About 40 feet away they measured the angle of elevation for the rocket and parachute to be 33°. She is standing at the point directly underneath the parachute. How long a pole does she need to retrieve her rocket and parachute?

10. ROCKET TO THE MOON

Sharla shot off her rocket. Delbert and Melissa were in charge of figuring out the height. The line from where Delbert was standing to the rocket made a 73° angle from the ground. From where Melissa was standing, 50 feet behind Delbert, it was a 66° angle. How high did the rocket go?

11. TRANSVERSING THE TRIBUTARY WITH CANINES

Rover and his doggy pals are standing on the other side of the river starting to wade in to swim across. You are slightly upriver from the dogs, and your line of sight to the dogs makes an 80° angle with the bank. You then walk about 30 yards downstream and sight again. This time you are down river (compared to the dogs) and it is about a 65° angle. How far across the river must the dogs swim?

12. DELBERT'S LAUNCH

When Delbert shot off his rocket, the friends tried different vantage points. Melissa stood about 100 yards away from Sharla with the launching pad between them on a straight line. The rocket went pretty much straight up, and Sharla measured a 43° angle from the ground to the rocket, and Melissa measured a 35° angle. How far up did Delbert's rocket go?

13. FLYING PAPER AIRPLANES

Melissa and her friends decide to fly their paper airplanes out of the window of a tall building (one that has windows that open). Delbert is part of the ground crew, and Janet is the launch director. Delbert sights the window at a 75° angle from the ground, then backs up 25 feet and sights it again, this time at a 64° angle. How high is the window?

14. JANET'S PAPER AIRPLANE

Janet, one of Delbert's friends, launches the first paper airplane. (See the previous problem, Flying Paper Airplanes.) She watches where it lands. From her perspective, the angle from the side of the building to where it lands is about 68°. How far away from the building does the airplane land?

I.   BOXCARS

Jared works switches in a train yard. He has to get cars from a portion of the train in the right order. He has an engine, a boxcar, a flatcar, a gondola car, and a tanker in that order. He needs to change the order to engine, tanker, boxcar, gondola car, and flatcar. He only has the following section of track to work with:

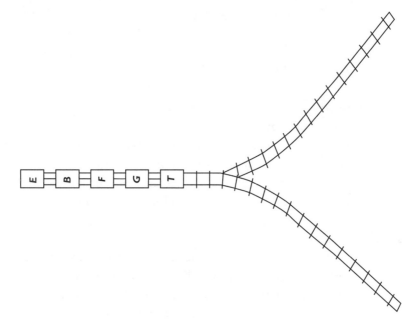

Note that Jared cannot convince the cars to get off the tracks and move into position; he must use conventional railroad backing, unhitching, hitching, switching and driving forward in order to accomplish this. How is it done most efficiently?

2.   THEY'RE TWINS

Sisters Lynn and Laurie play on The QueenAirs basketball team. Last month they had some amazing statistics: They each scored the same number of points. Together, they had the same number of free throws (1 point) as field goals (2 points), and this was also the number of 3-pointers. Lynn had three times as many free throws as she had field goals. Laurie had 5 times as many field goals as she had 3-pointers. They scored less than 350 points total. How many of each type of score did they each make?

3. RUDY'S ROOT BEER

Rudy likes his root beer. Sometimes he has it in the morning, sometimes he likes it in the afternoon. If he drinks it in the morning, he puts ice in it, if he drinks it in the afternoon, he puts ice cream in it. On vacation, Rudy had root beer on 19 different days. If there were 8 afternoons with no root beer and 15 mornings with no root beer, what is the fewest number of days his vacation could be?

4. DIGGING A TUNNEL

Two crews digging a tunnel through a mountain start on opposite sides of the mountain 120 feet apart. The first crew is making about 5 feet of progress per day, and the second crew is making about 4 feet of progress per day. After 4 days, the surveyor discovers that they are digging parallel tunnels, which, if they continue, would be about 35 feet apart. At this point each crew turns toward the other and continues digging. When will the two crews meet?

5. TOASTER SERIAL NUMBER

Crustee Toasters issues serial numbers consisting of two digits, then a letter, then two more digits and a letter. For example, 23UF51T is a valid serial number. The last letter advances consecutively with each new toaster, so 23UF51T is followed by 23UF51U, and 23UF51V, all the way to 23UF51Z. Once Z is reached, the last letter resets to A and the number in the next column to the left increases by one. So the toaster after 23UF51Z would carry the number 23UF52A. How many more toasters will be made after 98BA76Z before all digits and letters in the serial number are different again?

Problem Set B, Version 3

1. BEDTIME

It was late and I was tired and the kids were still up hopping around. I told them to get in bed, but my daughter Alyse said, "It's not time yet." I replied that it was 9:58, but she said "No, it's 8:56." (She was looking at the clock upside down.) How many times in a day can a regular 12 hour digital clock be read upside down and still give a valid time? (Ignore where the colon is or should be.)

2. CLASSIC CAR CLUB

In the newsletter of a classic car club, a note was inserted describing the 16 cars owned by members of the club. Every car is described with at least one of these statements. Among the 16 cars, there were:

1. At least one red convertible.
2. More blue sports cars than red sports cars.
3. Fewer convertibles than sports cars.
4. More blue convertibles than blue sports cars.
5. No convertible sports cars.

Unfortunately, one of cars was destroyed in a garage fire. However, the note in the bulletin was still accurate. What is the description of the car that was destroyed?

3. BACK IN SHAPE

Jody seriously needed to get back in shape. She also had a lot of yard work to do, so she decided to combine the two needs into one project. She decided to dig and move wheelbarrows full of dirt. On the first day, she dug and moved ½ a wheelbarrow full. On the second day, she dug and moved ⅓ of a wheelbarrow full and then ⅔ of a wheelbarrow of dirt. That was enough work. On the third day, she dug and moved dirt by fourths of a wheelbarrow: She moved ¼ as a warm-up, and then ²⁄₄ and ¾ as her exercise. She continued doing this, building up the denominator and starting with light loads as warm-ups and coming close to moving one full wheelbarrow on the last move, but never quite making it. The fourth day she dug and moved ⅕, ⅖, ⅗, and ⅘ wheelbarrow loads. She did this for a total of 47 days. How many wheelbarrow loads of dirt did she dig and move in that time?

4. THE WEDNESDAY CLUB

The Wednesday Club was named for the day of the week it met. Soon after it formed, however, the Wednesday Club also started another meeting on Tuesday for members and prospective members who could not make the Wednesday meetings. Since the club was so flexible, it soon expanded to Thursday, and some members who came to the Wednesday meetings or Tuesday meetings started coming to the Thursday meetings. Others went to either the Wednesday, Tuesday, or Thursday meetings only, some went to two meetings and some went to all three. Well, obviously a club this good couldn't be kept a secret, and membership and demand expanded the club to all days of the week. And on some days there were even different sections meeting. For example, the Wednesday Club Book Section met Friday at 1:00 and the Wednesday Club Skateboarders Section met Tuesday at 2:00. The Wednesday Club Movie Section met on Mondays at 4:00 and so on—I think you get the picture. (Occasionally the Wednesday Club even got together on Friday to watch a videotape of Monday Night Football: Thursday Edition.) Well, as it turned out, in one particular week every member attended at least one meeting. One member attended all meetings, and no identical set of members attended any two of the same meetings during the week. There were 8191 meetings during that week. What is the minimum number of members needed to accomplish this amazing occurrence?

5. WOLF MOUNTAIN SKIER'S PLAN

Weekend skiers at Wolf Mountain can register under a "frequent skier" program to receive 3 points towards a free lift ticket. Weekday skiers receive 10 points towards a free lift ticket. Julie, Justin, and Jamie together received 101 points this last season. Each skied the same number of days, but they didn't all go on the same days. How many weekdays and how many weekend days did they collectively ski?

Problem Set B, Version 4

1. HUESOS DE GALLO

My word has exactly two letters in common with each of these words. What is my word?

blaze   gravy   quilt   ghost   chump

2. WOLFIES ON THE RUN

The offense for the Wolfies is bad. They scored a touchdown in each of 13 different football games, but they never scored a touchdown in both halves of any game. Touchdowns in the first half were followed by scoreless second halves and touchdowns in the second half only occurred if the first half was scoreless. There were 11 scoreless first halves and 12 scoreless second halves in all. How many games did the Wolfies play this season?

3. WHEAT FIELD

County Road 12 runs straight north-south from Brighton to Chester. John is on County Road 17 (which runs east-west) about 3 miles from the intersection of the two roads and is going to walk home. Her house is 5 miles south of the intersection. John cuts across the wheat field to a point on County Road 12 so that half of her trip is through the wheat field and half is on County Road 12. How far does she go using this route?

4. DIGITAL CLOCK

In my bathroom, there is a mirror. If I look through the mirror while I am shaving, I can see my digital clock. The clock is a 12 hour clock. Sometimes the time that I see in the mirror causes me to panic because I think it is the actual time, when in fact it is actually a different time. For example, 852 when reflected in the mirror becomes 528, which is a legitimate time, but not the real time. (I can't see the colon that separates the hour from the minutes.) How many times per day (24 hours) does the clock in the mirror read a time that could be a real time but is not the actual time?

5. PERFECT SHUFFLE

A perfect shuffle is defined as follows: You separate the deck of cards into two equal piles with the top half of the deck in the left pile. Then you intersperse one card from each pile throughout the whole deck. So after the shuffle is over, the top card of the left pile is on top, with the top card of the right pile under it. The third card is the second card from the left pile, the fourth is the second card from the right pile, then third card from left pile, third card from right pile, and so on throughout the deck. How many perfect shuffles does it take to get a 52 card deck back into the order it was in before you started shuffling?

final exam options

YOU MAY OR MAY NOT choose to give a final exam, depending on whether you think it would be useful and whether your school's schedule allows you to give students adequate time. You and your students should not view this final in the same way you might view final exams in traditional courses. Whereas final exams are typically used strictly to evaluate students' accumulation of knowledge over a semester and account for a large part of students' grades, the problem-solving final is designed more to provide students with a final chance to apply what they've learned to a new situation: Most problems on the final are different (some are quite difficult) from those students have solved before and for the first time students will be solving problems under a time constraint. As students have worked in groups all year, we allow them to work in groups on the final. (There's no way to allow students enough time to do a final unless they work in groups. If you don't want to give a group final, we suggest you don't give a final.) In this way too the final is different in that students receive a group grade. We count the final as just 10% of a student's grade so students see evaluation as an important, but not overriding goal of the final; they take it seriously, but they don't feel the same level of pressure they might associate with finals in other classes. In fact, students look forward to the final as a chance to "show their stuff" and see for themselves what they've gained from the course. Many students have told us that the final was a fun way to end the semester.

Give students several days before the final to form groups of five or four people with whom they want to work on the final. As groups work on the final, they'll find their own efficient ways of working together, but you might suggest students start by tackling the problems in pairs and presenting a solution to the rest of the group to check the work. It should be obvious to students that every group member has a stake in questioning and checking the work of their peers.

We have not included here a ready-to-copy final exam that you can give your students. Instead we present families of problems from which you can choose. We chose six problems of which students had to do five in a 2-hour exam period. If you choose to use these problems, you'll either have to retype them or cut and paste. We felt this format, though perhaps inconvenient mechanically, would make it easiest for you to choose problems appropriate for your class. Likewise, you'll probably want to write your own directions for the final. These are the directions we use for the final when we give it:

Directions

You may use this paper to do scratch work, but any work that you want me to read for credit must be on the group paper with all of the names of members of your group. Write up one solution to each problem for your group. The problems are worth 10 points each and will be graded the way problem sets are graded, so be sure to show and explain all work and strategies used.

You only have to do five of the six problems. Do a good job on those five. If you have time, you may write up the other problem for 5 points extra credit. If you do turn in all six problems, clearly indicate which problem should be considered extra credit. Relax, have fun, and work together.

When you make the final, make a version with all of the problems on one or two pages and make enough copies for individual students. Also make a version with one problem to a page and space at the top of each page for four or five group member names. Each group gets one copy of this six-page version. They will turn in their work on these pages. If you copy each problem on a different colored paper you'll find them easier to sort and you can grade every group's solution to one problem at a time. If you do this (and even if you don't) make sure group member's names appear on every page!

The problems are arranged in families, which are separated by lines. Don't pick more than one problem from a family. The idea is that you can pick a different problem from a given family the next time you give a final. The problems are also rated by difficulty on a scale of 1 to 4, with 1 being easy and 4 being hard. Try to pick a mixture of difficulties.

Strategies are suggested for each problem, but don't suggest strategies to the students. The strategies are here for you so you can pick a variety of strategies for the problems for the final. Don't tell students the difficulty factor either.

RIVER CROSSING

A group of 24 adults and 36 children comes to a river that they wish to cross. They find a small boat that will hold 1 adult or 2 children. Everyone is able to row the boat. How many trips will it take for everyone to get across the river?

Strategies: manipulatives, act it out, look for a pattern, easier related problems, maybe finite differences, although finite differences aren't necessary
Difficulty: 2
Answer: 165 trips

RIVER CROSSING

A group of 34 adults and 27 children comes to a river that they wish to cross. They find a small boat that will hold 1 adult or 2 children. Everyone is able to row the boat. How many trips will it take for everyone to get across the river?

Strategies: manipulatives, act it out, look for a pattern, easier related problems, maybe finite differences, although finite differences aren't necessary
Difficulty: 2
Answer: 187 trips
Note: trips = $4a + 2c - 3$

MATH MAGIC

A man has 11 cards. On each card, he has written a positive whole number. He then asks you to say any whole number from 1 to 2000. You tell him a number. He then shows you a certain number of the cards he is holding. The numbers on the cards he shows you will add up to exactly whatever number you said. This always works, for any number you say from 1 to 2000. What numbers are on the cards?

Strategies: look for a pattern, systematic list, eliminate possibilities, work backwards
Difficulty: 3
Answer: Cards should be numbered 1, 2, 4, 8, 16, 32, etc. up to 1024. The last card can actually be less than that as long as the sum of all cards is greater than or equal to 2000.

In a precalculus class at the University of Nevada Las Vegas there were 75 students. Every student in the class had a calculator. Every calculator was either a Casio or a Texas Instruments (TI). There were nine more TIs than Casios. Four times as many students had non-graphing calculators as had graphing calculators. Ten students had graphing TIs. How many students had non-graphing Casios?

Strategies: Venn diagrams, systematic list, algebra, organize information
Difficulty: 2
Answer: 28

PARTY

There are 48 people at a party. There are 7 times as many adults as children. There are twice as many females as males. If there are 5 girls (female children) at the party, how many men (male adults) are there?

Strategies: Venn diagrams, systematic list, algebra, organize information
Difficulty: 1
Answer: 15

TOY CAR RACE

Jack, Jill, and Tom each have a battery operated toy car. The cars always travel in a straight line at a constant rate of speed. They decided to have a race. Each car started at the same time at the beginning of a straight race course. When Jill's car crossed the finish line it was ahead of Jack's car by 24 inches and was ahead of Tom's car by 32 inches. When Jack's car crossed the finish line it was ahead of Tom's car by 10 inches. How many inches long is the race course?

Strategies: draw a diagram, work backwards
Difficulty: 2
Answer: 120 inches

LETTUCE EATING SNAILS

Judy has 3 African snails named Sluggo, Pokey, and Lag. Each of the snails loves to eat lettuce. One day, Judy gave each snail the same number of heads of lettuce. The snails started munching away. Each snail ate at a constant rate of speed. When Sluggo finished all of his heads of lettuce, Pokey had 17 heads left and Lag had 26 heads left. When Pokey finished all of his lettuce, Lag had 12 heads left. How many heads of lettuce did each snail start with?

Strategies: draw a diagram, work backwards
Difficulty: 2
Answer: 68 heads

LOTSA NINES

What number times 434782608695652173913 gives all 9's for an answer?

Strategies: eliminate possibilities, look for a pattern, work backwards, guess and check
Difficulty: 3
Answer: 23

A WHOLE BUNCH OF THREES

What number times 17543859649122807 gives all 3's for an answer?

Strategies: eliminate possibilities, look for a pattern, work backwards, guess and check
Difficulty: 3
Answer: 19

DIGIT SWITCH

A bored accountant was sitting at her desk with nothing to do, so she started playing around with her computer. She entered the number 5739216507 and divided it by 2 and noted the remainder. She also divided 5739216507 by 3 and noted the remainder. She also divided it by 4, then by 5 and then by 6, and noted the remainder each time. Finally she divided it by 7 and noted the remainder. Then, since she was still bored, she reversed a pair of adjacent digits in the original number and went through the whole process again dividing by 2,3,4,5,6, and 7, noting the remainder each time. Then she again started with the original number and reversed another pair of adjacent digits and divided and noted the remainders. She did this for every possible pair of adjacent digits. Surprisingly, for one pair of adjacent digits all the remainders were the same as those reached with the original number. Which pair of adjacent digits caused this to happen?

Strategies: guess and check, solve an easier related problem, look for a pattern, eliminate possibilities
Difficulty: 2
Answer: the 9 and the 2

LARGE MATRIX

The matrix below is 100 by 100. Find the sum of all the numbers in the matrix.

6	10	14	18	22	26 ...
15	25	35	45	55	65 ...
24	40	56	72	88	104 ...
33	55	77	99	121	143 ...
.	.	.	.	.	.
.	.	.	.	.	.
.	.	.	.	.	.

Strategies: look for a pattern, finite differences, easier related problem
Difficulty: 3
Answer: 153,510,000

WHAT DO I NEED FOR A "B"?

In Mrs. Stinson's math class, student Mary Taylor (sometimes called MT for short), figured out that her average in the class was 76% right before winter vacation. Up to this point there had been 900 points in the class. Mary really wants a B in the class, so she wants to figure out what her average has to be for the 300 points after winter vacation in order for her to end the semester with an 80% average for all 1200 points. What does her average have to be for the 300 points after vacation for her to get her B?

Strategies: subproblems
Difficulty: 2
Answer: 92%

BATTING AVERAGE

One baseball season, Jose Canseco had been at bat 472 times as of September 1 and had a batting average of .286. He figured that he would have 108 times at bat during the rest of the season. He wanted to finish the season with a .300 batting average. What is the lowest batting average he can maintain for the rest of the season in order to end up with a season average of at least .300?

Strategies: subproblems
Difficulty: 2
Answer: .361

BATTING AVERAGE

A baseball player has been at bat 439 times so far this season and has a batting average of .278. He figures that he will have 171 times at bat during the rest of the season. What batting average does he have to maintain for the rest of the season in order to end up with a whole season average of at least .300?

Strategy: subproblems
Difficulty: 2
Answer: .357

FREE THROW PERCENTAGE

A few years ago, Magic Johnson of the Los Angeles Lakers had shot 200 free throws after 37 games. He had a free throw percentage at that time of .835. There were 45 games remaining to be played in the season, and Magic figured that he would shoot about the same number of free throws per game in those games as he had been shooting in the first 37 games. What free throw percentage did he have to maintain for the 45 remaining games in order to end up with an entire season percentage of .900 (and fulfill the incentive clause in his contract)?

Strategy: subproblems
Difficulty: 3
Answer: .955

STAMPS

The post office is changing over to only 3 denominations of stamps: 19 cents, 8 cents, and 5 cents. What is the largest amount of postage that cannot be made using these denominations?

Strategies: systematic list, pattern
Difficulty: 4
Answer: 22

STAMPS

The post office is changing over to only 3 denominations of stamps: 17 cents, 9 cents, and 5 cents. What is the largest amount of postage that cannot be made using these denominations?

Strategies: systematic list, look for a pattern
Difficulty: 4
Answer: 21

SHUTTLE

A new team sport has been created called Shuttle. In this game, there are 3 ways to score points. A troi is worth 13 points, a gorn is worth 10 points, and a crusher is worth 6 points. What number represents the largest score that cannot be made in this game?

Strategies: systematic list, pattern
Difficulty: 4
Answer: 27

PET STORE

I visited the pet store last week and found two kinds of pets for sale: rabbits for $5 and parakeets for $9. If I had $14 to spend, I could buy one rabbit and one parakeet. If I had $24 to spend, I could buy 3 rabbits ($15) and 1 parakeet ($9) which would be exactly $24. However, if I had $13 to spend, there would be no combination of rabbits and parakeets that would cost $13. Assuming that money is no concern, what is the largest amount of money that I could have and not be able to spend all of it on some combination of rabbits and parakeets?

Strategies: systematic list, pattern,
Difficulty: 3. This seems to be the most understandable of the four problems in this family.
Answer: $31

CCC

Three Civilian Conservation Corp members, Richard, Nancy, and John, are building a rock wall. They have 21 boulders to move across a field. Seven of the boulders are large, weighing 25 pounds. Seven of the boulders are medium sized, weighing 20 pounds. Seven of the boulders are small, weighing 15 pounds. Each worker has a wheelbarrow. They agree to share the task equally. Each person will carry the same number of boulders and the same number of pounds. How did they manage to do this?

Strategies: draw a diagram, manipulatives, subproblems
Difficulty: 1
Answer: There are many ways to do this.

MILK BUCKETS

You have two buckets: a 5-quart bucket and a 3-quart bucket. You need exactly 4 quarts of milk. You go to the store to get milk. They have a large vat of milk and you can fill up your buckets and also pour milk back into the vat. By pouring milk back and forth between the vat and your buckets, how can you measure out exactly 4 quarts of milk to take home? You may not use any other measuring device.

Strategies: draw a diagram, patterns, systematic list
Difficulty: 2
Answer: There are many ways to do this.

MILK CONSUMPTION

Mrs. Robinson has three kids: Alex, Betty, and Chris. Alex can drink a quart of milk in two days. Betty can drink a quart of milk in three days. Chris can drink a quart of milk in three days. The kids are expecting five guests for two days next week. How much milk should Mrs. Robinson expect to need for the eight kids? (Assume that the milk preferences of three children are representative of the five guests' milk preferences.)

Strategies: systematic list, draw a diagram, subproblems, unit analysis
Difficulty: 2
Answer: 6 2/9 quarts

MEXICAN DINNER

For Mandy's graduation her family and friends all went out to dinner at a Mexican restaurant. The restaurant served a bowl of chips for every three people, a bowl of salsa for every two people, and a bowl of guacamole for every four people. There were seven more bowls than people. How many people were at the dinner?

Strategies: systematic list, subproblems
Difficulty: 2
Answer: 91 people

MATH MASTERS

Two contestants were playing the new TV game show Math Masters. Both of them were excellent mathematicians. The host gave them each a positive whole number and told them that the product of their numbers was either 15, 20, 24, or 28. The first contestant to determine the other's number would be the winner. Neither contestant was able to determine the other's number immediately. Both contestants thought about it, made some notes, and finally one contestant was able to determine the other contestant's number. What was the loser's number?

Strategies: systematic list, eliminate possibilities, act it out
Difficulty: 4
Answer: 5

BLACK OR WHITE

Five logicians got together one evening to play some logic games. Their first game involved four players and one emcee who ran the game. The four players were Ryan, Torrey, Michael, and Bonnie, with Janet acting as the emcee. Janet told the other four that she was shuffling four white hats and three black hats and was going to put a hat on each of their heads. Each person would be given a chance to tell what color hat he or she had on. Janet told everyone to close their eyes. She then put a hat on each head and lined people up in single file facing in the same direction. Ryan, the person in the back, could see all the other heads when he opened his eyes. Janet asked him if he knew what color hat he had on. He did not know and said so. Torrey was next in line. She could not see Ryan, but could see the other two. She also said she did not know her hat color. Michael could only see Bonnie, and he said that he did not know either. Bonnie, who was in front and could see no one else, knew the color of the hat on her head and announced it correctly. What color was her hat and how did she know?

Strategies: systematic list, eliminate possibilities
Difficulty: 3
Answer: Bonnie's hat is white

Four people each hold a piece of paper with a positive whole number written on it. Each number is different. The sum of the four numbers is prime. Each pair of numbers has a greatest common factor greater than one. Each of these greatest common factors is different. What is the smallest set of numbers that fit these conditions?

(A greatest common factor is exactly what is sounds like, the largest number that is a factor of the two numbers in question. For example, the numbers 8 and 32 have a greatest common factor of 8. The numbers 114 and 116 have a greatest common factor of 2.)

Strategies: eliminate possibilities, systematic list, patterns, guess and check
Difficulty: 4
Answer: 6, 10, 15, 30

MARCHING BAND

Alyse, Bonnie, Chris, Daniel, Ed, Frank, Gary, Hilda, Irma, Jennifer, Karen, Lucille, Michael, Nam, Olga, Porky, Quincy, Rick, Stefan, Tom, Ulysses, Victoria, Wilma, Xue, and Yentl are all members of the River High School Marching Band. Their band director, Mr. Ryan, wants them to practice a particular maneuver over and over on the practice field. They begin in a five by five square as shown below. Then they execute the maneuver, which leaves them in the positions shown below center. They then execute the maneuver again, which leaves them in the position shown below right. They keep executing this maneuver over and over, and eventually they find that they are all in their original positions. How many times did they execute the maneuver?

Start					After 1 maneuver					After 2 maneuvers				
A	B	C	D	E	K	E	G	B	O	P	O	F	E	S
F	G	H	I	J	L	F	A	C	J	H	L	K	G	J
K	L	M	N	O	P	H	I	N	S	Q	A	C	N	D
P	Q	R	S	T	Q	R	M	D	T	R	M	I	B	T
U	V	W	X	Y	Y	X	V	W	U	U	W	X	V	Y

Strategies: subproblems, draw a diagram, manipulatives, look for a pattern, change the representation
Difficulty: 3
Answer: 60 times

TRIKES FOR TIKES

Two 3-year-olds, Bob and Ray, traveled to a nearby playground with their trikes. They decided to ride back and forth across the playground. Both of them ride at a constant speed (although their speeds are not equal to each other) and they each take no time to turn around at each end of the playground. Bob starts at the west end and Ray starts at the east end of the playground. They start at the same time and ride towards each other. They meet and pass each other 30 feet from the east end of the playground. When they reach the opposite end of the playground, they turn around and ride back towards each other. They meet again 14 feet from the west end of the playground. What is the length of the playground?

Strategies: draw a diagram, work backwards, algebra
Difficulty: 4
Answer: 76 feet

JOGGING ON THE FOOTBALL FIELD

Mike and Troy were jogging out on the football field. The football field is 100 yards long and 50 yards wide. They started at opposite ends of the field, in the corners on the same side of the field. They ran towards each other. Each boy ran at a constant speed, although Mike ran faster than Troy. Mike passed Troy after Mike had run 60 yards and Troy had run 40 yards. They each continued on, and ran all the way around the field, passing each other again at some point. It took Mike 15 seconds to finish his lap after he passed Troy the second time. How long did it take Troy to run around the field?

Strategies: diagram, pattern, unit analysis, maybe act it out
Difficulty: 3
Answer: 112.5 seconds

LONG BLOCK

I was taking a walk one day when I noticed two people walking toward me. I started counting seconds when they were passing a fire hydrant up ahead. From that point it took me fifteen seconds to pass them and another twelve seconds to reach the fire hydrant. Ten minutes after I passed them the first time, I passed them again. I realized that we were each walking around the block in opposite directions. I know that I walk 1 yard per second. What is the distance all the way around the block?

Strategies: unit analysis, draw a diagram
Difficulty: 2
Answer: 1080 yards

On the planet Rigel VII, there are time units of minutes, hours, days, weeks, months, and years. Of course, since Rigel is in a different solar system, the length of time for each unit is different than it is on Earth. The following information refers to these time units on Rigel VII.

There are twice as many weeks in a month as there are days in a week. There are as many days in a month as there are months in a year. There are half again as many hours in a day as there are minutes in an hour. There are 11 times as many hours in a day as there are days in a week. There are 235224 minutes in a year. How many hours are in a week?

Strategies: unit analysis, subproblems
Difficulty: 4
Answer: 99 hours in a week

WALKING TO SCHOOL

Kim walks her daughter Whitney to school every day. Kim's friend Denny also walks his daughter Brooke to school every day. Kim and Denny live next door to each other. It takes each of them x minutes to get to school (and x minutes to get back home) because they walk at the same speed. Normally they leave at the same time and walk together, but today Kim was in a rush and left her house y minutes before Denny left his. Kim got to school, dropped off Whitney and walked back home. At some point along the way, she met Denny walking Brooke to school. At what point did they meet? (Your answer should be in terms of x and y, and clearly state whether your answer is from school to home or from home to school.)

Strategies: easier related problem, draw a diagram, act it out, algebra
Difficulty: 3
Answer: $0.5y/x$ of the way from school to home

PIE EATING CONTEST

Wesley and Gordon had a pie eating contest. Wesley had won the contest last year, so he started with a handicap: he had to start with three more pies than Gordon. To partially offset this handicap, however, he was allowed to start eating 10 minutes earlier. Assume each boy's pie eating rate remains the same throughout the contest (they don't necessarily eat at the same rate as each other). Wesley started eating at 12:30. Gordon started eating at 12:40. They each had the same number of uneaten pies left at 1:00. Gordon finished eating his pies at 1:15. Wesley finished eating his pies at 1:20. How many pies did each boy have left at 1:05?

Strategies: subproblems, algebra, diagram
Difficulty: 3
Answer: At 1:05 Wesley had 13½ pies and Gordon had 12 pies

ANSWERS TO PROBLEM SETS

Chapter 1, Problem Set A

1. WORM JOURNEY
10 days

2. THE UPS AND DOWNS OF SHOPPING
13 floors

3. FOLLOW THE BOUNCING BALL
460 feet

4. FLOOR TILES
320 tiles

5. COUNTING ON NINJA TURTLES
22 turtles

6. DANGEROUS MANEUVERS
Feline to 39 to Bovine, 15 miles
Lupine to Feline to 39, 17 miles
Canine to Lupine to Feline, 14 miles
Arachnid to Canine to Lupine, 18 miles; or Arachnid to 39 to Feline to Lupine, 18 miles
Canine to Arachnid to 39, 16 miles
Lupine to Canine to Bovine, 10 miles
Arachnid to 39 to Feline, 7 miles

7. RACE

Ursula, Alma (3 m behind), Cathy (3 m behind), Lani (2 m behind), Isabel (2 m behind), and Betty (2 m behind)

8. A WHOLE LOTTA SHAKIN' GOIN' ON!

15 handshakes

9. HAYWIRE

Cherlondia to Shirley to Darlene
Carla to Cherlondia to Al to Max
Sylvia to Henry to Carla to Cherlondia to Shirley to Darlene to Wolfgang
Henry to Carla to Cherlondia to Shirley to Darlene to Wolfgang
Shirley to Darlene to Sylvia to Henry
Max to Henry to Carla to Sylvia to Dalamatia
Cherlondia to Shirley to Darlene to Sylvia
Messages can't be routed from Dalamatia to Henry.

Chapter 2, Problem Set A

1. CARDS AND COMICS

Cards @ $1.20	Comics @ $.60
5	0
4	2
3	4
2	6
1	8
0	10

2. FREE CONCERT TICKETS

A = Alexis, etc.

ABCD	*BACD*	*CABD*	*DABC*
ABDC	*BADC*	*CADB*	*DACB*
ACBD	*BCAD*	*CBAD*	*DBAC*
ACDB	*BCDA*	*CBDA*	*DBCA*
ADBC	*BDAC*	*CDAB*	*DCAB*
ADCB	*BDCA*	*CDBA*	*DCBA*

3. IT SURE IS TOUGH TO GET AN APARTMENT THESE DAYS

In the ninth month Plan A costs more ($640 per month vs. $620 per month for Plan B). But for the whole year, plan B costs more ($6990 total vs. $6780 for Plan A).

4. STORAGE SHEDS

8 ft × 8 ft	*10 ft × 10 ft*	*12 ft × 12 ft*	*15 ft × 15 ft*
8 ft × 10 ft	*10 ft × 12 ft*	*12 ft × 15 ft*	
8 ft × 12 ft	*10 ft × 15 ft*		
8 ft × 15 ft			

5. MAKING CHANGE

10 ways

6. FINISHED PRODUCT

First #	Second #
4	90
5	72
6	60
8	45
9	40
10	36
12	30
15	24
18	20

7. KYLE CRAVES CANDY

Five	Ten	Fifteen	Total	Five	Ten	Fifteen	Total
1	0	0	5	7	0	0	35
				5	1	0	35
2	0	0	10	4	0	1	35
0	1	0	10	3	2	0	35
				2	1	1	35
3	0	0	15	1	3	0	35
1	1	0	15	1	0	2	35
0	0	1	15	0	2	1	35
4	0	0	20	8	0	0	40
2	1	0	20	6	1	0	40
1	0	1	20	5	0	1	40
0	2	0	20	4	2	0	40
				3	1	1	40
5	0	0	25	2	3	0	40
3	1	0	25	2	0	2	40
2	0	1	25	1	2	1	40
1	2	0	25	0	4	0	40
0	1	1	25	0	1	3	40
6	0	0	30				
4	1	0	30				
3	0	1	30				
2	2	0	30				
1	1	1	30				
0	3	0	30				
0	0	2	30				

There are 40 ways (or 41 if you count not spending any money).

Chapter 3, Problem Set A

1. SQUARES ROOTS

   66 and 92

2. HOW MANY LINES

   Notice that no upper limit is given. The students should figure out what a reasonable upper limit is. Answer: 47

3. EGGS IN A BASKET

   119

4. DARTBOARD

   23, 58, 31, 6, 15

5. FIND THE NUMBER

   2178 × 4 = 8712; Answer: abcd is 2178

6. WOW WOW, SO COOK!

   757 + 757 + 45 = 1559; W = 7, O = 5, S = 4, C = 1, K = 9

7. NELSON + CARSON = REWARD

   526485 + 197485 = 723970
   D = 0, C = 1, E = 2, W = 3, S = 4, N = 5, L = 6, R = 7, O = 8, A = 9

8. THE THREE SQUARES

   Chris is 19, Phyllis is 23, Bob is 28.

9. TO TELL THE TRUTH

   Dog 1 is undetermined.
   Dog 2 is a truthteller.
   Dog 3 is a liar.

10. RANKINGS

	Height	Age	Weight
1.	Thuy	Jerel	Nick
2.	Miguel	Thuy	Jerel
3.	Nick	Miguel	Thuy
4.	Jerel	Nick	Miguel

Chapter 3, Problem Set B

1. **THE SIDEWALK AROUND THE GARDEN**
172 feet

2. **A NUMBER OF OPTIONS**
24 ways

3. **GOOD DIRECTIONS?**
Go 2 blocks east and one block south.

4. **HIGH SCORERS**
Heather: 25; Sara: 23; Martina: 19; Donna: 17; Kellene: 11

5. **WAYS TO SCORE**
14 ways

Chapter 4, Problem Set A

1. **SCHEDULES**

a. *Jill's schedule*
   1. *Band*
   2. *PE*
   3. *Science*
   4. *Math*
   5. *Lunch*
   6. *English*
   7. *History*

b. *Tom's schedule*
   1. *PE*
   2. *Math*
   3. *Drama*
   4. *Science*
   5. *Lunch*
   6. *English*
   7. *Typing*

c. *Leanne's schedule is impossible as she has to take both Math and PE during second period and has no class to take during seventh period.*

d. *Mea's schedule has many possibilities.*

e. *Part I: Jose's first schedule looks like this*
   1. *PE*
   2. *Math*
   3. *Drama*
   4. *Science*
   5. *Lunch*
   6. *English*
   7. *History*

Part 2: Because first period PE is closed, there is no way for Jose's schedule to work. He won't be able to take Drama because he will have to take Science third period to make his schedule work. So he must pick another elective, either Band or Typing.

Part 3: Now with the new sixth period science class, Jose's schedule will work.

   1   English

   2   Math   *(Note: Math and PE can be switched.)*

   3   Drama

   4   Lunch

   5   PE

   6   Science

   7   History

2. THE FISHING TRIP

Sally first, Larry second, Woody third, Marta fourth

3. CABINET MEMBERS

Georgianne, President; Norma, Vice President; Inez, secretary of state; Paula, secretary of education; Colleen, secretary of treasury

4. VOLLEYBALL TEAM

Elaine, outside hitter, freshman
Kelly, setter, junior
Shannon, middle blocker, sophomore

5. MUSIC PREFERENCES

Jack Mullin, country western; Mike Hardaway, rock; Adele Higgins, jazz; Edna Richmond, classical

6. SUSPECTS

Connie Wilde, purple hair; Pat Theeves, scar; Robin Steele, tall and blonde; Cary Fleece, birthmark

7. ANNIVERSARIES

Jorge married Lorna in May, 11 years ago.
Ahmed married Tori in July, 12 years ago.
Pete married Nylia in June, 13 years ago.

Chapter 4, Problem Set B

1. PHONE NUMBER

492-2804

2. WORTHY SUITOR

14 ways

3. SPORTING EVENTS

> *Ed, baseball, Monday*
> *Judy, frisbee, Tuesday*
> *Mama, golf, Thursday*
> *Lisa, soccer, Friday*

4. THE BILLBOARD

> *7 lines*

5. THOSE AMAZING NAMES

```
    E  L  I  S  A              E  L  I  S  A
    1  9  5  6  8              1  4  5  6  8
 +  A  J  U  D  Y      or   +  A  J  U  D  Y
    8  4  3  0  2              8  9  3  0  2
    ─────────────              ─────────────
    E  D  U  A  R  D           E  D  U  A  R  D
    1  0  3  8  7  0           1  0  3  8  7  0
```

Chapter 5, Problem Set A

1. SEQUENCE PATTERNS

a. 2, 5, 10, 17, **26**, **37**, **50**
   Add next odd number. Or, each term is 1 more than a perfect square.

b. 64, 32, 16, 8, 4, **2**, **1**, **1/2**
   Divide by 2. Or, each term is a descending power of 2.

c. 5, 10, 9, 18, 17, 34, 33, **66**, **65**, **130**
   Multiply by 2 and then subtract 1.

d. 1, 3, 7, 13, 21, **31**, **43**, **57**
   Add the next even number.

e. 2, 3, 5, 9, **17**, **33**, **65**
   *Add the next power of 2. Or, 2, 3, 5, 9, **16**, **27**, **43**. The difference of the differences increases by 1. There are probably other answers.*

f. 1, 5, 13, 26, 45, 71, **105**, **148**, **201**
   Starting with 4, the difference of the differences increases by 1.

g. 1, 2, 6, 24, 120, 720, **5040**, **40320**, **362880**
   Multiply by the next higher number. Or, each term is just n! (n factorial).

2. AIR SHOW

> *400*
> *The pattern is the square of the number of rows.*

3. RECTANGULAR DOTS

$34 \times 35 = 1190$

4. PENTAGONAL NUMBERS

425

Add together a triangular number and a square number. The triangular number has one fewer dots per side than the square number.

5. LAST DIGIT

2^{57} *ends in 2. The pattern goes 2,4,8,6, …*

6. FUNCTIONS

R: rule is subtract 6   S: rule is multiply by 5, then subtract 1
   $5 \rightarrow -1$ $5 \rightarrow 24$
   $712 \rightarrow 706$ $63 \rightarrow 314$

T: rule is to square and then add 1
   $5 \rightarrow 26$
   $895 \rightarrow 801026$

7. SPREADSHEET

A: $x + y$; B: $y - x$; C: $3x$; D: $2x + y$; E: $2x - y$; F: $x + y + 3$; G: $-2y$

8. BEES

231

This is a Fibonacci sequence added up.

9. PASCAL'S TRIANGLE

1, 6, 15, 20, 15, 6, 1
1, 7, 21, 35, 35, 7, 1
1, 8, 28, 56, 70, 56, 28, 8, 1
1, 9, 36, 84, 126, 126, 84, 36, 9, 1

10. OTHER PATTERNS IN PASCAL'S TRIANGLE

Answers will vary.

11. COIN FLIPS

three coins: HHH, HHT, HTH, HTT, THH, THT, TTH, TTT
With 4 coins there are 16 ways.

   If you just look at the number of heads (or the number of tails) the numbers show up in Pascal's triangle. For example, with three coins, there is one way to get three heads, three ways to get two heads, three ways to get one head, and one way to get zero heads for a total of eight ways. The 1, 3, 3, 1 row of Pascal's triangle describes possible 3-coin combinations.

Chapter 5, Problem Set B

1. GOLF MATCH

Diana will tee off second.

2. LEGAL EAGLES

Ostrom, tan, first
Savidge, burgundy, fifth
Stetson, black, fourth
Neumann, blue, second
Schoorl, silver, third
Neumann is a man.

3. COMIC OF THE MONTH

$22.42

4. RUDY'S CLOTHES RACK

7/11

5. ROO AND TIGGER

Roo by 4 feet

Chapter 6, Problem Set A

1. DIMES AND QUARTERS

8 quarters, 13 dimes

2. MARKDOWN

$34.30

3. TAX

$14.49

4. REFINANCING

36 months

5. NEW CONTRACT

32 starts

6. CHECKING ACCOUNT

39 checks

7. WEIRD NUMBER

There are many possible answers. Any two-digit number whose digits add to 12 will work.

8. BASEBALL CARDS

35 cards

9. STAMPS

five 16-cent stamps and seven 7-cent stamps

10. A BUNCH OF CHANGE

14 dimes, 25 nickels, 19 quarters

11. BOYS AND GIRLS

1380 girls

12. HOW OLD ARE RONNIE AND ALAN?

Ronnie is 31. Alan is 47.

13. TRAVELING TO MOM'S HOUSE

40 miles

14. RIDING A HORSE

3 miles per hour

15. FARGO

53.6 miles per hour

16. TELEPHONE SOLICITOR

65, 66, 67 calls all work

17. EQUAL VOLUME

6.75 inches

18. FREE THROWS

There are several possible answers. The "best" (most exact) is 245. Several other answers also work due to rounding: 237, 238, 244, 246, 251, 252, 258

Chapter 6, Problem Set B

1. DAILY ROUTINE

144 days. To double he can switch hands.

2. AFTER THE FOOTBALL GAME

15 people

3. CATS

201 cats

4. THE STOCK MARKET

Nita McDonald, Ford, lost $300
Tina Kortright, IBM, made $200
Luann Edwards, Xerox, made $400
Denise McElhatton, AT&T, made $700

5. LARRY LONGWAY AGAIN

3, 3, and 8

Chapter 7, Problem Set A

1. COFFEE

6 ounces

2. SHARING EXPENSES

Many answers are possible. Each person's share is $8.16. Leroy needs $5.84; Max needs 84¢; Alex owes $5.16; Kulwinder owes $1.16; Bobbi owes 36¢.

3. AIRPLANE SEATS

240 seats

4. SIX SQUARES

42 feet

5. SHADED AREA

$100 - 25\pi$ or 21.46. Note: the ¼ circles are all supposed to be the same size.

6. SAVINGS PLAN

12%

7. TEST AVERAGE

94%

8. CAR TRIP

36 minutes

9. TEST TRACK

8 hours

10. BOX

1620 in.³

11. STYROFOAM CUP

$\frac{19\pi}{3}$ or 19.9 in.³

12. **RED ROAD**

82.5 square units

Chapter 7, Problem Set B

1. **WHO WEIGHS WHAT?**

Phil, 180; Frank, 168; Tom, 173; Devon, 155; John, 164

2. **FAMILY DAY**

23 sections (or 22 sections and 4 rows)

3. **CARROT JUICE**

112 quarts

4. **HRUNKLA APARTMENT HOUSES**

a. Ride belt to SE corner.
b. Ride to eighth floor (or fourth or twelfth).
c. Ride North to NE corner.
d. Ride to seventh floor (or third or eleventh).
e. Ride W to NW corner.
f. Ride to ninth floor.
g. Ride E to friend's floor.

Note: Different routes are possible

5. **NIGHTMARES**

Oct. 31 (Boo!)

Chapter 8, Problem Set A

1. **UNIT CONVERSIONS**

a. 114.8 ft	*b. 51.8 m*	*c. 241.4 km*
d. 29.2 mi	*e. 121.9 cm*	*f. 34.3 in.*
g. 1371.5 mm	*h. 14.3 m/sec*	*i. 18.95 l*
j. 16.9 qrts		

2. **CHRISTINA'S TRIP**

a. 51.6 mi/hr	*b. 29 mi/gal*	*c. $1.19/gal*
d. 75.6 ft/sec	*e. $2.12/hr*	*f. 0.12 qt/min*
g. 3.5 cents/min	*h. 4.1 cents/mi*	
i. 24.4 mi/$	*j. 1.8 gal/hr*	

3. ANOTHER LONG COMMUTE

a. 2.5 gal	b. 1.75 hrs	c. 73.3 ft/sec
d. $1.89/hr	e. $1.32/gal	f. $1.10/pass
g. 3.87 cents/mi	h. 262.5 pass-mi	
i. 105 pass-mi/gal	j. 1.3 cents/pass-mile	

4. RULE OF THUMB

88 mi/hr, 58.7 mi/hr, 73.3 mi/hr
The rule of thumb is to multiply by 1.5.

5. PROJECTILE

a. 102.3 mi/hr   b. 164.6 km/hr

6. PAINTING CHIPMUNKS

Alvin, $24; Simon, $19; Theodore, $18

7. READING RATE (PART I)

0.44 pg/min

8. READING RATE (PART II)

about 20 or 21 books (20.58)

9. NURSING

8.4 cc/hr (would probably need to be a whole number, either 8 or 9)

Chapter 8, Problem Set B

1. WANT A SMOKE?

14 years, 213 days, 1 hour, and 30 minutes (using 365.25 days/yr)

2. SESAME STREET LIVE

17 adults, 13 junior, 90 children

3. CHAIN LETTER

98415 letters

4. WHO WAS SNOOZING?

Charlton was the snoozer.

5. VOLLEYBALL LEAGUE

Buckeyes beat Bombay Bicycle and lost to Sacto Magazine and Red Skeletons.

Chapter 9, Problem Set A

1. DIAGONALS

275 diagonals

2. SUM OF ODDS

25 million

3. TV TRUCK

504 TV sets

4. POTATOES

63 pounds of potatoes; 7 soldiers

5. SQUARE AND HEXAGON

$h + p = T/6 + 4S$

6. TWENTY-FIVE MAN ROSTER

12 infielders/outfielders, 6 starting pitchers, 4 relievers, 3 catchers

7. ODD AND EVEN

500

8. LAST DIGIT

6

9. FIFTY-TWO CARD PICKUP

$2^{52} - 1$

Chapter 9, Problem Set B

1. COVERING THE GRID

30 tiles

2. TUPPERWARE PARTIES

20,475 parties

3. ADDING CHLORINE

$1\frac{1}{4}$ oz

4. JOGGING AROUND A TRACK

every 40 seconds

5. NINE POINTS

84 triangles

Chapter 10, Problem Set A-1

1. THREE ADULTS AND TWO KIDS

13 trips, starting with the two kids going across

2. THE DOG, THE GOOSE, AND THE CORN

There are two solutions, which are virtually identical:

He must take the goose across first, leave it, and go back for the corn. He then takes the goose back to the first side, leaving it and taking the dog across. He leaves the dog with the corn and returns across the river to retrieve the goose.

He must take the goose across first, leave it, and go back for the dog. He then takes the goose back to the first side, leaving it and taking the corn across. He leaves the corn with the dog and returns across the river to retrieve the goose.

3. HOOP RITUAL

45 handshakes

4. SWITCHING JACKALS AND COYOTES

5 trips, the boat starts with the jackals

5. THE HOTEL BILL

The bellhop has $2 that the women had paid. The hotel has $55 from the women, and the bellhop has $2. The women each paid $19, and out of that total, the bellhop has $2 and the hotel has $55. There is no missing dollar.

6. PERSIS' GIFT SHOP

Persis either lost $25 or $32, depending on whether you cost the figurines at $6 or $13.

7. BUCKINGHAM PALACE

a. 16 moves   b. not possible

Chapter 10, Problem Set A-2

8. TWO JACKALS LOSE THEIR LICENSE

13 river crossings. The key to this problem is trading the jackal who can row with one of the other jackals in the middle of the problem.

9. JACK-QUEEN-DIAMOND

Jack of Diamonds, Queen of Hearts, and Queen of Diamonds

10. BASEBALL SEATING

Aisle, Mom, Alyse, Dad, Kevin, Jeremy (or put Mom on the other side of the aisle)

11. MAGIC TRIANGLE

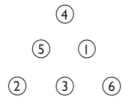

12. MAGIC SQUARES

1	8	3
6	4	2
5	0	7

There are actually a number of possible solutions. Some of the others can be found by switching columns with columns or rows with rows.

13. TRUE EQUATIONS

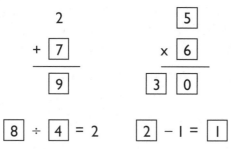

$$8 \div \boxed{4} = 2 \qquad \boxed{2} - 1 = \boxed{1}$$

Switching the 4 and 8 with the 3 and 6 respectively yields another solution.

14. THREE-ON-THREE BASKETBALL

	Team 1	Team 2	Team 3
Center	Horace	Ingrid	Jerome
Forward	Sasha	Tiffany	Taunia
Guard	Leon	Weston	Kathryn

Taunia is the forward on Kathryn's team.
Leon plays guard on Sasha's team.
Tiffany plays forward for a team including Ingrid and Weston.

15. CUBIST

E, right side up in normal orientation (Note: I appears twice.)

16. FOLDING CUBES

Answers will vary.

17. COED VOLLEYBALL

The problem as stated contains contradictory information. One or more constraints will have to be ignored.

18. CHEMICALLY UNBALANCED

$$HCl + Zn \longrightarrow ZnCl_2 + H_2$$
$$2 \quad 1 \qquad\qquad 1 \quad 1$$

$$Na + Cl_2 \longrightarrow NaCl$$
$$2 \quad 1 \qquad\qquad 2$$

$$Al + O_2 \longrightarrow Al_2O_3$$
$$4 \quad 3 \qquad\qquad 2$$

$$Na + H_2O \longrightarrow NaOH + H_2$$
$$2 \quad 2 \qquad\qquad 2 \quad 1$$

Chapter 10, Problem Set A-3

19. VATS THE PROBLEM

There's the same amount of water in the alchohol as there is alchohol in the water.

20. TRAINS FROM SALT LAKE CITY

4 hrs 36 min after first train left

21. CATCHING REMZI

2 o'clock

22. INCHWORM

3 minutes

23. CAN DO

nine 6-packs and three 8-packs

24. SODA

See student lists. There are 27 possible combinations.

Chapter 10, Problem Set B

1. DECREASING NUMBERS

   1013

2. WHITE SALE

   $65.40. She shouldn't have been so happy.

3. KDOG TV

   43.4 hours per week or 43 hours 24 minutes

4. THUNDER AND LIGHTNING

   In 5 seconds sound travels 1.028 miles. The rule of thumb is within 3% accuracy.

5. STATE FAIR

   Foot Massage, empty (ladder sellers), Hot Spas, Computer Horoscope, Encyclopedia Antarctica, empty (vaccum sellers), Slice-It-Dice-It-Veggie-Peeler

Chapter 11, Problem Set A

1. LOSING STREAK

   $9200

2. GENEROSITY

   $252

3. WHAT'S MY NUMBER

   6

4. THE MALL

   She started with $124. She spent $18 on a CD, $53 on a dress, $11 for lunch, $14 on a book, $12 for gas, and $4 on a tape. She gave her sibling $2.

5. USED CAR

   $6000

6. HOCKEY CARDS

   Jack 25, Jill 15

7. DONUTS

   19 donuts

8. GOLF CLUBS

   13 golf clubs

Chapter 11, Problem Set B

1.   HOW MUCH DOG FOOD?
$74.40

2.   THE LUGGAGE RACK
$1.30, and it would take 18 extra minutes

3.   CROSSING THE RIVER WITH DOGS
Odd-numbered trips cross over. Even-numbered trips cross back.
1. *L-Dog, M-dog, P-dog*
2. *L-dog*
3. *L-dog, J-dog*
4. *L-dog*
5. *Mama, Papa, Judy*
6. *Mama, M-dog*
7. *Lisa, L-dog*
8. *Papa, P-dog*
9. *Papa, Mama, Ed*
10. *L-dog*
11. *L-dog, E-dog, M-dog*
12. *L-dog*
13. *L-dog, P-dog*

4.   DON'T FEED THE ANIMALS
62 bags of peanuts

5.   LOST IN PURSUIT OF PEANUTS
north, 45 hours, 10 full bags and 16 peanuts left

Chapter 12, Problem Set A

1.   SENIOR CLASS
45 students

2.   HAMBURGERS AND HOT DOGS
45 like neither.

3.   ROCK BAND
11 band members

4.   EATING VEGETABLES
1, 4, 4, 0, 6

5. THE FIELD TRIPS

88 children

6. FAMILY REUNION

5 cousins were neither nieces nor aunts.

7. JUST WHAT ARE THESE THINGS, ANYWAY?

53 ENAJS are neither DERFS nor ODIFS.

8. BLOOD LINES

76, 12, 4, 24

9. MANY PENNIES

Jason, 18; Matt, 13; Critter, 6

10. BOTTLE CAPS

25 cola, 45 orange, 55 root beer; 125 total

Chapter 12, Problem Set B

1. HOLIDAY PASTRIES

84 total. Papa 30, Ed 15, Lisa 15, Judy 10, Mama 4, Dogs 10

2. PRESENTS, OH BOY!

Judy, 59", plastic bag, Legos
Gail, 62", pillowcase, shoes
Randy, 65", newspaper, picture
Lisa, 68", box, belt
Ed, 71", towel, candy

3. LEGO MY PYRAMID

bumps showing, 400; Legos needed, 385

4. THE HOLIDAY PARTY

30 cousins that weren't nephews or uncles, 10 uncles that were cousins but not nephews

5. HOLIDAY DINNER

19 meals

Chapter 13, Problem Set A

1. ALGEBRA THIS TIME

Answers will vary.

2. **MORE COINS**

27 nickels, 19 dimes

3. **SUPPLEMENTS**

58 and 122 degrees

4. **BIKE RIDE**

13⅓ miles per hour

5. **CHAMPIONSHIP GAME**

179 students

6. **FISHING POLES**

Daniel, 8 poles; Gary, 5 poles

7. **CAR WASH**

12 minutes

8. **INTEREST**

$7567.57 (Any answer between $7567.30 and $7567.83 rounds to the correct amount of interest.)

9. **CHEMISTRY**

29.41 gallons of 24% and 20.59 gallons of 41%

10. **LADDER**

about 16 feet

Chapter 13, Problem Set B

1. **ALL IN THE FAMILY**

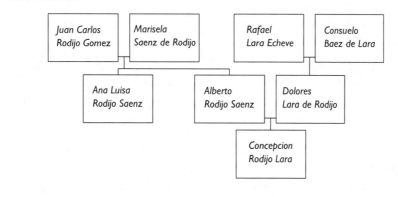

2. **HOW MANY ZEROS?**

1249 zeros

3. VALLEY SPRINGS

4 to 11

4. FORMING PENTOMINOES

12 different pentominoes

5. WHEN I'M SIXTY-FOUR

Start with one, then make sure any subsequent choice of yours and your opponent add up to 9.

Chapter 14, Problem Set A

1. EIGHT FUNCTIONS

a. $y = 7x + 6$
b. $y = x^2 + 5x + 6$
c. $y = 2x^2 - 3x + 4$
d. $y = -4x + 5$
e. $y = x^3 + 3x^2 + x - 2$
f. $y = 6x - 14$
g. $y = x^2 + 2x - 5$
h. $y = 2x^3 - 4x + 1$

2. TRIANGULAR NUMBERS

$y = (\frac{1}{2})n^2 + (\frac{1}{2})n$

3. PENTAGONAL NUMBERS

$y = (\frac{3}{2})n^2 - (\frac{1}{2})n$

4. DIAGONALS

$D = (\frac{1}{2})n^2 - (\frac{3}{2})n$

5. THE GREAT PYRAMID OF ORANGES

22100 oranges

Chapter 14, Problem Set B

1. CELEBRATION TIME

$46.00

2. WILSHIRE BOULEVARD

$A — 27 — B — 15 — C — 21 — D — 48 — E$ *(A = Ardith, etc. The numbers represent blocks between houses.)*

3. FIVES AND ONES

Carol $8, Monica $6, Tomás $5, Andy $4, Jurmaii $2

4. REGIONS IN A CIRCLE

5051 regions

5. CUBS WANT PETS

The second sign (above cat cage) was wrong and a cat costs $27.75. (Fish cost $8 and dogs cost $50.)

Chapter 15, Problem Set A

1. COFFEE STAIN

Adults are $13, children are $7. The 58 should be 53, 57 should be 54, and 110 should be 118.

2. THE THREE OTHER SQUARES

33, 18, 24

3. TWO BILLS

40, 41, 42, or 43

4. FAIR AIRFARE

$198, $204, or $213

5. AHSME

Under both systems, guess on any question you can narrow down to two choices. Under the old system, also guess on any question you can narrow down to three or four choices.

6. TWO-INPUT FUNCTION

$4x + y^2$

Chapter 15, Problem Set B

1. ALGEBRA AND FRENCH

3, 9

2. LOTSA FACTORS

1050 factors

3. DICEY DIFFERENCES

1 occurs in 10 ways

4. MOVIE THEATER

35 moves

5. AREA AND PERIMETER

5 by 20; 6 by 12; 8 by 8

Chapter 16, Problem Set A

1. MORE DOTS

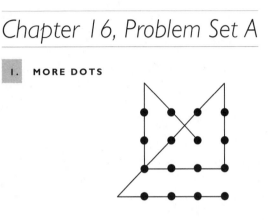

2. FEARLESS FLY

12.5 miles (Change the focus to how long the fly is flying.)

3. TOOTHPICKS

A tetrahedron will form 4 equilateral triangles. (A square with the diagonals is acceptable if you recognize that the diagonals are longer than the sides.)

4. PERFECT SQUARES

97

5. COMPLEMENTARY EVENTS

a. roll a die and not get a six.
b. roll a die and get an even number.
c. roll a die twice and get at least one six.
d. roll a die five times and don't get six every time.
e. There are 40 people in the room and at least two have the same birthday.

6. PAY DAY

$222.50

7. THE LIKELIHOOD OF BEING LATE

Your chances of being late are 6.9%

8. ANOTHER CARD ARRANGEMENT

Put the cards in order from top to bottom: 3, 8, 7, A, Q, 6, 4, 2, J, K, 10, 9, 5

9. **KNIGHT MOVES**
> *a. 16 moves*
> *b. impossible*

Chapter 16, Problem Set B

1. **COMPUTER ERROR**
> *959 numbers*

2. **THE AMAZING RESTIN**
> *STYLE*

3. **BOAT TRIP**
> *15 weeks*

4. **PALINDROME CREATOR**
> *188 numbers*

5. **MULTIPLES**

Chapter 17, Problem Set A

1. **REFRIGERATOR**
> *The major brand refrigerator would be cheaper after 20 months. Refrigerators are expected to last far longer than that, so the major brand should be the most cost effective. She may also want to look at repair records for the two brands.*

2. SODA

restaurant about $.90; mini-mart about $.82

3. LETTUCE

about 4 days

4. APPLE ORCHARD

2.4 hr; 20 hr; answers will vary, around 9 to 12 people

5. JEANNE'S ORIGAMI BOX

44 books

6. CUBIC EQUATION

approximately -3.1, 1.0, 6.1

7. CHRISTMAS TREE LOT

50 feet by 100 feet gives the maximum area of 5000 square feet.

8. BOX

about 66 in.³

9. JAWS

about $5 million

10. MORE PHONE CALLS

day	evening	night
$0.42 $0.33	$0.30 $0.26	$0.22 $0.18

11. BIG PROBLEMS

about 20 weeks

12. SAILING

about 55 minutes

13. YOUR BEDROOM

Answers will vary.

14. TELEPHONE POLE

28 feet

15. STADIUM POLE

73 feet

16. HOW WIDE IS THE RIVER

70 feet

17. **FRISBEE ON THE ROOF**

30 feet, 25 feet

18. **KITE STRING**

97 feet

Chapter 17, Problem Set B

1. **SODA JERK**

21; ¹¹⁄₂₁

2. **LICENSE PLATES**

3024 (The 3025th will have all different letters and digits.)

3. **KAYAKING**

3¼ miles

4. **THE DIGITAL CLOCK AND THE MIRROR**

22 times per day

5. **THE LATTICE**

138 feet

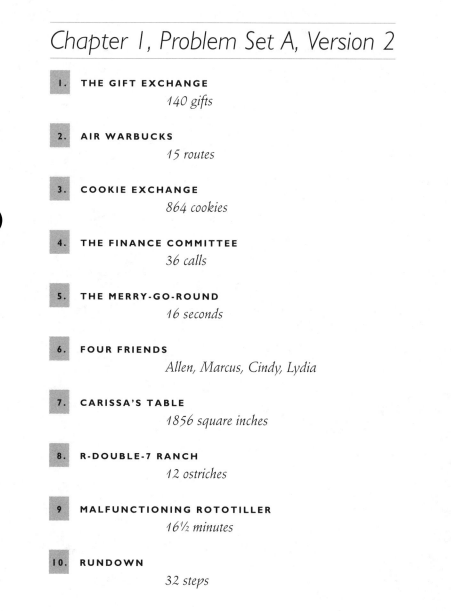

Chapter 1, Problem Set A, Version 2

1. THE GIFT EXCHANGE
140 gifts

2. AIR WARBUCKS
15 routes

3. COOKIE EXCHANGE
864 cookies

4. THE FINANCE COMMITTEE
36 calls

5. THE MERRY-GO-ROUND
16 seconds

6. FOUR FRIENDS
Allen, Marcus, Cindy, Lydia

7. CARISSA'S TABLE
1856 square inches

8. R-DOUBLE-7 RANCH
12 ostriches

9. MALFUNCTIONING ROTOTILLER
16½ minutes

10. RUNDOWN
32 steps

11. THE DOG WHO LIKES TO RUN

6975 feet

12. TRAVELING ART SHOW

30 cities

13. GEORGETOWN RACE

Dusenberg - 8 sec - Model T - 4 sec - Edsel - 3 sec - Studebaker - 7 sec - Pierce.

14. CLASSROOM CEILING

144 panels

15. ARKANSAS CITIES

From Malvern to Pine Bluff: *50 miles by way of Sheridan*

From Camden to Pine Bluff: *72 miles by way of Fordyce*

From Benton to Arkadelphia: *72 miles by way of Malvern and Sheridan*

From Fordyce to Malvern: *95 miles by way of Pine Bluff and Sheridan (remember Fordyce to Sheridan is closed)*

From Benton to Camden: *122 miles by way of Malvern, Sheridan, Arkadelphia and Gurden*

16. WILDERNESS CAMP

They can't get a message to Eugenia because Carl has only found Glenda's camp and she has not found anyone else's.

Hank can send a message (by way of Carl) by sending it to Adrienne, to Freda, then to Carl.

    a. You can't.

    b. Route it through DuJannie and Bart to Glenda or Freda, Carl to Glenda.

    c. You can't.

    d. Route it to Bart, Eugenia, Hank, Adrienne to Freda, or Hank, Adrienne, to Freda.

    e. Send it through DuJannie, Hank, Adrienne, and Freda to Carl, or send it through Eugenia, Hank, Adrienne, and Freda, to Carl.

    f. You can't.

Chapter 2, Problem Set A, Version 2

1. RIDE TICKETS

29 ways

2. LEARNING THE HARD WAY

18 ways

3. RENTING A CAR

The second plan is cheaper up to day 8. He should probably choose that one.

4. WAYLON'S CANDY

11 ways

5. FENCING WITH NEIGHBORS

7 ways

6. ARCADE

The possible scores are 55, 60, 65, 70, 75, 80, 85, 90, 95, 100, 105, 110, 120, 125, 130, 140, 150. (All the multiples of 5 from 55 to 150 except 115, 135 and 145.)

7. RUDY'S SHOT TOTALS

10 ways

8. SKIING BIKERS

34 ways

9. SUBJECT-VERB-OBJECT

168 sentences

Chapter 3, Problem Set A, Version 2

1. SITTING IN THE PARK

14 or 74 people

2. DANCING IN PE

61 students

3. A CUBE ROOT

41

4. LOVE LETTERS

L is 1, B is 9, O is zero. The other digits cannot be definitely determined. The possibilities are summarized below.
If E = 2, then V = 3. Then A = 7, 5, 8, 4 and U = 5, 7, 4, 8.
If E = 3, then V = 4. Then A = 5, 8 and U = 8, 5.
If E = 4, then V = 5. Then A = 8, 6 and U = 6, 8.
If E = 5, then V = 6. Then A = 7, 8 and U = 8, 7.

5. SHUTOUT

	S	O	C	C	E	R
	5	2	3	3	4	0
+	G	O	A	L	I	E
	7	2	9	8	6	4
N	O	S	C	O	R	E
1	2	5	3	2	0	4

four answers but basically they are the same
C and L are interchangeable
E and I are interchangeable

6. THE SECRET TO MONOPOLY

```
  H  O  U  S  E  S     S
  8  7  9  6  4  6     6
+ H  O  T  E  L  S     S
  8  7  3  4  2  6     6
─────────────────────────
C  O  N  T  R  O  L
1  7  5  3  0  7  2
```

very tough
This is the only solution.

7. SCHOOL DAZE GRID

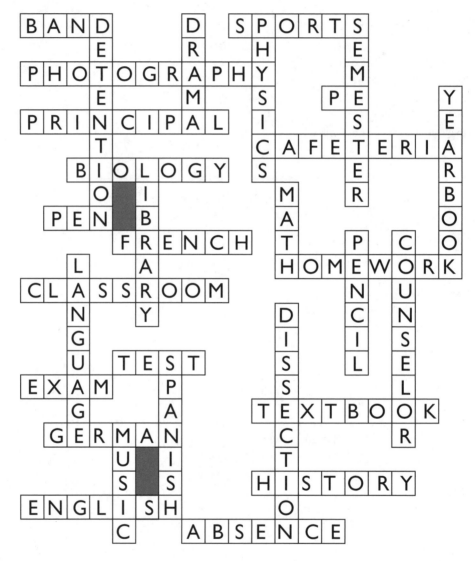

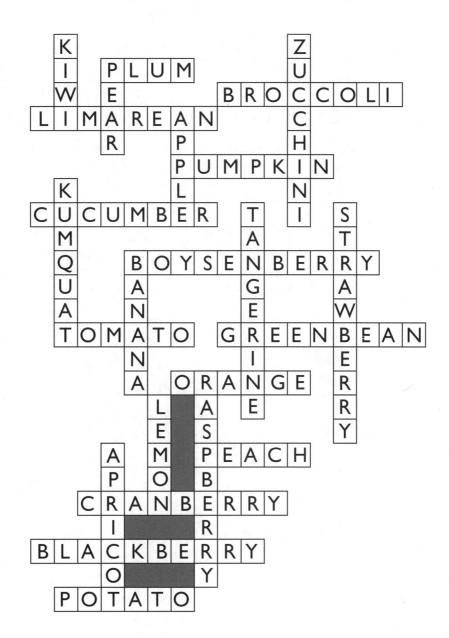

Chapter 3, Problem Set B, Version 2

1. LOG CUTTING

> *12 minutes*

2. WEIRD WORDS

> *30 or 36, depending on if you include* y

3. GETTING AROUND TOWN

> *2 blocks east to 15th, turn left. Go 5 blocks north to I, turn left. Go 3 blocks west to 12th, turn left. Go 2 blocks south to K and you are there.*
>
> **Or**, *2 blocks east to 15th, turn left. Go two blocks north to L, turn left. Go 4 blocks west to 11th, turn right. Go 2 blocks north to J, turn right. Go 1 block east to 12th, turn right. Go 1 block south to K and you are there.*
>
> *Both routes are 12 blocks. First way has fewer turns (3 instead of 5).*

4. SLEEPY BABIES

   BABY = 8781, and YAWNS = 17562

5. VIDEO GAMES

   14 ways

Chapter 3, Problem Set B, Version 3

1. THE BIKEPATH AROUND THE LAWN

   212 feet

2. FAST FOOD

hamburger, fries, coffee	*hamburger, onion rings, coffee*
hamburger, fries, milk	*hamburger, onion rings, milk*
hamburger, fries, soda	*hamburger, onion rings, soda*
hamburger, fries, milkshake	*hamburger, onion rings, milkshake*
chicken nuggets, fries, coffee	*chicken nuggets, onion rings, coffee*
chicken nuggets, fries, milk	*chicken nuggets, onion rings, milk*
chicken nuggets, fries, soda	*chicken nuggets, onion rings, soda*
chicken nuggets, fries, milkshake	*chicken nuggets, onion rings, milkshake*
hot dog, fries, coffee	*hot dog, onion rings, coffee*
hot dog, fries, milk	*hot dog, onion rings, milk*
hot dog, fries, soda	*hot dog, onion rings, soda*
hot dog, fries, milkshake	*hot dog, onion rings, milkshake*

   24 ways

3. A DARING CATFISH

   9 days and 9 nights

4. FIND MY NUMBERS

   13, 17, 19, 23, 25

5. FOOTBALL SCORES

   18 ways

Chapter 3, Problem Set B, Version 4

1. TRAILERS

   24

2. TRAILER PAD

   $35\frac{1}{3}$ ft^3 or 61056 in^3

3. KITE CHASING

8 steps to the right of original position

4. FIELDING PRACTICE

22 ways

5. SLEEPING IN THE TENT

8458 + 1984 = 10442

Chapter 4, Problem Set A, Version 2

1. THE HOBBYISTS

Lisa, model airplanes; Elaine, model railroading; Consuelo, rocketry; and Brittney, tropical fish

2. MIXED DOUBLES TENNIS

Mark Katricz and Sherry Blue Cloud vs. Timothy Amaya and Diana Ostergard

3. SUMMER JOBS

LaTisha, lifeguard; Zack, bagger; Steve, food server; Michelle, construction worker

4. SPORTS IS ALL RELATIVE

Bonnie and Michael, basketball; Ryan, tennis; Stefan, bowling

5. MATH DEPARTMENT MEETING

Fara, statistics; Laurie, finite; Elaine, algebra; Maile, calculus; Cliff, tech math

6. NEXT YEAR AT COLLEGE

Jenny Oslowski, Penn Valley; Akinte Reynoso, Saint Mary's; Chuck Penigar, University of Memphis; Norma Van Hee, Sierra Tech

7. LOOMIS DAY PARADE

first, Wayne, Baton
second, Stacy, Band
third, Mort, Dance
fourth, Cloe, Equestrian

8. STUDENT ACHIEVEMENT AWARDS

Matt Kinsella, Math; Ginny Perata, Computers; Clyde Macomber, English; Velma Sholseth, Physics

9. NOVEMBER ELECTIONS

Margurite Hardy, Governor; Darcie Cusack, Assembly; Brent Tomfohrde, Senator; Amir Wyckoff, President

Chapter 4, Problem Set B, Version 2

1. PACIFIC RIM

28 routes

2 PRIME JACKS

most - Dawn 79 and Ellen 89 can combine for 168 jacks which can be separated into same sized piles in 16 ways.
least - Betty 29 and Ellen 89 combine for 118 jacks which can be separated into same sized piles in only 4 ways.

3. RELATIONSHIPS

John is Mary's grandson; Tina is Bob's daughter in law.

4. TO TELL THE TRUTH

Abe. This is the only thing you can tell for sure.

5. THE ACTION NEWS TEAM

Alex, producer, 20 years
Chris, director, 10 years
Pat, anchor, 5 years
Sam, sports, 15 years

Chapter 4, Problem Set B, Version 3

1 DOOR IN AND DOOR OUT

30 ways

2 JERRY'S AGE

44

3. KLINGONS LIKE WORD ARITHMETIC TOO

	C	R	E	K	L	G
	1	8	4	0	6	5
+R	U	T	A	N	G	
	8	7	2	3	9	5
C	K	G	L	E	L	K
1	0	5	6	4	6	0

4 **THE SHADOW KNOWS**

He needs to walk 8 miles with his shadow in front of him and 2 miles with his shadow on his right.

5 **THE NEW FALL SEASON**

Wall Street Blues, Tuesday, variety
All in Favor, Thursday, news
Murphy's Law, Wednesday, drama
50-50, Monday, comedy

Chapter 4, Problem Set B, Version 4

1. **LUCKY SVEN**

30 prices

2. **LETTER PUZZLE**

0 1 2 3 4 5 6 7 8 9
M A G Y H C W R L D

3. **TWO GUARDIANS**

Door 2

4. **RELATIVES**

Half siblings are Tom and Phillip, Phillip and Jeannine, Jeannine and Nancy, Nancy and Woody.
Step siblings are Tom & Jeannine, Jeannine and Woody.

5. **WAYNES'S WORLD**

Dana Campbell, keyboard; Mike Algar, guitar; Garth Carvey, drums; Wayne Myers, bass

Chapter 5, Problem Set A, Version 2

1. **SEQUENCE PATTERNS #2**

a.	20, 23, 26	Explanations may vary. Add 3 to get the next term.
b.	9, 11, 13	Add 2 to get the next term.
c.	17, 23, 30	Add 1, add 2, add 3, and so on.
d.	19, 31, 50	Fibonacci sequence: Add 2 consecutive terms to get the next term.
e.	22, 35, 57	Fibonacci sequence: Add 2 consecutive terms to get the next term.
f.	20, 16, 25	Double series: One is adding 5, the other is adding 3.
g.	13, 19, 26	Add consecutive numbers to get the next term: (Add 1, then add 2, add 3, . . .)
h.	67, 131, 259	Add consecutive powers of 2.

2. **SPREADSHEET #2**
   - a. $2x$
   - b. $y - x$
   - c. $3y$
   - e. $x + 4$
   - f. $2y - 3$
   - g. $x + y + 1$
   - h. xy (multiplication)
   - i. $x(y - 1)$

3. **FUNCTIONS**

   15 and 435; $I = 3H$

   9 and 322; $R = Q + 4$

   9 and 153; $X = 2W - 1$

4. **THE GREAT SALE**

   717160 people, not including Asa

5. **MMM MACARONI AND CHEESE**

   1/3 of the macaroni and cheese

6. **BIRD AND BEEF**

   2450 customers

7. **MAILING LISTS**

   305,175,781 catalogs

8. **THE ANTS COME MARCHING IN**

   55 ants

9. **PARTY TIME**

   6 weeks (730 parties)

10. **YOUR OWN SEQUENCES**

   Answers may vary. Students can set up the problems as in the text and exchange papers in order to check each others' sequences.

Chapter 5, Problem Set B, Version 2

1. **SOMETHING BUT THE TRUTH**

   Rick, innocent; Louise, accomplice; Manny, main burglar

2. **YALE RECORD CLUB**

   $6.99 for each CD, $3.87 for shipping, and 38 CD's cost $269.49

3. TEN POSTS

600 meters

4. PET STORE CONTEST

$^{11}\!/_{24}$

5. WORLD WIDE WIDGETS

Woody, Wichita, bookkeeper
Ned, Dodge, manager
Gus, Concordia, vice president
Dick, Lawrence, window washer
Jake, Belleville, mailroom

Chapter 5, Problem Set B, Version 3

1. BURBANK NEIGHBORS

Stanley, maroon, fourth
Neuerburg, red, second
Frick, yellow, fifth
Wahhab, blue, third
Stump, green, first

2. KANGA AND ROO

Roo won by 8 feet.

3. BUCKS FOR CLUCKS

Choose egg 3. It's a winner if egg 3 has the true statement and it has a 50% chance of being a winner if egg 1 has the true statement.

4. DOG AND TREES

568 meters

5. PRODUCT OF OUR TIMES

16 times

Chapter 5, Problem Set B, Version 4

1. NEW CAR OPTIONS

53 styles

2. SHEET CAKE

row 5, column 5

3. PLANET THREA

1/5

4. CAMP SACRAMENTO

Lisa Horlick, rings; Danny Horlick, slide; Jaime Walker, tire swing; Justin Walker, monkey bars; Jacob Bland, rock

5. PLAYING DETECTIVE

Joe turned off the light switch.

Chapter 6, Problem Set A, Version 2

1. QUARTERS, DIMES, AND NICKELS

4 quarters, 12 dimes, 16 nickels

2. CHANGE

7 nickels, 10 dimes, and 13 quarters

3. ROCKS

Christopher has 22 rocks, Gordon has 9 rocks.

4. LONG JOURNEY

75 miles. Answer to alternate question: 1½ hours

5. HEALTH CLUB

15 months

6. T-SHIRTS

$7.80

7. CENTRAL VIRGINIA COLLEGE

522 sophomores, 609 freshman; 87 more freshmen

8. MUTUAL FUNDS

$78,300

9. COMPACT DISKS

11 compact disks

10. STICKERS

Cici started with 18 stickers. Amatina started with 54.

Chapter 6, Problem Set B, Version 2

1. SPARE CHANGE

8 ways (or 4 if you don't include 50-cent pieces)

2. THE MATH TEST

1, 30; 2, 15; 3, 10; 5, 6

3. SKI TRIP

$840

4. EXPENSIVE MISSILE

$3,596,182,074

5. COLLEGE ROOMMATES

Glory Alder, black, Chemistry
Helen Carlson, brown, Physics
Joan Daniels, blonde, Accounting
Irene Bonds, red, English

Chapter 6, Problem Set B, Version 3

1. READY FOR "THE SHOW"

3/11

2. BIKE RACE

11 volunteers

3. STORKE TOWER

21 minutes and 12 seconds

4. FAMILY OUTINGS

Erin, President's Day, amusement park, hot dogs
Andy, Memorial Day, zoo, pizza
Jenny, 4th of July, museum, burgers
Phillip, Labor Day, county fair, deli sandwich

5. LUNCH MONEY

He spent $2, $3, and $16.

Chapter 6, Problem Set B, Version 4

1. GRANDPA'S ATTIC

21 grandchildren

2. FROG CHORUS

1908 seconds

3. ROCK, SCISSORS, PAPER

Bonnie wins

4. THE AYER FAMILY

Lucy, 14, August, Monday
Paul, 7, July, Wednesday
Lawrence, 11, January, Thursday
Don, 15, November, Saturday

5. POOR SCORE

Hole	1	2	3	4	5	6	7	8	9	Total
Bob A	4	4	7	2	3	4	4	5	3	36
Bob B	3	4	4	4	5	3	3	4	6	36

Chapter 7, Problem Set A, Version 2

1. MAGNET SCHOOL

$6\frac{2}{3}\%$

2. ORANGES

10 oranges

3. BOYSENBERRIES

$5.76

4. STEREO SALE

$127.58 (or $127.575)

5. LIFE'S NECESSITIES

8 sodas

6. AN "A" IN MATH

She can't. (She would have to get 104.2%)

7. SOIL AND SAND
40 cubic yards

8. ONE HUNDRED SIXTY-EIGHT INCHES OF STRING
360 square inches

9. JUAN'S CHURCH
10.9375%

10. A LOT OF STUFF
7 pounds, 13 ounces

11. SHOOTING PERCENTAGE
60% (12 out of 20)

12. CAMP STOVE
22 minutes

13. ROAD RALLY
32.7 miles per hour

Chapter 7, Problem Set B, Version 2

1. USED CARS
"Lemons cheap and no green people."

2. THE NATURAL LOOK
11/26

3. TYPESETTING
He runs out after 162.

4. A FAMILY MAN
daughter, 23; son, 18; man, 45

5. HOW TO AVOID FALLING ASLEEP IN A MEETING
There were 25 people.

1 left after counting by 6's
1 left after counting by 7's
1 came back after counting by 8's
1 came back after counting by 10's

Chapter 7, Problem Set B, Version 3

1. WHO'S ON THE BENCH

There were 17 people on the bench; the team came in after counting by 3's.

2. GAMUSE PLAYGROUND

Takes slides down to 9th, then 7th, then 5th floor. Take tube up to 8th floor. Take escalators up to 10th, then 12th floor.

3. SIERRA SLUGGERS

KC, 150; Mark, 138; Larry, 149; Jack, 131; Chris, 140

4. BICYCLE TRAINING

20 mph

5. PRIZE MONEY

10th and 11th place win $25,963 each.

Chapter 7, Problem Set B, Version 4

1. MILEAGE SIGN

61 miles

2. A NEW VERSION OF SCRABBLE

A = 2, E = 1, I = 4, O = 6, U = 3, B = 11, G = 1, L = 2, M = 4, N = 5, P = 6, R = 10, S = 3, T = 9, V = 14, W = 8

PROBLEM-SOLVING = 986

3. SLIDE

504 seconds later

4. THREE DIMENSIONAL CHESS

It takes three moves. (There are many ways to make the moves.)

5. LEAKY SINK

21.5 seconds

Chapter 8, Problem Set A, Version 2

1. **MORE CONVERSIONS**

        a. 147.6 ft   *b. 85.3 m*   *c. 402.3 km*

        d. 19.3 mi   *e. 152.4 cm*   *f. 9.4 in.*

        g. 1219.1 mm   *h. 22.4 m/sec*   *i. 11.4 liters*

        j. 21.1 qts

2. **WHAT'S UP DOC?**

        a. $.07/carrot   *b. 7 cents/carrot*

        c. 3.2 ounces/carrot   *d. 5 carrots/lb*

3. **MASON'S TAXI SERVICE**

        a. 33 gal   *b 150 mi/hr*   *c. 220 ft/sec*

        d. $16.65/hr   *e. 16.7 mi/gal*   *f. $15.26/pass*

        g. 11.1 cents/mi   *h. 2200 pass-mile*

        i. 66.7 pass-mi/gal   *j. 2.8 cents/pass-mi*

4. **MARCEL'S TRIP**

        a. 14 gal   *b. 7 hrs*   *c. 88 ft/sec*

        d. $2.32/hr   *e. $1.16/gal*   *f. $2.71/pass*

        g. 3.9 cents/mi   *h. 2520 pass-mi*   *i. 180 pass-mi/gal*

        j. 0.64 cents/pass-mi

5. **COMMUTER FLIGHT**

        a. 9.2 mi/min   *b. 806.7 ft/sec*   *c. 32000 pass-mi*

        d. 44000 pass-mi/hr   *e. 733.3 pass-mi/min*

6. **A SHOT IN THE DARK**

        a. 134.2 mi/hr   *b. 216 km/hr*

7. **IT'S ABOUT TIME**

    Each person gets $30 except Jeannette, who gets $36.

8. **AFTER THE DEADHEADS**

    Sassafras, $27.37; Moonshine, $14.49; Peace, $19.32; Harmony, $28.98; Chynna, $38.64

9A. **WHERE'S THE RUE?**

    6 miles/hr

9B. **WHERE'S THE VACHE?**

    95.8 times/yr

10. MANUSCRIPT

        a. *357 words/min*   *b.* *43 pgs/hr*

11. EVENING EXERCISE

        20 holes/walk

Chapter 8, Unit Conversion Worksheet

    1. *190.3 yd*   *2.* *190080 inches*
    3. *1836 inches*   *4.* *135.5 miles*
    5. *504 hours*   *6.* *4320 min*
    7. *83.3 days*   *8.* *20160 min*

Chapter 8, Unit Analysis: Worksheet 2

    a. *54 mi/hr*   *b.* *28.8 mi/gal*
    c. *$1.29/gal*   *d.* *79.2 ft/sec*
    e. *$2.42/hr*   *f.* *$1.08/passenger*
    g. *4 cents/min*   *h.* *4.5 cents/mi*
    i. *26.4 yds/sec*   *j.* *172.8 pass-mi/gal*
    k. *22.3 mi/dollar*   *l.* *1.875 gal/hr*
    m. *0.7 cents/pass-mi*

Chapter 8, Unit Analysis Practice Quiz

    1. *51 mi/hr*   *2.* *25 mi/gal*
    3. *$7.82*   *4.* *$2.35/hr*
    5. *4.6 cents/mi*   *6.* *0.85 mi/min*
    7. *74.8 ft/sec*   *8.* *2.04 gal/hr*
    9. *33.3 mi/gal*   *10.* *58.1 mi/hr*
   11. *85.3 ft/sec*   *12.* *126 mi*
   13. *$1.23/gal*   *14.* *50.4 mi/hr*
   15. *73.9 ft/sec*   *16.* *Vida, $10.66; Von, $8.67; Vera, $6.67*
   17. *240 pass-mi*   *18.* *4.25 cents/pass-mi*
   19. *Jerome and Hoppy, $4.08 each; Francien, $2.04*
   20. *5.0 m*   *21.* *3.5 mi*
   22. *0.53 gal*   *23.* *0.95 l*
   24. *23.7 m/sec*   *25.* *14.3 m/sec*

Chapter 8, Unit Analysis Test

1. 23.1 m
2. 3.98 mi
3. 4.8 gal
4. 17.1 l
5. 24.6 m/sec
6. 10.75 labor-hours
7. $5.20/labor-hour
8. $26.00
9. $18.20
10. $11.70
11. 52.8 mi/hr
12. $11.52
13. 27.5 mi/gal
14. 77.4 ft/sec
15. 2.91 cents/mi
16. 244 mi
17. $0.82/gal
18. 48.8 mi/hr
19. 122 pass-mi/gal
20. 0.67 cents/pass-mi

Chapter 8, Problem Set B, Version 2

1. I CAN SEE FOR MILES AND MILES

1 hour, 41 minutes and 15 seconds

2. GENEROUS FRIENDS

Each glass was half full.

3. AN AGE OLD PROBLEM

Kevin is 35, Lee is 57, and Kate is 51.

4. FILLING THE PLANTER BOX

26⅔ trips or 27 trips

5. CROSS NUMBER PUZZLE

```
3 8 1        2 6 4
7 8 4   or   3 2 4
7 2 9        3 4 3
```

Chapter 8, Problem Set B, Version 3

1. DISCOUNT HARDWARE

3 hammers, 11 screwdrivers, 86 nails

2. LIFE SPAN

73 years, 343 days

3. COIN COLLECTION

2 dimes and a nickel

4. THE GOAT PROBLEM

2156.25π square feet, or approximately 6774 square feet

5. CROSS SUMS

Chapter 8, Problem Set B, Version 4

1. WEIRD WALLY'S WEIRD WINE

1908, 1917, 1926, 1935, 1944, 1953, 1962

2. HOOVER LAKE FLOODS THE MOJAVE DESERT

2.97 ft

3. VCR

I: Record at LP; will have 10 minutes left.
II: Switch after 10 minutes.

4. SPRINKLERS

57%

5. CROSS NUMBER PUZZLE

6, 1
4, 7

Chapter 9, Problem Set A, Version 2

1. **LAST DIGIT AGAIN**

   The last digit is 1.

2. **DIAGONALS OF A POLYGON**

   77 diagonals

3. **SUM NUMBERS - LOTSA NUMBERS**

   96,012,000

4. **AIR FARE**

   1 hour and 50 minutes

5. **SEASON TICKET PLANS**

   $2^{42} - 1$

6. **ONCE A YANKEES FAN, ALWAYS A YANKEES FAN**

   $2^{25} - 1$

7. **CLASSIC MUSTANGS**

   Travis, 6; Sandra, 3; narrator, 2

8. **VIVE LA DIFFERENCE!**

   125,750

9. **RICARDO & MARITZA**

   Maritza saved $19.84 more than Ricardo.

10. **BUSINESS CARDS**

    132860

Chapter 9, Problem Set B, Version 2

1. **COVERING THE PATIO**

   401 nails

2. **LIKE A WILDFIRE**

   16,376 people (including the 8 firefighters who started the program)

3. **SUM OF TEN**

   282

4. **LAPPING JOGGERS**

   Jan ran 3 miles, and Silvia ran 3.75 miles

5. **THE PHOON BROTHERS**

   Each Phoon pays $11.73, Helen pays $3.91 or Phoons each pay $11.95 and Helen pays $3.25. Some rounding is needed to assure that all the money gets paid.

Chapter 9, Problem Set B, Version 3

1. **PYRAMID SCHEME**

   24,570 people had invested

2. **LOSING TIME**

   20 days later on a Saturday

3. **DRIVE ME WILDE**

   F, K & W pay $5.20; D pays $4.01; Mildred pays $.74

   Other answers: F, K & W each pay $5.07; D pays $4.19; M pays $.94. Some rounding is necessary to assure that all the money gets paid.

4. **SOCCER LEAGUE**

TEAM	WINS	LOSSES	TIES
A	1	8	1
B	5	5	0
C	10	0	0
D	5	4	1
H	7	2	1
T	0	9	1

   Allosaurus tied Triceratops. Dimetrodon tied Hypsilophodon. Brontosaurus and Dimetrodon split their games.

5. **RUNNING ERRANDS**

   120 different sets of errands

Chapter 9, Problem Set B, Version 4

1. **TWO VEHICLES**

   The van has driven 17,000 miles.

2. **DIGITAL CLOCK**

   5:02

3. WATCH YOUR SPEED

60 miles per hour

4. TWO LANE HIGHWAY

100 passing periods

5. PEDESTRIAN

28 miles per hour

Chapter 10, Problem Set A, Version 2

1. HANUM'S ISLAND

nine trips

2. MAGIC TRIANGLE #2

There are several possibilities. One is shown below.

	5	
3		1
4	2	6

3. ROOKIE PURCHASE

Max lost $1500.

4. LAWN CHAIR AND BARBEQUE

Marc made $2, Wilma lost $1, and presumably Sammie lost $1, though he currently owns the chair and grill and could make or lose more money on them.

5. STAMPS

seven different ways

6. FIVE TILES

twelve ways

LETTER CUBE

Place the letters as shown on the folded-out cube. The answer is N (right side up).

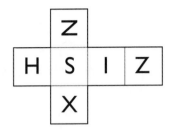

8. **SIX AND FOUR**

three rotations on the left die, three rotations on the right one

9. **A HEART IN THE RIGHT PLACE**

Two of Diamonds, Three of Hearts, and Six of Diamonds

10. **TWO DICE**

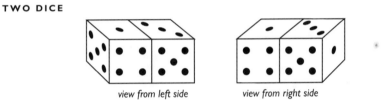

view from left side   view from right side

11. **JUST A PEW KIDS**

This is impossible, unless you want to split the family across an aisle.

12. **LONG TABLE**

20 ways

13. **MAGIC SQUARE**

2	6	7
10	5	0
3	4	8

14. **CARDS IN TWO ROWS**

From left to right, there is a Jack with a Queen on top of it, an Ace with a King on top of it, and a Queen with an Ace on top of it.

15. BLUEGRASS AT DINNER

Fiddle	*Banjo*	*Guitar*
Emily	Ben	Lucille
Sue	Marty	Kathleen
George	Irving	Kris

Sue plays violin in Marty's group. Ben plays banjo in Emily's group. George plays violin, and Irving and Kris are also in his group.

16. GOOD NEWS FOR CUBES

All three combinations form cubes.

Chapter 10, Problem Set B, Version 2

1. DUELING PINS

Lani and Hank Wojic, 290 and 217 pins
Fawnda and Bill Carson, 258 and 211 pins
Rhonda and Mark Sanchez, 281 and 243 pins
Wojics beat Sanchezes 290 to 243
Sanchezes beat Carsons 281 to 211
Carsons beat Wojics 258 to 217

2. STOPLIGHTS

You will have to stop at the eighteenth light after you started (counting the starting light as number 1) so you make it through 17 intersections counting the first.

3. TICKET PRICES

$7, $10, $16, $28

4. CAPICUA NUMBERS

1098 or 1089 (not counting 1 to 9)

5. A FAST(?) SPACESHIP

308 years

Chapter 10, Problem Set B, Version 3

1. ODD-ODD NUMBERS

19530

2. THE BRIDGE TOURNAMENT

Dave and Mary Hatfield, 880 points
Jim and Jean Friedrich, 680 points
Anne and Randy Muir, 490 points

3. DISCOUNT TICKETS

22 children's tickets

4. DRIVING ON THE FREEWAY

8.8 car lengths

5. CAKE RECIPE

3⅓ cups cake flour
2¹³⁄₁₆ teaspoons baking powder (2¾ is more realistic)
2½ cups sugar
1¼ cup butter
1¼ cup milk
5 eggs

Chapter 10, Problem Set B, Version 4

1. BATTING AVERAGE

.261 during vacation

2. PYRAMIDS

listed from light to heavy: Lori, Kelly, Diane, Debbie, Barbara, Carmella, Lisa, Kate

3. STEP ON A CRACK AND BREAK YOUR BACK

3/11

4. START YOUR ENGINES

perfect squares 1,4,9,etc. to 144

5. RODGERS AND HAMMERSTEIN

Press disc skip once, then once, then twice, then twice, then twice, then twice, exchanging each time.

Chapter 11, Problem Set A, Version 2

1. MARY'S CAR LOT

20 cars

2. ORANGE YOU HUNGRY?

36 oranges

3. TURNPIKE

$13

4. THE MONOPOLY GAME

$250

5. BROWN THUMB

23 plants

6. JELLY BEAN RABBITS

30 jelly beans. Lily ate 17; I ate 13.

7. WINNING GOLDFISH

5 goldfish

8. PRETTY FISHY

24 fishbowls

9. LOST HIS MARBLES

20 marbles

Chapter 11, Problem Set B, Version 2

1. CHICKEN EGGS

48 eggs

2. HEARTBEATS

4,828,950 fewer heartbeats for Joanne in a year

3. PENNIES IN THE SAND

started with 50 pennies, lost 53

4. JOGGING

between 5.0 and 5.2 mph

5. THE BRIDGE OVER RAT-TONGUE RAVINE

Odd numbers are trips across, even numbers are trips back:

1. *Thunder and Eagle go over*
2. *Eagle*
3. *Three Rattlers and Dragons*
4. *Thunder*
5. *Three Rattlers and Eagle*
6. *Eagle*
7. *Thunder and Eagle*

Chapter 11, Problem Set B, Version 3

1. **HOT DOG**

   48 hot dogs

2. **FRATERNITY OUTING**

   11 trips (there is more than one possible way to arrange the 11 trips.) Odd numbers are trips to the contest; evens are trips back.

   1. *J, TR, BZT, NK*
   2. *J, TR, NK*
   3. *J, TR, EP*
   4. *J, TR*
   5. *J, TR, 2PPP*
   6. *J, TR, BZT*
   7. *J, TR,BZT,1PPP*
   8. *J, TR, BZT*
   9. *J, TR, 2PPP*
   10. *J, TR*
   11. *J, TR, BZT, NK*

3. **WHICH CAR SHOULD THEY TAKE?**

   $2.13 one way; $4.26 round trip

4. **HOT DOG AGAIN**

   45 hot dogs

5. **LOST IN GRIDLOCK**

   2 blocks east, 5 blocks south

Chapter 11, Problem Set B, Version 4

1. **LOST CARDS**

   140 cards when she left for school

2. **FENCE PAINTING**

   23⅓ fences

3. **JOHN AND MARCIA**

   330 ways

4. **WALKING**

   287.46 feet

5. WEDDING RECEPTION

There are many legal ways. Here's one:

1. JR, Mina, Brian, Jerri
2. Jerri
3. Len, Phil, Jerri
4. Jerri
5. Amanda, Kevin, Walter, Jerri
6. Brian, Jerri
7. Jerri, Brian, Jill, Lincoln

Chapter 12, Problem Set A, Version 2

1. JUNIOR PROM

36 juniors

2. SODA SURVEY

209

3. COMPANY BARBEQUE

a. *1 person*
b. *4 people*
c. *3 people*
d. *0 people*
e. *6 people*

4. SPIRIT OF WOODSTOCK

1 member

5. COUNTRY CLUB

115 members

6. EAST PARKING LOT

18 white vehicles

7. SPLIT TICKET

70 people

8. BRAVE ALL-STARS

36 people

9. EARTHQUAKE DAMAGES

4 houses; 4 houses

Chapter 12, Problem Set B, Version 2

1. THE TREASURE OF SIERRA MARBLES

Tom, 69; Huck, 5; Becky, 40

2. TOOTHPICK SQUARES

220 toothpicks

3. THE FRESHMAN CLASS

14 students

4. THE SANDWICH SHOP

79 different sandwiches

5. FINE ARTS

Alan Innis, symphony, publisher
Chris Hatfield, musicals, reporter
Bev Gunderson, jazz, engineer
Doreen Jackson, art, doctor
Ernie Fillmore, ballet, dentist

Chapter 12, Problem Set B, Version 3

1. HUNGRY BROTHERS

55 cookies

2. LET GO MY LEGO

Legos, 220; bumps, 440

3. COUNTRY MUSIC

8 songs

4. HOW MUCH STEREO CAN YOU AFFORD?

18 ways

5. POLITICAL PARTIES

Maria Lamson, Bus, The Bronx
Walter Peterson, bike, Queens
Valerie Archer, Car, Seaside
Jasper Doyle, walk, Manhattan
Teresa Sinderson, subway, Long Island

Chapter 12, Problem Set B, Version 4

1. FOUR FRIENDS

driver, Areatha, soup, lemon lime
front seat passenger, Mark, spaghetti, cola
back seat left, Sara, chili, orange soda
back seat right, Roberto, macaroni & cheese, root beer

2. SOCCER TEAM

Four people play goalie. Three people play fullback and forward only.

3. ORANGE TREASURE

160 oranges at start

Ahab, 73; Bluebeard, 46; Hook, 35; monkeys, 6

4. PENTAGON

35 triangles

5. DIGIT 8

600,000

Chapter 13, Problem Set A, Version 2

1. MORE AND MORE COINS

11 quarters, 6 dimes

2. COMPLEMENTS

29° and 61°

3. MARYLOU'S INVESTMENTS

$5000 at 8% and $4000 at 5%

4. A SMALL WOODWORKING COMPANY

17 small packages and 9 large packages

5. SPEEDING TIX

The speed limit is 25 miles per hour; Chris was going 48 miles per hour.

6. DAD GETS LOTS OF HELP

93⅓ minutes

7. MOM GETS HELP?

-120 minutes (What does a negative answer mean on a problem like this?)

8. TAXING BERNICE

$40,500 was taxed at 7%, and $1500 was taxed at 9%.

9. TERRY'S BOOBOO

1³⁄₇ gallons of concentrate

10. ALGEBRA AREA

595 square cm

11. MICHEALA'S SEASON

17 singles, 3 doubles, and 4 triples

12. GOLD COUNTRY TIRE

29 customers bought 2 tires; 6 customers bought 4 tires.

13. CLARENCE AND STEPHANIE ARE THINKING

Clarence, 16; Stephanie, 6

14. SUGAR PUNCH

Add 4.4 liters of water.

15. SLED RUN

about 293.2 feet

16. CAFE STANDARDS

50,000 cars

Chapter 13, Problem Set B, Version 2

1. THE DRAMA PRODUCTION

A, G, B, J, C, H, D, L, E, I, F, K (A = Augie, etc.)

2. SELLING STEAK

Karl is charging $6 and there are 10 boxes.

3. DICEY PRIMES

15 to 13

4. ICE CREAM COUPONS

both are juniors

5. HALFWAY LINES

Switch the 7 and the 10, draw a vertical line between the 2nd and 3rd columns; the horizontal line goes below the 2nd row.

Chapter 13, Problem Set B, Version 3

1. LATE TO THE GATE

4.5 mph

2. CARD ARRANGEMENT

from top: 1, 6, 2, 10, 3, 7, 4, 9, 5, 8

3. RECTANGLE RATIOS

length, 15; width, 3

4. TRIOMINOES

12 figures

5. NEMATOAD

Match every pick-up with your opponent's to total five. (If the opponent picks up 3, for example, you pick up 2.)

Chapter 13, Problem Set B, Version 4

1. AMAZING NUMBERS

right to the 4, diagonally downright to 6, left to 1, diagonally upright to 4, down to 5, right to E

2. LID ASTRAY

There are a few completely different strategies. Look for efficiency.

3. RADIATOR

4.16 quarts

4. LSAT TEST

14 ways

5. LARGE POWER OF TWO

797

Chapter 14, Problem Set A, Version 2

1. **A COVEY OF FUNCTIONS**
   - a. $y = 4x + 3$
   - b. $y = -5x + 4$
   - c. $y = 4x^2 - 2x + 3$
   - d. $y = (\frac{1}{2})x + 7$
   - e. $y = -2x + 2$
   - f. $y = 2x^2 + 3x + 7$
   - g. $y = 2x^3 + 3x^2 + 7x - 1$
   - h. $y = (-\frac{3}{2})x - 2$

2. **BLOCK PYRAMID**
   2381 blocks visible

3. **A BEVY OF FUNCTIONS**
   - i. $y = 2x + 1$
   - j. $y = -x^2 + 4x$
   - k. $y = 4x - 7$
   - l. $y = x^2 + 4x - 3$
   - m. $y = -3x + 1$
   - n. $y = (\frac{1}{2})x^2 - 6x - 2$

4. **HEXAGONAL NUMBERS**
   $y = 3x^2 - 3x + 1$

5. **A GAGGLE OF CUBIC FUNCTIONS**
   - p. $y = -2x^3 + 3x^2 + 6x + 23$
   - q. $y = -x^3 + 4x^2 + 8$
   - r. $y = x^3 + 4x^2 - 3x - 5$
   - s. $y = (\frac{1}{2})x^3 - 6x^2 - 2x + 5$

Chapter 14, Problem Set B, Version 2

1. **WORMS**
   144 cases (actually 143.4) or 143 cases with 144 worms left over

2. **PRODUCE**
   5 apples

3. **ANTIFREEZE**
   17.3 quarts

4. STRANGE NUMBER

85714

5. TWO SEQUENCES

tied on 54th term; passed on 55th

Chapter 14, Problem Set B, Version 3

1. OLD CHEVY

228.48 miles

2. COUNTY FAIR

$116.20

3. HOW MANY SEGMENTS?

½ n² − ½ n

4. MYSTERY SUM

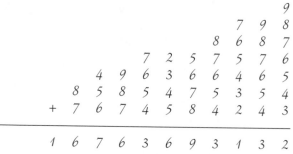

```
                              9
                        7  9  8
                     8  6  8  7
               7  2  5  7  5  7  6
         4  9  6  3  6  6  4  6  5
         8  5  8  5  4  7  5  3  5  4
    +  7  6  7  4  5  8  4  2  4  3
   ─────────────────────────────────
    1  6  7  6  3  6  9  3  1  3  2
```

5. HOLLYWOOD SQUARES

Top Row: Gregorio Wilson, Della Jefferson, Howard Taft
Middle Row: Isabel Kennedy, Betty Nixon, Clara Madison
Bottom Row: Ellen Pierce, Frank Lincoln, Anh Roosevelt

Chapter 14, Problem Set B, Version 4

1. ANTS

25 inches

2. SEQUENCE RACING

221 terms

3. CORNER CAFE

>*Clockwise around the table:*
>
>*Gil, french toast, sausage*
>*Stan, omelette, hashbrowns*
>*Karen, eggs, muffin*
>*Donna, pancakes, strawberries*

4. THE GREAT NUMBERINI'S NUMBER

>*38095*

5. SKIING ARIZONA

>*11; 11*

Chapter 15, Problem Set A, Version 2

1. THE CLASSIC HOMEWORK EXCUSE

>*doughnuts, $.45; coffee, $.65*
>
>*5 coffees and 7 doughnuts should be $6.40*
>*6 coffees and 11 doughnuts should be $8.85*
>*9 coffees and 5 doughnuts should be $8.10*
>*10 coffees and 8 doughnuts should be $10.10*

2. SON OF TWO-INPUT FUNCTION

>*a. $2x + y$*
>*b. $3y - x$*
>*c. $y - x$*
>*d. $2x - y$*
>*e. $2x + 3y$*
>*f. $x^2 + y$*

3. DOLORES' AGE

>*11 to 13 years old*

4. LOG RIDE

>*youngest, 14; oldest, 33*

5. COMPUTER PRINT-OUT

>*Child, $4; Adult, $6*

6. STAMP COMBINATIONS

>*3, 7, 8, 10, 11, 13, 15, 17, 18, 20, 21, 25, and 28 cents*

7. GOOD AND YUMMY RESTAURANT

a.

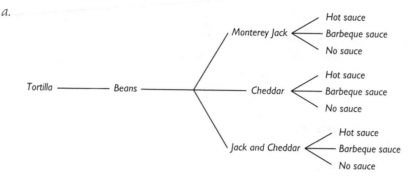

b.

Jack Cheese	Cheddar Cheese	Hot Sauce	Barbeque Sauce
X			
	X		
X	X		
X		X	
	X	X	
X	X	X	
X			X
	X		X
X	X		X

Chapter 15, Problem Set B, Version 2

1. ALONA'S FENCE

162.5 fence boards

2. STOCKS

Cayla, $15; Billie Jo, $19; Alex, $57; Derwood, $60

3. ZNORS

44 Zmuds; 8 are also Zlogs and Zorfs

4. CONFERENCE

from Topeka to Peoria

5. **FOUR BY FOUR**

7	16	13	5
15	9	2	12
4	1	10	14
11	6	8	3

Chapter 15, Problem Set B, Version 3

1. **DEAR OLD DAD**

   Uncle Pedro is 24; Aunt Jasmine is 37. (Dad is 36 and Grandma is 58.)

2. **SIXTEEN CANDLES**

   PBPBPBPBGYGYGYGY or reverse

3. **REAL DOLLS**

   14 male, non-Cabbage Patch dolls

4. **WHH**

   pairs in order (h, w): (0, 0) (1, 2) (1, -1) (-9, -3) (-8, -4) (-9, -6)

5. **ONE HUNDRED FACTORS**

   45360

Chapter 15, Problem Set B, Version 4

1. **MARBLES**

   51

2. **COUSINS**

   Many arrangements are possible. This is one:

   Day 1

Hike:	1	2	3	4	5
Gleane:	Tom	Bonnie	Janet	Stefan	Michael
Jenick:	Ryan	Torrey	Will	Daniel	Gary

   Day 2

Hike:	1	2	3	4	5
Gleane:	Michael	Tom	Bonnie	Janet	Stefan
Jenick:	Torrey	Will	Daniel	Gary	Ryan

   Day 3

Hike:	1	2	3	4	5
Gleane:	Stefan	Michael	Tom	Bonnie	Janet
Jenick:	Will	Daniel	Gary	Ryan	Torrey

Day 4

Hike:	*1*	*2*	*3*	*4*	*5*
Gleane:	*Janet*	*Stefan*	*Michael*	*Tom*	*Bonnie*
Jenick:	*Daniel*	*Gary*	*Ryan*	*Torrey*	*Will*

Day 5

Hike:	*1*	*2*	*3*	*4*	*5*
Gleane:	*Bonnie*	*Janet*	*Stefan*	*Michael*	*Tom*
Jenick:	*Gary*	*Ryan*	*Torrey*	*Will*	*Daniel*

3. ANT GRAPEVINE

28 days

4. LONG LIST OF NUMBERS

two thousand two hundred two

5. ALPHABET SOUP

shape (or phase)

Chapter 16, Problem Set A, Version 2

1. BASIC HEX

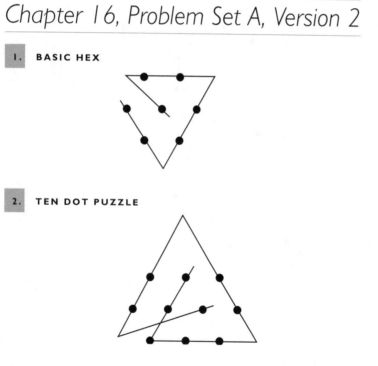

2. TEN DOT PUZZLE

3. FOURTEEN DOT PUZZLE

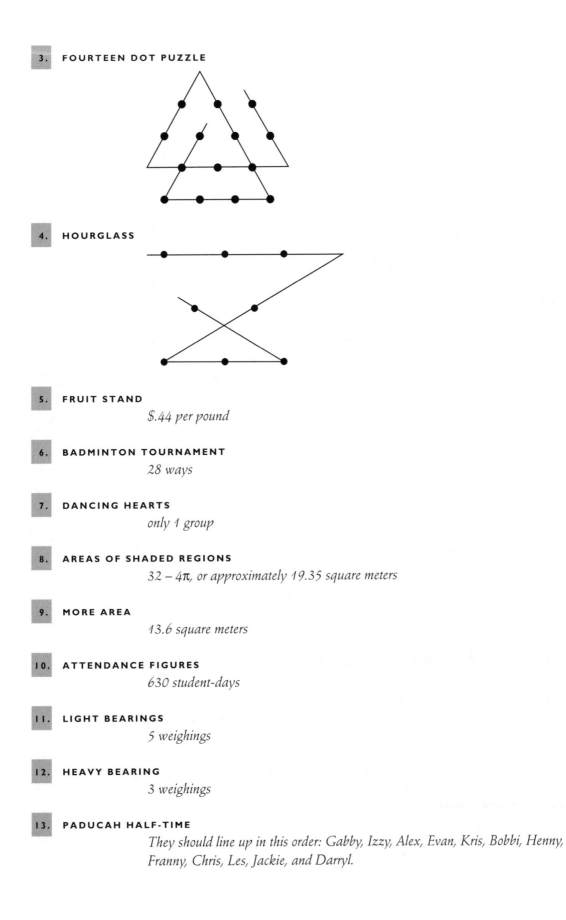

4. HOURGLASS

5. FRUIT STAND
$.44 per pound

6. BADMINTON TOURNAMENT
28 ways

7. DANCING HEARTS
only 1 group

8. AREAS OF SHADED REGIONS
32 − 4π, or approximately 19.35 square meters

9. MORE AREA
13.6 square meters

10. ATTENDANCE FIGURES
630 student-days

11. LIGHT BEARINGS
5 weighings

12. HEAVY BEARING
3 weighings

13. PADUCAH HALF-TIME
They should line up in this order: Gabby, Izzy, Alex, Evan, Kris, Bobbi, Henny, Franny, Chris, Les, Jackie, and Darryl.

14. **WALKING HOME FROM SCHOOL**

13.5 miles

15. **MORE TOOTHPICKS**

16. **PERFECT CUBES**

211 perfect cubes

17. **SOME COMPLEMENTARY EVENTS**

a. A family has three children, at least one is a boy.

b. They watch three movies, two or less have Friday the Thirteenth in the title.

c. You find six coins, and at least one is a dime.

d. You meet four new people, and three or fewer are from Pennsylvania.

18. **RUNNING GEORGE**

26.5 miles

19. **IS SHE, OR ISN'T SHE**

63.2%

20. **ALPHABET FLASH CARDS**

The cards should be in this order: I O A S J B Y P C K V D T L E Q Z F M X G R N H U W

21. **ORGAN TRANSPLANTS**

Survival chances are about 50%.

Chapter 16, Problem Set B, Version 2

1. **RECTANGULAR TILES**

Many arrangements are possible. The large rectangle is 23 × 31

2. **CONSECUTIVE INTEGERS**

all powers of 2 below 600: 1, 2, 4, 8, 16, 32, 64, 128, 256, 512

3. **ALPHABETICAL NUMBERS**

669

4. **SAY THE MAGIC WORD**
   WIND

5. **WHERE SHOULD YOU STAND?**
   189th position

Chapter 16, Problem Set B, Version 3

1. **LARGE CORPORATION**
   72.2%

2. **MOVIE STARS**
   Bill Preston, red striped
   Ted Reaper, green checkered
   Don Logan, blue print
   Grim Thanes, yellow plain

3. **SUMSUMS**
   448

4. **WRESTLING NEWSLETTER**
   LUNGE

5. **THREE DIGIT TRIANGLES**

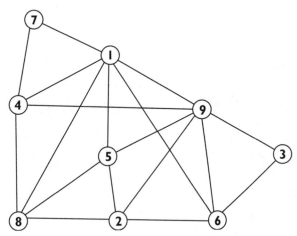

Chapter 16, Problem Set B, Version 4

1. **REUNION**
   61 mph

2. BAND

   5 × 12 or 6 × 8

3. POKER

   Hand 1: 6D, 6H, 6C, KD, KH
   Hand 2: Straight flush, 7, 8, 9, 10, J of diamonds
   Hand 3: 8H, 9H, 10H, JH, QD
   Hand 4: 2H, 2D, 3H, 3D, 4D
   Hand 5: Flush: 4, 5, 7, Q, A of hearts

4. DICE PRODUCTS

   8/11

5. BOOK CHOICE

   M

Chapter 17, Problem Set A, Version 2

1. DENISE'S AUTO REPAIR

   a. 12 hour return, $120/hour
   b. 60-hour return, $24/hour
   c. 72-hour return, $20/hour

2. RUNNING ON M.T.

   a. 198 minutes
   b. about 8.5 miles

3. KATHY'S CATERING SERVICE

   Answers will vary. About $14.00 each for 10–19 people, about $13.00 each for 20–29 people, and about $13.50 each for 30–39 people.

4. GROUND TURKEY

   Answers will vary.
   a. 15 hours
   b. 6 months
   c. 47 degrees

5. SELLING SODAS AT THE PARADE

   2 six-packs

6. ANOTHER CUBIC

   approximately -1.23

7. PIZZA

About $3.00 calculating it by diameter, about $7.00 calculating by area

8. THE CHICKEN COOP

120 feet by 60 feet

9. LAUNCHING ROCKETS

26 feet high

10. ROCKET TO THE MOON

360 feet

11. TRANSVERSING THE TRIBUTARY WITH CANINES

47 yards

12. DELBERT'S LAUNCH

373 yards

13. FLYING PAPER AIRPLANES

31 feet

14. JANET'S PAPER AIRPLANE

76 feet

Chapter 17, Problem Set B, Version 2

1. BOXCARS

1. Back up right, unhitch gondola and tanker, and drive forward.
2. Back up left, unhitch flatcar, drive forward.
3. Back up right, pick up gondola, drive forward.
4. Back up left, unhitch gondola and boxcar, drive forward.
5. Back up right, pick up tanker, drive forward.
6. Back up left, pick up boxcar, gondola, and flatcar, and he's done.

2. THEY'RE TWINS

Lynn: 46 three-pointers, 6 field goals, 18 free throws
Laurie: 10 three-pointers, 50 field goals, 38 free throws

3. RUDY'S ROOT BEER

21 days

4. DIGGING A TUNNEL

$10\frac{1}{9}$ days

5. **TOASTER SERIAL NUMBER**

3224 toasters (The 3225th will have all different letters and digits again.)

Chapter 17, Problem Set B, Version 3

1. **BEDTIME**

306 times per day

2. **CLASSIC CAR CLUB**

Red sports car

3. **BACK IN SHAPE**

564 loads

4. **THE WEDNESDAY CLUB**

13 members

5. **WOLF MOUNTAIN SKIER'S PLAN**

8 weekdays, 7 weekend days

Chapter 17, Problem Set B, Version 4

1. **HUESOS DE GALLO**

laugh

2. **WOLFIES ON THE RUN**

18 games

3. **WHEAT FIELD**

6.8 miles

4. **DIGITAL CLOCK**

124 times

5. **PERFECT SHUFFLE**

8 shuffles